T0320044

The Regional Impact of National Policies

The Regional Impact of National Policies

The Case of Brazil

Edited by

Werner Baer

Lemann Professor of Economics, University of Illinois at Urbana-Champaign, USA

Edward Elgar

Cheltenham, UK • Northampton, MA, USA

Published by
Edward Elgar Publishing Limited
The Lypiatts
15 Lansdown Road
Cheltenham
Glos GL50 2JA
UK

Edward Elgar Publishing, Inc.
William Pratt House
9 Dewey Court
Northampton
Massachusetts 01060
USA

A catalogue record for this book
is available from the British Library

Library of Congress Control Number: 2012930606

ISBN 978 0 85793 669 1

Typeset by Servis Filmsetting Ltd, Stockport, Cheshire
Printed and bound by MPG Books Group, UK

Contents

Contributors

Roberto Cavalcanti de Albuquerque is Technical Director of the National Forum, founded in 1988, and sponsored by Brazil's National Institute of Advanced Studies.

Eliseu Alves is Researcher and former Director-President of Embrapa, Brazil.

Edmund Amann is Reader in Development Economics at the University of Manchester, UK.

Carlos Roberto Azzoni Professor of Economics at the University of São Paulo, Brazil; former Dean of the Faculty of Economics, Administration and Accounting.

Carlos José Caetano Bacha is Professor of Economics at the University of São Paulo in Piracicaba (Esalq), Brazil.

Werner Baer is the Lemann Professor of Economics, University of Illinois at Urbana-Champaign, USA.

Alexandre Rands Barros is Professor of Economics, Federal University of Pernambuco, Brazil.

Luiz Ricardo Cavalcante is Researcher at the Brazilian Institute for Applied Economic Research (IPEA).

Elisio Contini is Researcher, Deputy Head of Strategic Studies and Training, Embrapa, Brazil.

Marcos C. Holanda is Professor of Economics at the Federal University of Ceara, Brazil.

Camila Kraide Kretzmann is a PhD student in Applied Economics at the University of São Paulo in Piracicaba (Esalq), Brazil.

André Matos Magalhães is Professor of Economics at the Federal University of Pernambuco, Brazil. He is also the editor of the *Revista Brasileira de Estudos Regionais e Urbanos*.

Geraldo B. Martha Jr is Researcher and Supervisor for Strategic Studies, Embrapa, Brazil.

Márcia Azanha Ferraz Dias de Moraes is Professor of Economics at the University of São Paulo at Piracicaba (Esalq), Brazil.

Charles C. Mueller is an Emeritus Professor of Economics at the University of Brasília, Brazil.

Fabíola Cristina Ribeiro de Oliveira is a PhD student in Applied Economics at the Department of Economics, University of São Paulo at Piracicaba (Esalq), Brazil.

Raul da Mota Silveira-Neto is Associate Professor of Economics at the Federal University of Pernambuco, Brazil.

Nicholas M. Trebat is Assistant Professor at IBMEC University, Rio de Janeiro, Brazil.

Thomas J. Trebat is Executive Director of the Institute of Latin American Studies and of the Institute's Center for Brazilian Studies, Columbia University, USA.

Simone Uderman is Professor in the Department of Human Sciences and of the MSc Program in Public Policy, Knowledge Management and Regional Development at the State University of Bahia, Brazil.

André Villela is Assistant Professor at the Graduate School of Economics, Fundação Getulio Vargas in Rio de Janeiro, Brazil.

1. Introduction

Werner Baer

It is well known that the benefits of Brazil's economic growth and development have been unevenly (some would say inequitably) distributed from a regional point of view. This is evident from the data in Table 1.1, where it will be noted that the Southeast of the country, with 42 percent of the population, produced 56 percent of the gross domestic product (GDP); whereas the Northeast, with 27.7 percent of the population, produced only 13 percent of the GDP.

There are many studies which have dealt with the phenomenon.[1] On occasion the central government has taken action to try explicitly to redress regional inequality: examples are the regional development

Table 1.1 Brazil: regional distribution of population and GDP

a. Brazil: regional population distribution

	1970	1996	2003	2006	2010
North	3.9	7.1	7.9	8.0	8.5
Northeast	30.3	28.5	27.8	27.6	27.7
Southeast	42.7	52.7	42.6	42.6	42.1
South	17.7	15.0	14.7	14.6	15.0
Center-West	5.4	6.7	7.0	7.2	6.7
Total	100.0	100.0	100.0	100.0	100.0

b. Brazil: regional distribution of GDP

	1970	1997	2003	2005	2008
North	2.2	4.4	5.0	5.0	5.1
Northeast	12.1	13.1	13.8	13.1	13.1
Southeast	65.0	58.6	55.2	56.5	56.0
South	17.4	17.7	18.6	16.3	16.6
Center-West	3.8	6.2	7.4	8.7	9.2
Total	100.0	100.0	100.0	100.0	100.0

Source: IBGE.

institutions (such as SUDENE for the Northeast of Brazil), regional development banks, and special tax incentives for firms investing in poorer regions. However, specific policies which deal directly with regional inequalities have only been sporadic, and long periods have passed when the country had almost no explicit regional policies.

This does not mean that in periods of non-explicit regional policies the actions of the central government were neutral as regards regions. It is thus important in a country of such continental proportions as Brazil to get an idea of how the government's general economic policies have influenced the regional distribution of economic growth. This was the purpose of a conference which was held in Porto de Galinhas, Pernambuco, Brazil on 18–20 November 2010. Most papers presented were concerned directly or indirectly with the regional impact of various policies, and form the basis for this book.

André Villela (Chapter 2) goes back in history and examines the regional impact of Brazil's first systematic program of import substitutions in the 1950s, also known as the Targets Program of President Kubitschek, finding that the program aggravated already existing regional disparities.

Roberto Cavalcanti de Albuquerque (Chapter 3) developed a social inclusion index which he uses to measure the extent of a recent process of increased social inclusion and how it manifested itself among various regions. The study by Silveira-Neto and Azzoni (Chapter 4) shows that the largest recent decline of regional inequality in per capita income is due to social programs, which have a large impact on reducing poverty in poor regions. On the other hand, Márcia Azanha Ferraz Dias de Moraes et al. (Chapter 5), in their analysis of Brazilian labor policies, show that these did not necessarily lead to convergence of salaries or job creation between regions.

Amann and Baer (Chapter 6) concentrate on Brazil's privatization programs in the 1990s and early 2000s, and conclude that their bias was to favor the more developed regions, where state enterprises had been more prominent. Cavalcante and Uderman's survey (Chapter 7) of Brazil's science and technology location and policies also shows a regional concentration which does not seem to be redressed. Holanda and Magalhães (Chapter 8) examine the regional impact of foreign direct investment (FDI) and find that there is no strong regional policy towards FDI, and that there is a strong concentration of FDI in the Southeast and South of the country. Alexandre Rands Barros (Chapter 9) analyzes various Brazilian stabilization plans and finds that they had only a negligible impact on changes in regional distribution of economic activities.

Three chapters deal with specific agricultural aspects of Brazil's economy which have regional implications. Bacha (Chapter 10) is mainly concerned with the destruction of forests and the difficulties involved in regulating and controlling deforestation in various regions. Mueller (Chapter 11) concentrates on one of the frontier regions of Brazil, Mato Grosso, analyzing how market forces have shaped the use of the land. Martha et al. (Chapter 12) analyze Embrapa, the Brazilian government's agricultural research corporation, which has made a substantial contribution to the modernization of the country's agricultural sector, but in its early days had few explicit regional goals.

A final chapter by Trebat and Trebat (Chapter 13) deals with Rio de Janeiro, both city and state. Although the federal government never had a specific regional policy for the city or state, its programs have had, and are still having, an enormous impact.

The conference was a collaborative effort of the following institutions: the Federal University of Pernambuco, Datametrica, the University of São Paulo, the Lemann Institute for Brazilian Studies of the University of Illinois. Support was also received from the Banco do Nordeste and Embrapa.

Special thanks go to Reese Hartmann for valuable editorial assistance.

NOTE

1. Werner Baer (2008), *The Brazilian Economy: Growth and Development*, 6th edition, Boulder, CO: Lynne Rienner Publishers, Chapter 11.

2. The regional impacts of Juscelino Kubitschek's Targets Program

André Villela[1]

2.1 INTRODUCTION

The Targets Program, launched in 1956 by President Juscelino Kubitschek, stands as a landmark in Brazilian history. The program served as a decisive instrument in the advancement of the import-substituting industrialization process, and ultimately would lead to important changes in the country's productive landscape.

Literature dealing with the program is proportional to its importance in the economic history of modern Brazil.[2] Nevertheless, most of these contributions focus on its political-ideological, macroeconomic or microeconomic aspects, and very little attention is given to its regional impact.[3] By the same token, work on the regional question in Brazil, while often analyzing the impacts of the Targets Program, does so from a long-term perspective in which the second half of the 1950s appears as one among several important subperiods.

This chapter seeks to assess the regional impacts of the Targets Program. It differs from previous work on at least two counts:

1. It assesses the extent to which the regional dimension was present not only in the program itself, but also in several earlier documents leading up to it.
2. It focuses mainly on the Targets Program during the period 1956 to 1961, but also examines the broader period from 1950 to 1970.

Analysis is based mostly on data gathered from secondary literature, although official documents of the program itself, often overlooked by previous work, have also provided invaluable information.

2.2 THE TARGETS PROGRAM: A BRIEF SUMMARY

While on the campaign trail, Juscelino Kubitschek promised the Brazilian people that if he were elected, he would implement a set of measures aimed at boosting economic development. These measures would later take shape in the 1956 Targets Program. Once in office, Kubitschek took advantage of a benign international environment – characterized, inter alia, by the existence of private capital flows and resources made available by international agencies – in order to put into practice his bold project of structural transformation of the Brazilian economy and society.[4]

With a view to implementing such a program within the confines of his five-year term, he created a parallel administrative structure, led by the Conselho de Desenvolvimento (Development Council), linked directly to the presidency, to which the different sector-specific "executive groups" (*grupos executivos*) would be attached.[5] Starting with projects elaborated years earlier by the Joint Brazil–United States Commission,[6] and combined with several new ones, the program consisted of 30 different targets, divided among five sectors: energy, transportation, agriculture, basic industry and education.[7]

Funds earmarked for the program were divided roughly as follows: two-thirds in national currency (totaling some Cr$300 billion[8]), and the remaining third in foreign currency expenditures on the importation of goods and services valued at US$2.2 billion.[9] The bulk of investments would be made in the energy and transport sectors (77 percent of the total in local currency and 65 percent of dollar-denominated expenditures), followed by basic industry (16 percent and 28 percent), with agriculture and education accounting for the remainder.

Sources of funds in domestic currency were distributed as follows: approximately 40 percent from the federal government budget; 10 percent from the states; 35 percent from publicly owned enterprises; and the remaining 15 percent from official agencies, such as the Bank of Brazil and the National Economic Development Bank (BNDE). Foreign currency funds would be provided by international institutions, such as the World Bank and the American Eximbank; official foreign-aid agencies; direct investment (often internalized without the need for foreign exchange cover, under the aegis of SUMOC Instruction No. 113); and suppliers' credits.[10]

The results of the program were generally positive, with a high degree of performance in areas such as road construction (138 percent of the original target being accomplished); extension of generating capacity in the electric energy sector (82 percent); the manufacture of cars and trucks (78 percent); and crude oil production (76 percent).[11]

On a broader level, the program proved decisive in accelerating the rate of growth of gross domestic product (GDP) during the Kubitschek administration. GDP growth reached on average 8.1 percent per annum between 1956 and 1960, compared to 6.7 percent in the previous five-year period. Moreover, the program constituted a new phase in the import-substituting industrialization process in Brazil, having involved a direct and decisive role of the state in the economic realm. The industrial sector advanced significantly and become more sophisticated, as measured by the increased share of the capital and durable consumer goods sectors in total manufacturing value added. Yet the program also lay at the root of a perverse legacy in the shape of rising inflation and a deterioration of both the fiscal and the external position of the country.[12]

2.3   THE REGIONAL DIMENSION OF THE TARGETS PROGRAM IN THEORY

In order to assess the regional impacts of the Targets Program, it is worth examining the intellectual development of the initiative, beginning with the work of the Joint Brazil–United States Commission and leading up to the campaign manifesto of the then presidential candidate Juscelino Kubitschek.

2.3.1   The Report of the Joint Brazil–United States Commission

The roots of Kubitschek's Targets Program can actually be traced to the second Vargas government (1951–54) and, more specifically, to the work of the Joint Brazil–United States Economic Development Commission (hereafter, the CMBEU, its acronym in Portuguese). The latter produced a noteworthy technical report,[13] which would serve as a starting point for projects financed by the BNDE, which was created in 1952.[14] Ultimately, the bulk of the projects outlined by the Joint Commission – in the areas of energy, transportation, ports and shipping, and basic industries – would be revised and updated before being incorporated into the Targets Program.

The text of the CMBEU report reveals the technicians' full awareness of the regional aspect of Brazil's underdevelopment. As early as on pages 16 and 17, the high disparities in both inter- and intra-regional incomes are being highlighted, together with the significant gap separating rural and urban living standards in 1950. Nevertheless, in the section entitled "Regional Aspects of the Joint Commission's Program" (pp. 80–81) the authors eschew any spatial treatment of the proposed projects, and instead prefer to stress that:

Table 2.1   *Regional distribution of recommended investments for railroads, ports and power – share in recommended Joint Commission's Program (%)*

Regions of Brazil	Share of total population in 1950	Share in 1950 national income	Share in gross value of industrial production in 1949	Railroad equipment	Port rehabilitation	Power expansion
South	32.7	48.3	60.4	46.5	52.2	71.2
East	36.4	36.6	30.9	40.5	26.0	19.3
Center-West	3.4	2.0	0.7	5.9	0.2	1.5
Northeast	24.0	11.3	7.3	7.1	17.5	8.0
North	3.6	1.8	0.7	–	4.1	–

Source: Joint Brazil–United States Commission (1953), p. 80.

> the recommended investments reflect the relative economic importance of the different regions of Brazil, involving no attempt to correct imbalances in regional rates of growth. Productivity and other priority criteria were the guiding considerations. (p. 80)

Later in the text, they admit to the potential socio-political problems resulting from such regional disparities in income and productivity. Yet they insist that the "limitations of resources" and their commercial nature (loans, and not grants), not to mention the terms of reference under which the commission operated, "rendered imperative a concentration of effort on obviously pressing priority problems".[15] In the eyes of the Commission, redressing regional imbalances did not qualify as a priority at the time. In line with this view, the investments recommended by the CMBEU follow the spatial distribution indicated in Table 2.1.

The table confirms – along the same lines pointed out by the report of the Commission itself[16] – that there was a marked concentration of infrastructure investments in the South and East,[17] where "rapid industrial development and increasing agricultural production have tended to create the most serious transport and power bottlenecks" (p. 81).

With a view to rationalizing the spatial allocation of resources, the report draws attention to the specific characteristics of each sector. For instance, in the case of investments in energy, it notes the greater amount of potential hydraulic generation sites in the South (and their easier access). In the case of railways, it contrasts the appalling state of the federally run network in the East – to be endowed with the greater share of investments in this sector – with the relatively good situation found in the *paulista* network (maintained by the state government and the private sector), which would naturally call for a lesser amount of investment.[18] Finally, it explains the disproportional allocation of resources in the North and Northeast dedicated to improving port infrastructure and the promotion of shipping. Both regions are highly dependent on both international and interregional trade.[19]

As noted, there was never any suggestion by the Joint Commission that its projects should somehow seek to redress pre-existing regional imbalances. Yet the technicians were well aware of the potential benefits of the construction of the Paulo Afonso hydroelectric power plant[20] and two accompanying power lines to a vast area in the poor Northeastern region. Projections estimated that the additional supply of new energy would be absorbed by the region's major coastal cities by as early as 1954, and the Commission was quick to show support for the expansion of the generating capacity of the Paulo Afonso plant. A third unit in the Paulo Afonso project, according to the CMBEU Report, would "preserve the truly developmental character of this undertaking by giving to the company the possibility of creating a sizeable cushion of extra power which should provide an important stimulus in attracting industrial undertakings to the Northeast".[21]

In addressing the expected economic and financial impacts of the investment program suggested by the Joint Commission, the report indirectly touched upon the regional question when it stated that greater decentralization of industry would lead "to a better balanced distribution of productive power" and would relieve "congestion in industrial centers" (p. 244). The latter reflected the fact that the cities of Rio de Janeiro and São Paulo jointly harbored as much as half of the manufacturing value added in Brazil in 1949, giving rise to several infrastructural bottlenecks in these two large urban areas (p. 226). However, the authors were also aware that providing stimulus to the expansion of the supply of energy and transport services beyond these two cities would not, in itself, ensure spatial decentralization of each and every type of industrial activity. They admitted that there are cases in which the existing pool of qualified labor, proximity to complementary industries, or a greater supply of banking and commercial services may attract new firms to traditional, more developed regions. Still, they also note that in other sectors a greater supply of energy and transport services could be decisive for firms contemplating investments outside the Rio–São Paulo axis (ibid.).

2.3.2 Kubitschek's Campaign Program

While campaigning for President in 1955, Juscelino Kubitschek circulated a document which would later be published in book form. It brought together "a collection of the first ideas of the governmental program I intend to implement as President of the Republic".[22] In it, the then candidate showed support for state intervention in the economy, promoting a National Development Program which would aim to "increase people's living standards, opening up opportunities for a better future" (pp. 37ff.). To achieve this goal, Kubitschek's plan outlined six primary objectives, one of which was named "Regional and urban planning". In one particular passage, he detailed his views on the spatial dimension of the economic development process:

> Regional and urban planning involves problems which must be addressed in a special manner by the public administration. The coordinated development of certain areas, in which geographic and historical factors play a decisive influence, must be programmed and supported by the government so as to bring us nearer to the ideal of a balanced evolution of every region of the country. Thus the problems of Amazonia, the São Francisco Valley, the Semi-arid, and of Central Brazil must be treated adequately, by adopting the methods that characterize modern regional planning. (p. 41)

In the fifth part of the book, Kubitschek elaborates his ideas on regional planning. After a short introduction, he presents a brief proposal for the "economic valorization of the Amazon". This would include incentives for the improvement of navigation services in the region, the connection by air of Manaus and Belém with the rest of the territory, and support for permanent industrial activities in the two great Amazonian cities, by means of "special stimuli necessary for the creation of certain local industries, especially through long-term credit" (p. 227).

The third section of this chapter, dedicated to regional issues, deals briefly with the "Renovation of the São Francisco valley". Here the text is vague, and goes no further than to defend plans and projects already on course in the region.

Kubitschek deals at greater length with questions related to the "Development of the Northeast". In this section, he states that the problems of the so-called "drought polygon" must be approached within the broader issue of economic development in the Northeastern region as a whole. Symptomatically, he argues that the problem of the semi-arid region depends, crucially, on the industrialization of the cities in the humid zones, without which any investments made in the dry regions would fail (p. 233). At the center of Kubistchek's strategy for the Northeast would be "a well-conceived plan for the creation of industrial conglomerates across the broad area of influence of the Paulo Afonso dam", to be created with "forceful governmental incentives" (p. 235).

Sections 5 and 8, in the final part of the book, deal succinctly with proposals for other disadvantaged regions, such as the Rio Doce Valley in the state of Minas Gerais; the "industrial conglomerate" in Santa Catarina; central Brazil; and the federal territories. In light of its anticipated spatial impacts, the text also emphasizes the projected transfer of the federal capital to Brasília and, from there, the planned construction of a road connecting it to Belém. Kubitschek believed that this road would "in the future become one of Brazil's most important lines of economic and geo-political integration" (p. 242).[23]

It is worth noting the inclusion of "regional and urban planning" as a primary objective of Kubitchek's government program. However, apart from the rather more detailed treatment of the economic potential of the Northeastern region – brought about by the Paulo Afonso power plant – the regional question did not seem to be at the heart of the government's economic development agenda. As shall become clear shortly, this impression would be confirmed when the Targets Program itself was disclosed.

2.3.3   The Targets Program

The authors of the Targets Program, in their introduction,[24] drew attention to both the operational and the political constraints that led the government to choose a "programming" effort over a more ambitious "planning" initiative. At the same time, they argued that the program should focus on key sectors, in a clear indication of the nature of the government's approach.

The sectoral approach notwithstanding, the document did not fail to allude explicitly to the regional question, thus echoing concerns which had been voiced earlier in Kubitschek's government program. In this respect, it singled out investments being made in "the most backward areas of the country, such as Amazonia, the São Francisco Valley, the 'Drought Polygon' and the southwestern border region . . . which only indirectly fall into the Targets Program", but that "tend to be guided by the techniques of regional planning in areas of early settlement and economic development" (p. 19).[25]

Planned investments in the transport sector – including roads, railways, ports and navigation – were perceived as instrumental in achieving greater territorial integration. The same might be said of projects in the energy sector (generation and distribution), particularly those connected to the Paulo Afonso power plant and reservoir, and its attendant impacts on the Northeastern region.

Observation of the spatial destination of the resources envisioned by the Targets Program offers a first glimpse of its regional impacts. Of the 30 targets into which the program was divided, only in nine cases are there indications as to the geographical destination of planned investments, namely: electric energy (Target 1), oil (Targets 4 and 5), railways (Targets 6 and 7), roads (Targets 8 and 9), steel (Target 19) and the automotive industry (Target 27). These targets involved approximately 73 percent of domestic currency resources and 65 percent of foreign currency investments.

As expected, targets for which one could find an indication of the spatial allocation of planned investments display a disproportionate concentration of funds in the most developed regions of the country, namely, the Southeast and South. This was the case in the energy sector (95 percent of resources), oil refining (67 percent), railway construction (67 percent), road building (78 percent), steel (100 percent), cement (69 percent) and automobiles (almost 100 percent).[26]

Having discussed the intentions of policymakers laid out in the report of the Brazil–USA Joint Commission, Kubitschek's campaign program, and the Targets Program itself, the next section examines the actual outlays and their spatial distribution, thus providing a first-order idea of their regional impacts. Proper assessment of the longer-term regional impacts of those investments requires a look at the behavior of state and regional-level indicators of income per capita over a longer time span. This task will be left to section 2.5 of this chapter.

2.4   THE REGIONAL DIMENSION OF THE TARGETS PROGRAM IN PRACTICE: DISBURSEMENTS UNDER THE PROGRAM

The four-volume report published by the Development Council in December 1960 allows one to assess the extent to which each of the 30 original targets in the program was met. Moreover – and just as in the case of the document of the Targets Program itself – it provides information indicating the spatial allocation of resources (in this case, where the investments were actually made). Below I provide and briefly analyze results on each of the targets discussed in the previous section:

2.4.1   Electric Energy (Target 1)

By the end of 1960, this target was 87.6 percent met in terms of planned capacity expansion. In the case of plants completed between 1956 and

1960, as well as those set to enter operation in 1961, the Southeast witnessed the greatest share of additional generating capacity (78 percent of the total), followed by the South (12.4 percent) and the Northeast (6.7 percent).[27]

2.4.2   Oil Refining (Target 5)

The revised version of this target called for an expansion of refining capacity to 308 000 barrels per day. Once the REDUC refinery in Duque de Caxias in Rio de Janeiro state started operating, total capacity in the country reached 308 600 barrels by 1961; it follows that this target was fully met. The 200 000 barrel per day expansion was derived mostly from refineries located in the Southeast (73.5 percent of the increase); the single refinery in the Northeast accounted for 22.3 percent; with the remainder being accounted for by small refineries in the Southern and Northern regions.

2.4.3   Railway Equipment (Target 6)

By the end of the 1956–1961 period, approximately 76 percent of this target had been met. Loans provided by the BNDE amounted to Cr$14 billion, of which some 20 percent had no clear geographical destination.[28] Of the remaining portion of the funds for which I have information, most was allocated to companies operating in the Southeast (68.5 percent), followed by the South (19.6 percent), Northeast (8.4 percent) and Center-West (3.6 percent).

2.4.4   Railway Construction (Target 7)

This was one of the areas in which the Program was clearly unsuccessful. Of the more than 1600 additional kilometers of railways planned to open for traffic, just 57 percent in the case of main lines and 60 percent of secondary lines were built. In the end, 826.5 kilometers of new track was laid, of which 52 percent was in the Northeast, 26.7 percent in the South, 19.5 percent in the Southeast and 1.5 percent in the Center-West.

2.4.5   Road Asphalting (Target 8)

This target was met almost entirely, reaching a total of 6650 additional kilometers of paved roads by September 1960. Looking at the location of the individual roads benefited by these investments, one notes a regional distribution which is slightly less skewed than in other targets: Southeast

(38.4 percent), South (35 percent), Northeast (16.7 percent), Center-West (9.6 percent) and North (0.3 percent).

2.4.6   Road Building (Target 9)

By September 1960, 13 557 kilometers of new roads had been opened,[29] indicating that the initial target had been exceeded by one-third. As was the case in Target 8, there was a fairly balanced distribution of these new roads across the Brazilian territory: 26.9 percent in the Center-West, 26.5 percent in the Southeast, 25.2 percent in the Northeast, 11.7 percent in the North and 9.7 percent in the South.

2.4.7   Steel (Target 19)

Total capacity in the steel industry increased by over 1.2 million metric tons and met the revised version of the original target. Geographical concentration is striking in this case, in terms of both resource allocation and new capacity. Indeed, just 3 percent of the US$350 million in foreign credit allocated to the steel sector was directed at plants lying outside the Southeast, while 98 percent of the additional capacity was located in that same region.[30]

2.4.8   Cement (Target 22)

The target for cement was 90 percent achieved: of the planned 1.34 million ton capacity expansion, 1.2 million tons were added. Of these, 83 percent referred to units located in the Southeast, 13 percent in the South and 4 percent in the Center-West.

2.4.9   Automobile Industry (Target 27)

The full US$330 million and Cr$17.3 billion invested in the automobile industry up to October 1960 involved manufacturers located in the Southeast.

Summary of Investments

Table 2.2 summarizes the above information and also includes data for the value of Targets Program resources loaned by the National Economic Development Bank in the 1956–60 period.

The table highlights the concentration of Targets Program investments in the wealthier regions (Southeast and South). The exceptions

Table 2.2   Targets Program: regional distribution of selected investments (%)

Variable	Unit	North	North-east	South-east	South	Center-West
Electric Energy	Generating Capacity (MW)	1.7	6.7	78.0	12.4	1.3
Oil Refining	Additional Capacity (bbl/day)	2.5	22.3	73.5	1.7	0.0
Railway Equipment	Km of track	0.0	8.4	68.5	19.6	3.6
Railway Construction	Km of track	0.0	52.3	19.5	26.7	1.5
Road Asphalting	Km of roads	0.3	16.7	38.4	35.0	9.6
Road Building	Km of roads	11.7	25.2	26.5	9.7	26.9
Steel	Additional capacity (tons)	0.0	0.0	98.2	1.8	0.0
Cement	Additional capacity (tons)	0.0	0.0	83.0	13.0	4.0
Automobile Industry	Investments (Cr$ and US$)	0.0	0.0	100.0	0.0	0.0
BNDE Loans	Cr$	0.9	6.2	76.8	13.3	2.8

Source: Author's calculations based on data in Brasil, Presidência da República (1960) and *Mémórias do Desenvolvimento* (2010), pp. 80–82.

are investments in transport (railways and roads) and oil refining, where the Northeastern region received a larger share of resources. Overall, the spatial allocation of Targets Program investments bore little resemblance to the regional distribution of population across the Brazilian territory. Instead, it showed a greater proximity to each region's share of total GDP, as shown in Tables 2.3 and 2.4.

Despite the fragmentary nature of the information provided in Table 2.2 (due to the limitations of the original source), it does allow a first approximation to the issue at hand, namely, a measure of the regional impact of the Targets Program. However, the results so far are short term. In order to assess the medium- to long-term impacts of the program, one needs to look at state and regional-level per capita income data over a longer period of time, which includes the years before, during and after Kubitschek's administration. The next section of the chapter will examine the statistical evidence produced in the regional economics literature.

Table 2.3   *Brazil: evolution of the regional distribution of population,*
1950–70 (%)

Region	1950	1960	1970
North	3.6	3.7	3.9
Northeast	34.6	31.6	30.3
Southeast	43.4	43.8	42.7
South	15.0	16.7	17.6
Center-West	3.4	4.2	5.5
Brazil	100.0	100.0	100.0

Source: Redwood (1978), p. 124.

Table 2.4   *Share of macro regions in Brazilian GDP, 1950–70 (%)*

Regions	1950	1956	1957	1958	1959	1960	1961	1965	1970
North	1.7	2.1	2.5	2.3	2.0	2.3	2.6	2.1	2.2
Northeast	14.5	13.2	13.4	12.8	14.2	14.5	13.8	15.0	11.9
Southeast	66.0	65.5	65.2	65.3	64.2	63.6	63.9	62.6	65.2
South	16.1	16.9	16.8	17.2	17.3	17.3	16.6	17.0	17.0
Center-West	1.7	2.3	2.1	2.4	2.3	2.3	3.0	3.3	3.6
Brazil	100.0	100.0	100.0	100.0	100.0	100.0	100.0	100.0	100.0

Source: Azzoni (1997).

2.5   LONGER-TERM REGIONAL IMPACTS OF THE PROGRAM

Investment projects were approached on an essentially sectoral as opposed to regional basis. As such, the program did not constitute an explicit, deliberate instrument of regional policy, in the sense that it did not contain well-defined guidelines with the final goal of redressing regional imbalances. Yet a set of investment projects on such a scale, concentrated in a relatively short period of time, was bound to have distinct regional effects. In this respect, the program definitely qualified as a case of implicit regional policy.[31]

A natural starting point for an assessment of the longer-term regional impacts of the program should examine the evolution of the spatial distribution of economic activity across the Brazilian territory. Since at least Furtado (1970), it has been a well-established fact that from the First World War onwards, the state of São Paulo would concentrate an

Table 2.5   Evolution of the regional distribution of total and sectoral product, 1949–70 (%)

Region	1949				1959				1970			
	Agric.	Ind.	Serv.	Total	Agric.	Ind.	Serv.	Total	Agric.	Ind	Serv.	Total
North	1.7	0.9	2.0	1.7	2.4	1.2	2.3	2.0	3.6	1.1	2.4	2.1
Northeast	19.3	9.7	13.0	13.9	27.9	7.5	12.7	14.4	20.3	5.8	13.1	11.6
Southeast	54.7	75.2	70.8	67.5	38.1	78.2	68.7	65.0	33.8	80.3	63.8	65.5
South	21.1	13.4	12.9	15.2	26.9	12.2	14.1	16.2	35.4	11.9	16.4	17.2
Center-West	3.2	0.7	1.4	1.7	4.6	0.8	2.2	2.4	7.0	0.9	4.4	3.6
Brazil	100.0	100.0	100.0	100.0	100.0	100.0	100.0	100.0	100.0	100.0	100.0	100.0

Source: Redwood (1978), p. 127.

increasing share of national output. Between 1920 and 1950, São Paulo's share of the industrial workforce increased from 29.1 percent to 38.6 percent, while in the Northeast it declined from 27 percent to 17 percent. According to Furtado, industrial concentration in São Paulo expanded even further following the Second World War, with the state's share of national manufacturing output increasing from 39.6 percent to 45.3 percent between 1948 and 1955 (Furtado, 1970, p. 238).

If we extend Furtado's time frame to 1959, to cover the early years of the Targets Program, census data become available, allowing for a more precise picture of the distribution of national output over time. Table 2.5 shows that between 1949 and 1959, the Southeast's predominance in the manufacturing domain continued in the 1950s. The Northeast's share of industrial output during the same decade declined from 10 percent to 7.5 percent of the total, possibly an early indication of the concentration of Targets Program investments in the wealthier regions of Brazil.

Moving into the 1960s, a starker picture of the Northeast's relative industrial decline emerges. Indeed, while the secondary sector increased its share of national output by almost 10 percentage points between 1949 and 1970 (from 22 percent to 30.4 percent), its share of the Northeastern economy remained roughly stable, having declined slightly between 1949 and 1959, but recovering by 1970. It was almost as if the rapid industrialization drive which characterized the Southeast (and, to a lesser extent, the South) over these two decades had altogether bypassed the Northeast.

The analysis up to this point can be enriched if attention is shifted to the behavior of per capita income indicators at both the state and regional levels, and how they varied over the 1950–70 period. Different rates of growth provide a measure of the extent to which income disparities within

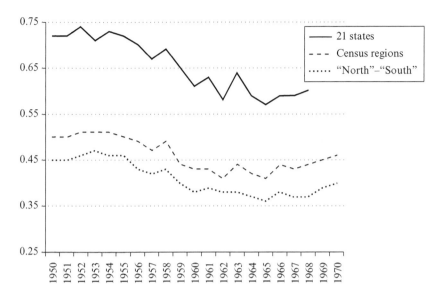

Figure 2.1   *Brazil: alternative measures of regional inequality in per capita GDP, 1950/1970 (Vw)*

and between regions have diverged or converged over time. Analysis of the post-1955 period allows one to infer the long-term impacts of the Targets Program, which complement the short-term effects discussed in the previous section of the chapter.

The literature on convergence and divergence between Brazilian states has established a few stylized facts concerning the evolution of income disparities in the 1950–70 period, and can be summarized as follows:

- 1950–55: relative stability, with variations (average GDP growth of 6.7 percent p.a.).
- 1955–61: sharp drop, except in 1958 (GDP growth of 8.1 percent p.a.).
- 1962–65: moderate reduction, with variations (GDP growth of 3.2 percent p.a.).
- 1965–70: increase (GDP growth of 8.6 percent p.a.).

From the standpoint of the present discussion, the most interesting subperiods are those which either coincided with the Targets Program (1955–61), or followed it (1962–65 and 1965–70). Figure 2.1 shows a sharp drop in all three indicators of regional inequality between 1955 and 1961.[32] This result brings with it an apparent paradox, however. As discussed earlier, the Targets Program intensified an earlier trend pointing towards greater spatial concentration of productive activity (especially industry) in the South and Southeast.[33] Yet the graph indicates precisely the opposite in terms of what one should expect: namely, that income disparities were falling instead of rising during the implementation of the investment plans of the program. How can these two stylized facts be reconciled?

For Redwood (1977), the reason behind this contradiction is apparent. Yes, he says, the program did lead towards a greater concentration of economic activity in the richer regions of Brazil and, as such, should have occasioned increasing – and not decreasing – intra-regional income disparities. However, contrasting behavior of the agricultural sector in different regions, and the impact of the Targets Program on migratory flows, combined to produce the counter-intuitive result captured by the falling curves in Figure 2.1.

Regarding the first of these two points, Redwood (1977) argues that the severe crisis which hit the São Paulo coffee sector in the mid-1950s caused a sharp decline in that state's agricultural output. At the same time, Northeastern agriculture grew at rates above the national average. The result of these two opposing trends in the primary sector was that the Northeastern economy grew at a higher pace than the country as a whole and, as a result, regional disparities in income per capita decreased.[34]

As for the second point – the intense shift of labor from the Northeast to the Southeast – the author reinforces an argument originally made by Graham (1969), which emphasizes the role migratory flows played as safety valves for the Northeastern labor market. Migration from the Northeast artificially increased the per capita income of those who stayed in the region, while the opposite took place in the Southeast.

A combination of a relatively better performance of the agricultural sector in the Northeast, with outmigration from that region in the second half of the 1950s, resulted in minor increases in both absolute and relative incomes in the Northeast, North and Center-West. Thus, a degree of convergence in regional income levels during the implementation of the Targets Program was experienced, as shown in Table 2.6.

From 1960, the Brazilian economy experienced a period of economic and political instability. We can identify an interlude characterized by slow growth extending from the short-lived Quadros administration (1961) until the start of the so-called "Economic Miracle" in 1967. There were multiple causes for this stagnation, and they involved a combination of: (1) political instability; (2) the effects of two stabilization programs (the Trienal Plan and PAEG, the Plano de Ação Econômica do Governo); and (3) the expected slowdown in capacity expansion in the wake of the Targets Program projects.

Table 2.6   Evolution of regional relative output ratios, 1949–70

Region	1949	1959	1970
North	0.49	0.55	0.55
Northeast	0.41	0.45	0.39
Southeast	1.59	1.49	1.53
South	1.03	0.98	0.97
Center-West	0.51	0.56	0.67
Brazil	1.00	1.00	1.00
NE/SE	0.26	0.30	0.25
NE/SP	0.20	0.22	0.19
SP/SE	1.32	1.40	1.35

Source: Redwood (1978), p.467.

As seen in Figure 2.1, this period of relative stagnation (when com-pared to the rapid growth witnessed in the Kubitschek years and during the "Miracle") was accompanied by an additional drop in the indicators of state and regional per capita income disparity.[35] In this respect, it con-tinued the trend which had begun in the mid-1950s, though at a slower rate. The reason for this continuation rests on different bases, however. Unlike what happened during the years of the Targets Program, it was the retraction in manufacturing activity in the more industrialized areas (most notably, São Paulo), that was responsible for the poor regions "catching up" economically.

After almost a decade and a half when state and regional income dis-parities fell, all indicators point to an increase by the late 1960s (see Figure 2.1, and Table 2A.1 in the Appendix). The reason for this was the start of a new cycle of rapid, manufacturing-led economic growth. The "Miracle", spanning from the late 1960s to the early 1970s, was based on a vigor-ous expansion of the durable goods sector (and, to a lesser extent, the capital goods and construction industries). As such, it ended up benefiting Southeastern states disproportionably, where the bulk of this sector was located. This was an additional, if indirect, effect of the Targets Program, in the sense that it had been responsible for the consolidation of São Paulo (and, more broadly, the Southeastern and Southern states) as the center for the production of capital goods and consumer durables. These were precisely the sectors that, years later, would lie at the heart of the tremen-dous industrial expansion of the "Miracle" years.

In closing, one may reasonably assert that the worsening of the regional income disparity indicators in the late 1960s was an indirect result of the Targets Program, given that it derived from the disproportionate growth during the "Miracle" period, of the very sectors that were at the heart of the program (and that were located in the Southeast/South). The aggravation of this trend was only avoided through the introduction, in the 1970s, of explicit regional policies, giving rise to a long period of reduction in regional disparities and the reversion and subsequent reconcentration of economic activity in Brazil.[36]

2.6　FINAL REMARKS

As discussed above, the document laying out the Targets Program, while mentioning the need to address the issue of regional imbalances, in practice repeated the same arguments found in the report of the Joint Brazil–United States Commission, which favored the allocation of scarce resources to richer regions. Examination of the geographical destination of Targets Program resources – both at the planning stage and in practice – revealed that most investments were channeled into the Southeastern and Southern regions, with the exception of the transport sector (rail and road), where geographical distribution of resources appears to have been more balanced. In this respect, one may confidently state that the Targets Program helped to aggravate earlier regional imbalances in Brazil.

The chapter argues that, in parallel to the concentration of manufacturing activity in the Southeast (a phenomenon which actually predated the Targets Program), there was a process of deconcentration of income among the different regions of Brazil. In other words – and contrary to what one would expect – there was actually a reduction in interregional income differences in the late 1950s, and this amid the increased concentration of the dynamic sectors of industry in the South and Southeast brought about by the Targets Program.

According to Redwood (1977), this counter-intuitive pattern derived, in part, from the different behavior of the agricultural sectors of São Paulo and the Northeast in the second half of the decade. In particular, the crisis which hit the *paulista* coffee sector during the Kubitschek administration caused the São Paulo economy to grow at a slower rate than other areas. When one adds to this the intense migratory flows into the Southeast, attracted by the projects included in the Targets Program, the additional channel through which per capita incomes in the poorer regions grew at a faster pace in this period becomes clear.

Such convergence of regional per capita incomes carried over into the 1960s, although at a slower pace. The explanation lies in the economic stagnation and political instability experienced by Brazil at this time. The poor performance of the economy – which hit the industrial sector particularly hard – ended up penalizing the South and Southeast, thus causing further reduction in inter-regional income disparities.

However, from the moment Brazil entered the new and vigorous manufacturing-led growth cycle of the "Miracle" years (1968–73), a renewed phase of widening income disparities arose. The previous concentration of manufacturing activity in the Southern and Southeastern states resulted in higher-than-average growth in these very same regions. Bearing in mind that industrial growth in the early years of the "Miracle" was based significantly on previously installed capacity inherited from Targets Program projects (that is, with little new investment), then it is not an overstatement to claim that the long-term impacts of the program – as with the short-term effects, discussed above – tended to reinforce spatial concentration of production and income. In this respect, the program contributed to a worsening of regional disparities from the turn of the 1960s to the 1970s.

In conclusion, it may be said that the regional impacts of the Targets Program were long-lasting and aggravated pre-existing regional income disparities. In the short run, the program helped to concentrate resources even further in the most developed regions. The longer-term impacts of this regional bias were felt during the "Miracle" years, when vigorous growth of the durable consumer goods sector helped to intensify disparities in regional income. On the other hand, periods that witnessed a decline in per capita income disparities between states and regions, such as in the periods 1955–61 and 1962–65, can be explained: in the former case, by an exogenous factor (São Paulo's agricultural crisis) coupled with internal migratory flows from the "periphery" to the "center"; and in the latter, by the stagnation that befell the manufacturing sector, which was already highly concentrated in the Southeast. With the exception of the coffee crisis in São Paulo, these were all phenomena directly or indirectly associated with the Targets Program.

NOTES

1. Comments from Rodrigo Simões and participants at the Porto de Galinhas Conference to an earlier version of the chapter are gratefully acknowledged. The usual caveats apply.
2. For detailed treatments of the Targets Program see Lessa (1982), Sikkink (1991), Sochaczewski (1993), Lafer (2002) and Leopoldi (2002).
3. Cano (1985) is an important exception, in that the author discusses in great detail the regional impacts of policies implemented during the so-called "heavy industry" period – which includes the Targets Program.
4. In this respect, see Sikkink (1991), especially Chapter 2.

5. On this latter point, see Lafer (2002).
6. The Joint Commission was set up in December 1950 and it operated between July 1951 and December 1953, after which it published its final report.
7. The construction of the new capital, Brasília, was considered by President Kubitschek as a "synthesis-target", and was not part of the 30-target program.
8. Given that during the period covered by the Targets Program Brazil operated under a complex – and changing – system of multiple exchange rates, it would be virtually impossible to provide correspondent figures in US dollars whenever investments are quoted in Cruzeiros in the text.
9. Officials estimated that these investments would amount to approximately 2.5 percent of Brazilian gross domestic product (GDP) in 1956, peaking at 7.6 percent in 1958 and declining thereafter to 4.1 percent in 1961 (Brasil, Presidência da República, 1958, Vol. 1, p.46). Since these estimates were based on the assumption that the economy would grow at the same rate as was observed between 1953 and 1956, and that the program actually allowed for a higher rate of GDP growth, the relative weight of those investments turned out to be lower than these original projections.
10. Brasil, Presidência da República (1958), Vol. 1, p.46.
11. See Orenstein and Sochaczewski (1989), p.180.
12. See Abreu (1994) and Villela (2005).
13. See Joint Brazil–United States Economic Development Commission (1953).
14. See Malan (1986).
15. Joint Brazil–United States Economic Development Commission (1953), p.80.
16. "the allocation of funds, on a project by project basis, actually led to a pattern of investment that reflected rather closely the real economic importance of the various regions of the Brazilian economy" Joint Brazil–United States Economic Development Commission, 1953, p.81.
17. Bearing in mind that, according to the official definition at the time, the South comprised not only the states of Rio Grande do Sul, Santa Catarina and Paraná, but also São Paulo. The Eastern region, in turn, was made up of the following states: Sergipe, Bahia, Minas Gerais, Espírito Santo, Rio de Janeiro and the Federal District (that is, the city of Rio de Janeiro). Unless otherwise indicated, this chapter will use the modern-day division of the Brazilian territory into five so-called macro regions, namely: North, Northeast, Southeast, South and Center-West.
18. According to the Commission, the few investments allocated to the rail network in the Northeast – despite its parlous state – was justified on the grounds that those resources were not aimed at overcoming a transport bottleneck in the region, but rather to averting, for security reasons, the complete breakdown of the local railway infrastructure.
19. Still, these two sectors did not account for more than 10 percent of investments in the 41 projects drawn up by the Commission.
20. This is the first stage of the project (now known as Paulo Afonso I), comprising two generating units with a combined capacity of 120 MW.
21. See Joint Brazil–United States Economic Development Commission (1953), p.221. As will be shown later, a similar argument was to be made in the document detailing the Targets Program.
22. See Kubitschek (1955), p.9. According to Campos (2004), Vol. I, p.267, this campaign document, later published in book form, had been ghost-authored by Roberto Campos himself and Lucas Lopes, later to become the chief economic officials in the Kubitschek government.
23. This point was emphasized by both Juscelino Kubitschek and Lucas Lopes, chief coordinator of the program, in interviews given years later to Celso Lafer. See Lafer (2002), pp.56–7.
24. See Brasil, Presidência da República (1958).
25. The case of Brasilia deserved a special mention in the text, which pointed out its "major economic significance, for it shall cause a broadening of the human occupation over vast areas of the hinterland, thus incorporating into the country's assets regions

of considerable economic potential. Several projects within the Targets Program, especially in the transport sector, are articulated into the plan for Brasília" (Brasil, Presidência da República, 1958).

26. This includes resources earmarked for roads connecting the Southeast to the Northeast (BR-4 e BR-5, or Rio-Bahia) and to the Center-West (BR-31, or Vitória-Cuiabá).

27. Percentages calculated from information furnished by Brasil, Presidência da República (1960), Vol. 1. Note that this proportion would increase to more than 85 percent were we to include the expected additional capacity to come on stream in 1963, provided by the Três Marias (Minas Gerais) plant and 50 percent of the expected potential from the Furnas plant in São Paulo and Minas Gerais.

28. These were funds channeled into the National Railway Department and the state-owned railway company, RFFSA.

29. This figure includes 1750 km of "other roads" for which the report of the Development Council does not provide further information.

30. Such concentration would be reinforced over the course of the 1960s, when new plants located in the states of São Paulo (Cosipa), Minas Gerais (Usiminas) and Espírito Santo (Cia. Ferro e Aço de Vitória) added another 1.2 million tons of capacity. Cosinor, located in the Northeast (Pernambuco state), would represent a mere 50000 additional tons when it started operations in 1965.

31. For the distinction between explicit and implicit regional policies, see Redwood (1978).

32. The only exception to this downward trend occurred in 1958, when a severe drought hit the Northeast, causing a brief deterioration of this indicator.

33. As already noted, among others, by Baer (1965), Baer and Geiger (1978), Lessa (1982) and Cano (1985).

34. In this regard, Redwood (1977, p. 523) finds strong (positive) correlation between the variables "real value of coffee output in São Paulo" and "annual values of the regional inequality indicator (Vw)".

35. This result had already been noted by Azzoni (1997). Econometric tests carried out by that author indicate that the rate of growth of national GDP causes the rate of convergence in per capita state-level income to decrease in a given five-year period, with convergence increasing again in the subsequent five-year period.

36. For details of this process, see Diniz (1993).

REFERENCES

Abreu, Marcelo de Paiva (1994), "Crescimento Rápido e Limites do Modelo Autárquico", in Bolívar Lamounier, Dionísio D. Carneiro and Marcelo de P. Abreu (eds), *50 Anos de Brasil: 50 Anos de Fundação Getulio Vargas*, Rio de Janeiro: Editora FGV, pp. 146–155.

Azzoni, Carlos Roberto (1997), "Concentração Regional e Dispersão das Rendas Per Capita Estaduais: análise a partir das séries históricas estaduais de PIB, 1939–1995", *Estudos Econômicos*, **27** (3), 341–393.

Baer, Werner (1965), *Industrialization and Economic Development in Brazil*, Homewood, IL: Yale University Press.

Baer, Werner and Pedro P. Geiger (1978), "Industrialização, Urbanização e a Persistência das Desigualdades Regionais no Brasil", in Werner Baer, Pedro P. Geiger and Paulo R. Haddad (eds), *Dimensões do Desenvolvimento Brasileiro*, Rio de Janeiro: Campus, pp. 65–110.

Brasil, Presidência da República, Conselho de Desenvolvimento (1958), *Programa de Metas*, 3 vols, Rio de Janeiro: O Conselho.

Brasil, Presidência da República, Conselho de Desenvolvimento (1960), *Relatório* do Conselho de Desenvolvimento sobre a Execução do Programa de Metas no Qüinqüênio 1956/1960, apresentado ao excelentíssimo Sr. Presidente da República, 4 vols, Rio de Janeiro: O Conselho.

Campos, Roberto de Oliveira (2004), *A Lanterna na Popa: memórias*, 4th edn, Rio de Janeiro: Topbooks.

Cano, Wilson (1985), *Desequilíbrios Regionais e Concentração Industrial no Brasil, 1930/1970*, São Paulo: Global.

Diniz, Clélio C. (1993), "Desenvolvimento Poligonal no Brasil: nem desconcentração nem contínua polarização", *Nova Economia*, **31** (1), 35–64.

Furtado, Celso (1970), *Formação Econômica do Brasil*, 10th edn, São Paulo: Cia. Editora Nacional.

Graham, Douglas H. (1969), "Padrões de Convergência e Divergência do Crescimento Econômico Regional e das Migrações no Brasil – 1940/1960", *Revista Brasileira de Economia*, **23** (3), 53–76.

Joint Brazil–United States Economic Development Commission (1953), *The Development of Brazil: Report*, Washington, DC: Institute of Inter-American Affairs, Foreign Relations Administration.

Kubitschek, Juscelino (1955), *Diretrizes Gerais do Plano Nacional de Desenvolvimento*, Belo Horizonte: Oscar Nicolai.

Lafer, Celso (2002), *JK e o Programa de Metas (1956–1961): processo de planejamento e sistema político no Brasil*, Rio de Janeiro: Editora FGV.

Leopoldi, Maria A. (2002), "Crescendo em Meio à Incerteza: a política econômica do Governo JK (1956–60)", in Angela Castro Gomes (ed.), *O Brasil de JK*, 2nd edn, Rio de Janeiro: Editora FGV, pp. 107–142.

Lessa, Carlos (1982), *Quinze Anos de Política Econômica*, 3rd edn, São Paulo: Brasiliense.

Malan, Pedro S. (1986), "Relações Econômicas Internacionais do Brasil (1945–1964)", in B. Fausto (ed.), *História Geral da Civilização Brasileira*, Tome III, Vol. 4, 2nd edn, São Paulo: Difel, pp. 51–106.

Mémórias do Desenvolvimento (2010), **4** (4), September.

Orenstein, Luiz and Antonio Claudio Sochaczewski (1989), "Democracia com Desenvolvimento: 1956–1961", in Marcelo de P. Abreu (ed.), *A Ordem do Progresso: cem anos de política econômica republicana, 1889–1989*, Rio de Janeiro: Campus, pp. 171–195.

Redwood III, John (1977), "Evolução Recente das Disparidades de Renda Regional no Brasil", *Pesquisa e Planejamento Econômico*, **7** (3), 485–550.

Redwood III, John (1978), "Implicit and Explicit Regional Policies in Brazil", Unpublished PhD thesis, University of California, Berkeley.

Sikkink, Kathryn (1991), *Ideas and Institutions: Developmentalism in Brazil and Argentina*, Ithaca, NY, USA and London, UK: Cornell University Press.

Sochaczewski, Antonio Cláudio (1993), *Desenvolvimento Econômico e Financeiro do Brasil: 1952–1968*, São Paulo: Trajetória Cultural.

Souza, Nali de Jesus de (1993), "Desenvolvimento Polarizado e Desequilíbrios Regionais no Brasil", *Análise Econômica*, **11**, 29–59.

Villela, André (2005), "O Governo JK e a Crise Não Resolvida (1956–63)", in Fabio Giambiagi, André Villela, Lavínia Barros de Castro and Jennifer Hermann (eds), *Economia Brasileira Contemporânea*, Rio de Janeiro: Campus, pp. 45–78.

APPENDIX

Table 2A.1   *Brazil: alternative measures of regional inequality in income per capita, 1939–85 (V_W coefficients of variation)*

Anos	State-level			Macroregions		State of SP/Rest of Brazil
	Williamson	Haddad/Andrade	N.J.Souza	Redwood III	N.J. Souza	N.J. Souza
1939	0.50	0.78	0.78	–	0.43	0.36
1947	0.69	0.70	0.71	–	0.45	0.40
1950	0.73	0.72	0.73	0.50	0.50	0.45
1955	0.69	0.72	0.71	0.50	0.50	0.46
1960	–	0.61	0.62	0.43	0.43	0.42
1965	–	0.57	0.59	0.41	0.39	0.41
1970	–	–	0.65	0.46	0.49	0.52
1975	–	–	0.60	–	0.47	0.47
1980	–	–	0.53	–	0.43	0.41
1985	–	–	0.44	–	0.37	0.30

Source: Souza (1993), Table 2.

3. Regional imbalances in Brazil according to social inclusion

Roberto Cavalcanti de Albuquerque

3.1 INTRODUCTION

The purpose of this chapter is to conceive and construct a composite development indicator, the Social Inclusion Index. It aims at measuring and analyzing both the extent of the recent process of accelerated social inclusion which prevailed in Brazil, and its impact on spatial inequalities among regions, states and rural, urban and metropolitan areas.

3.2 THE MEANING OF SOCIAL INCLUSION

Modern democracy is based on three fundamental principles. The first of them is the popular sovereignty, by which, as Montesquieu says, "the people as a body" (the political commonwealth) "has the sovereign power".[1]

The second principle, representation, legitimates the partial transfer of political power by the people (the electorate) through a regulated decision process (the elections) to their elected representatives, with mandates limited in time and periodically renewable. The authors of *The Federalist* (1787–88), Alexander Hamilton, James Madison and John Jay, call this system a "popular government" or "republican government".[2] John Stuart Mill prefers to name it "representative government", considering it, "ideally, the best form of governing".[3] For him, "there ought to be no pariahs in a full-grown and civilized nation; no persons disqualified, except through their own default".[4]

According to the third principle of modern democracy, political power, besides being exercised directly or indirectly by the people, must be employed to their benefit. This principle was announced by Pericles in 430 BC when he said that Athens was a democracy because its government was beneficial to the many and not to the few.[5] A direct democracy, the Athenian, where the "people" included only males 20 years and over, excluding women, slaves, foreigners: this represented around 30 000 citizens in the time of Pericles, a mere 12 percent of the 250 000 inhabitants of Attica.[6]

The eighteenth century's thinkers considered a minimum of economic sufficiency an essential condition for the right to vote and therefore for democracy. Hamilton affirms that "a power over a man's subsistence amounts to a power over his will".[7] In the same vein, Kant says that the vote "presupposes the independence or self-sufficiency of the individual citizen".[8]

Based on these principles, the nineteenth century's political thinking has evolved to consider that democracy must also be accomplished in the economic and social dimensions, thus avoiding, or discouraging, inequalities and injustices which may contaminate political liberty.[9]

As a corollary of this conceptual evolution, governments were asked to provide a fully inclusive educational system, capable of assuring a minimum level of schooling for all. From the viewpoint of the eighteenth and nineteenth-century philosophers, "liberal education" only – liberal because oriented towards the formation of "good judgment" and critical conscience, is able to qualify the individual for democratic practice in general and the right to vote in particular.[10] Equal educational opportunity for all became thus a state obligation.[11]

During the twentieth century the idea and practice of political, social and economic democracy spread throughout the world, viewed as capable of amply guaranteeing participation rights in open societies, and of ensuring productive inclusiveness and sufficient income. By the end of the century, a new globalization wave, emerging with informatics and telematics, announced a society and an economy based on knowledge and information.[12]

The concept of social inclusion is rooted in these ideas and practices. For the purposes of this chapter, it is nonetheless advisable to capture its three essential dimensions. The first is economic inclusiveness. It occurs by means of a stable productive occupation, socially protected and able to provide an income sufficient to the attainment of the individual's or family's basic needs, in a dynamic economy where income and wealth are well distributed.

The second dimension is educational inclusiveness. It implies the acquisition of the abilities and skills necessary for living and participating in an economy and society based on knowledge and information.

The third and last dimension is digital inclusion, that is, access to information and telematics tools, which supposes competence, acquired through specific training, in the codes, languages and skills that are deemed necessary by society.

3.3   THE SOCIAL INCLUSION INDEX (SII)

The Social Inclusion Index (SII) was calculated for Brazil as a whole, its five great regions, the three household situations (rural, urban and metropolitan) and the 27 states, the Federal District of Brasília included among them (see Figure 3.1). It aims at measuring the phenomenon of social inclusion as already conceived. It is a composite and comprehensive index, integrated by three components and 12 subcomponents.

The first component, employment and income, corresponds to the Economic Inclusiveness Index. It is formed by four subcomponents or indicators: (1) the occupation rate, that is, the percentage of the economically active population (EAP), which is occupied; (2) the rate of employment formalization, that is, the percentage of the remunerated employees formally contracted and socially protected by the national social security

Figure 3.1   Brazil, its regions and states

system; (3) the proportion of non-poor in the population; and (4) the coefficient of equality, that is, the complement to one of the Gini coefficient.

The second component, education and knowledge, corresponds to the Educational Inclusiveness Index. It is also formed by four indicators: (1) the rate of literacy of the population 15 years old or more; (2) the percentage of persons 15 years old or more and with four years and more of schooling; (3) the percentage of persons 20 years old or more and with nine years and more of schooling; and (4) the percentage of persons 24 years old or more and with 12 years and more of schooling.

The third and last component, information and communication, corresponds to the Digital Inclusion Index. It is formed by four other indicators: the percentage of households with: (1) at least one microcomputer; (2) access to the Internet; (3) a television set; (4) a telephone set, fixed or mobile.[13]

For the construction of the SII a database was formed from special tabulations of IBGE's PNADS for 2001, 2008 and 2009.[14] An estimate of the SII for 2010 was made by projecting the tendency verified between 2001 and 2008–09.

3.4   THE SII: AN OVERVIEW

Table 3.1 constructs a decreasing scale of social inclusion for Brazil (total, rural, urban and metropolitan), its regions (total, rural, urban and metropolitan) and states in 2009. Thirteen of these social situations obtain levels of social inclusion considered medium-high (SII lower than 8.50 and equal to or higher than 7.00); 27 situations have social inclusions considered medium-low (SII lower than 7.00 and equal to or higher than 5.00); and ten other situations have social inclusions considered low (SII lower than 5.00).[15]

The best grade goes to the southern state of Santa Catarina, with an SII of 8.14, followed by the metropolitan South (which corresponds to the metropolitan areas of Curitiba in the state of Paraná, and Porto Alegre in the state of Rio Grande do Sul) with an SII of 8.12; and by the urban South with a SII of 7.88. The Federal District (which corresponds to the metropolitan Center-West) comes in the 4th place, with an SII of 7.80, followed by the state of São Paulo, with an SII of 7.78.

Brazil as a whole occupies 21st place, with an SII of 6.51; metropolitan Brazil, 13th place (grade 7.37); urban Brazil, 17th place (grade 6.68); and rural Brazil, 48th place (grade 4.10).

The rank of regions according to the SII is headed by the South (grade 7.63, 6th place), followed the Southeast (grade 7.38, 12th place),

Table 3.1   The Social Inclusion Index (SII), 2009–10: Brazil, regions, areas and states

Rank, SII 2009	Brasil, regions, areas, states	2009	Growth* 2001–09	SII 2010 (estimated)	
Medium-high social inclusion: SII of 2009 lower than 8.50 and equal or higher than 7.00					
1	Santa Catarina	8.14	3.8	8.46	SC
2	Metropolitan South	8.12	3.7	8.43	SUM
3	Urban South	7.88	4.0	8.21	SUU
4	Federal District**	7.80	4.0	8.23	DF
5	São Paulo	7.78	3.9	8.09	SP
6	South	7.63	4.2	7.96	SU
7	Metropolitan Southeast	7.63	3.9	7.93	SDM
8	Urban Southeast	7.50	4.3	7.83	SDU
9	Paraná	7.49	4.9	7.86	PR
10	Rio Grande do Sul	7.48	3.9	7.78	RS
11	Rio de Janeiro	7.40	4.0	7.70	RJ
12	Southeast	7.38	4.3	7.70	SD
13	Metropolitan Brazil	7.37	4.0	7.67	BRM
Medium-low social inclusion: SII of 2009 lower than 7.00 and equal or higher than 5.00					
14	Espírito Santo	6.86	5.4	7.24	ES
15	Urban Center-West	6.73	5.3	7.09	COU
16	Center-West	6.69	5.5	7.07	CO
17	Urban Brazil	6.68	4.8	7.01	BRU
18	Minas Gerais	6.66	5.1	7.01	MG
19	Mato Grosso do Sul	6.62	4.9	6.95	MS
20	Mato Grosso	6.51	6.3	6.94	MT
21	Brazil	6.51	4.8	6.82	BR
22	Goiás	6.42	5.7	6.78	GO
23	Metropolitan North	6.34	4.4	6.63	NOM
24	Rondônia	6.17	4.7	6.46	RO
25	Metropolitan Northeast	6.16	5.0	6.48	NEM
26	Roraima	6.14	5.7	6.51	RR
27	Acre	5.97	4.1	6.22	AC
28	Amapá	5.86	2.0	6.00	AP
29	Rural South	5.79	5.5	6.13	SUR
30	Amazonas	5.78	3.3	5.97	AM
31	Urban North	5.77	5.1	6.07	NOU
32	Tocantins	5.74	9.6	6.32	TO
33	North	5.45	4.3	5.69	NO

Table 3.1 (continued)

Rank, SII 2009	Brasil, regions, areas, states	2009	Growth* 2001–09	SII 2010 (estimated)	
Medium-low social inclusion: SII of 2009 lower than 7.00 and equal or higher than 5.00					
34	Sergipe	5.23	5.6	5.53	SE
35	Rio Grande do Norte	5.22	4.9	5.49	RN
36	Rural Southeast	5.15	7.1	5.53	SDR
37	Urban Northeast	5.13	6.2	5.45	NEU
38	Rural Center-West	5.03	7.6	5.50	COR
39	Ceará	5.02	7.3	5.39	CE
40	Pará	5.01	3.9	5.21	PA
Low social inclusion: SII of 2009 lower than 5.00					
41	Pernambuco	4.88	5.9	5.17	PE
42	Bahia	4.86	7.8	5.24	BA
43	Northeast	4.82	7.0	5.16	NE
44	Paraíba	4.81	5.6	5.08	PB
45	Piauí	4.51	7.9	4.88	PU
46	Alagoas	4.41	8.2	4.77	AL
47	Maranhão	4.40	8.2	4.77	MA
48	Rural Brazil	4.10	8.4	4.52	BRR
49	Rural North	3.92	. . .	3.98	NOR
50	Rural Northeast	3.27	7.9	3.59	NER

Notes: * Average annual growth (%). ** Or metropolitan Center-West.

Sources: IBGE's PNADs (2001, 2008, 2009) (special tabulations from micro data).

the Center-West (6.69, 16th place), the North (5.45, 33th place) and the Northeast (4.82, 43th place).

The rural Northeast is at the bottom of the scale (grade 3.27, 50th place), being preceded by rural North (3.92, 49th place), rural Brazil (mentioned above) and the northeastern states of Maranhão (4.40, 47th place), Alagoas (4.41, 46th place) and Piauí (4.51, 45th place).

Figure 3.2 shows the scale of social inclusion for Brazil, its regions, states and metropolitan, urban and rural areas in 2009, making evident the dominance of medium-low levels of social inclusion.

The average annual growth of the SII for Brazil in 2001–09 was 4.8 percent, significantly superior to its real gross domestic product (GDP) per capita in the same period, which was 2.1 percent.[16] It is clear from

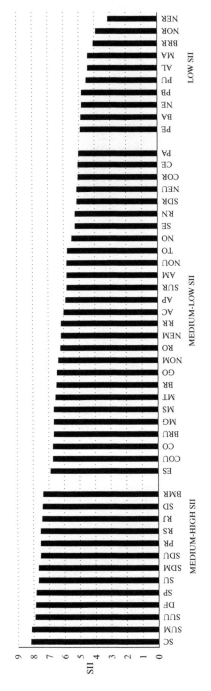

Figure 3.2   The scale of social inclusion in Brazil, 2009

Table 3.1 that there is an inverse correlation between the SII grades and their growth rates. For the SIIs higher than 7.00, for example, they vary from 3.7 percent to 4.9 percent; for the SIIs lower than 5.00, from 5.9 percent to 8.4 percent.[17]

Table 3.1 also presents the SIIs estimated for 2010. According to them, the state of Espírito Santo (SII of 7.24), urban Center-West (7.09), the Center-West as a whole (7.07), urban Brazil (7.01) and the state of Minas Gerais (7.01) would be included in the medium-high group. The states of Bahia (SII of 5.24), Pernambuco (5.17), the Northeast (5.16) and the state of Paraíba (5.08) would be included in the medium-low group.

3.5   BRAZIL'S SII AND ITS COMPONENTS

Table 3.2 and Figure 3.3 shows Brazil's SIIs and their three components for 2001 and 2009, measuring the respective growth rates.

They show that the Brazilian SII increased 46 percent between 2001 and 2009 or 4.8 percent per year, going from grade 4.46 to grade 6.51. The information and communication component, that is, the Digital Inclusion Index, increased more, jumping 63 percent or 6.3 percent yearly. The two other components – employment and income, or the Economic Insertion Index: and education and knowledge, or Educational Insertion Index – show performances which are inferior both to the SII and to the Digital Inclusion Index: 39 percent and 36 percent, respectively, or 4.2 percent, and 3.9 percent annually.

Table 3.2   Brazil: the Social Inclusion Index (SII) and its components, 2001 and 2009

SII and Components	2001	2009	Variation (%) 2001–09	Growth* 2001–09
Social Inclusion Index, SII	4.46	6.51	45.9	4.8
Component: employment and income	4.32	6.02	39.3	4.2
Component: education and knowledge	4.62	6.29	36.3	3.9
Component: information and communication	4.43	7.20	62.5	6.3

Note: * Average annual growth (%).

Sources: IBGE's PNADs (2001, 2009) (special tabulations from micro data).

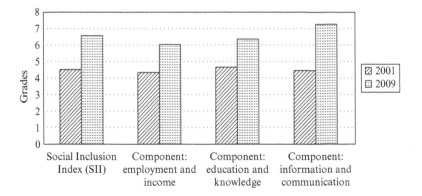

Figure 3.3   Brazil: SII and components, 2001 and 2009

3.6   REGIONAL INEQUALITIES (I): THE SII AND COMPONENTS

Brazil's spatial inequalities, measured by the SII and its three components, are presented in Table 3.3. They tend to be larger in 2001 when compared with 2009, thus confirming the historical tendency for convergence already observed when other development indicators – GDP per capita, for instance – are used.

In 2001, the lowest regional SII, that of the Northeast, corresponded to 63 percent of Brazil's SII; the Economic Insertion Index, to 66 percent; the Educational Insertion Index, to 62 percent; and the Digital Inclusion Index, to 62 percent. In 2009, these percentages were, respectively, 74 percent, 74 percent, 73 percent and 75 percent.

On the other hand, the highest SII, that of the South, was in 2001 23 percent superior to Brazil's; the Economic Insertion Index, 53 percent; the Educational Insertion Index, 9 percent; and the Digital Inclusion Index, 9 percent. For 2009 these figures were, respectively, 17 percent, 34 percent, 8 percent and 11 percent.

This means that social inclusion increased more rapidly in the poorer Northeast than in the richer South. As a matter of fact, it may be said that this applies to the two least developed regions, the Northeast and the Center-West when compared with the two most developed ones, the South and the Southeast.[18] Between 2001 and 2009, the SIIs of the Northeast and the Center-West grew, respectively, at 7.0 percent and 5.5 percent annually, while those of the South and Southeast grew at 4.2 percent and 4.3 percent. As may be seen in Table 3.3, these differentials are similar for the three SIIs components.

Table 3.3   Brazil: regional inequalities measured by the SII and components, 2001 and 2009

SII and components, by region	Grades		Variation, %	Growth*	Brazil = 100	
	2001	2009	2001–09	2001–09	2001	2009
Social Inclusion Index, SII						
Brazil	4.46	6.51	45.9	4.8	100	100
North	3.88	5.45	40.4	4.3	87	84
Northeast	2.81	4.82	71.7	7.0	63	74
Southeast	5.28	7.38	39.9	4.3	118	114
South	5.48	7.63	39.1	4.2	123	117
Center-West	4.37	6.69	53.3	5.5	98	103
Component: employment and income						
Brazil	4.32	6.02	39.3	4.2	100	100
North	3.67	5.35	46.0	4.8	85	89
Northeast	2.84	4.45	56.8	5.8	66	74
Southeast	4.96	6.76	36.3	3.9	115	112
South	6.62	8.07	21.9	2.5	153	134
Center-West	3.96	5.84	47.4	5.0	92	97
Component: education and knowledge						
Brazil	4.62	6.29	36.3	3.9	100	100
North	4.35	5.60	28.7	3.2	94	89
Northeast	2.85	4.58	60.6	6.1	62	73
Southeast	5.50	7.17	30.4	3.4	119	114
South	5.01	6.81	35.8	3.9	109	108
Center-West	4.85	6.61	36.2	3.9	105	105
Component: information and communication						
Brazil	4.43	7.20	62.5	6.3	100	100
North	3.63	5.40	48.9	5.1	82	75
Northeast	2.73	5.43	98.6	9.0	62	75
Southeast	5.38	8.22	53.0	5.5	121	114
South	4.82	8.01	66.1	6.6	109	111
Center-West	4.29	7.41	72.9	7.1	97	103

Note: * Average annual growth (%).

Sources: IBGE's PNADs (2001, 2009) (special tabulations from micro data).

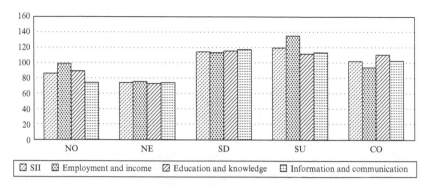

Figure 3.4   SII and its components, 2009 (Brazil = 100)

There was thus in this period a significant reduction in regional disparities as measured by SII. In 2001–09, the coefficient of variation, V, for the SII fell from 24.9 percent to 19.1 percent (falling 23 percent), with Vs for the components of employment and income, and education and knowledge, declining more quickly (from 32.9 percent to 22.7 percent in the first case, a reduction of 31 percent; and from 22.5 percent to 17.1 percent in the second, a reduction of 24 percent). It fell less than the SII for the information and communication component: from 22.7 percent to 20 percent, a reduction of 19 percent.

Figure 3.4 shows the SIIs and their components for the regions in 2009, when Brazil's equaled 100. While those of the Northeast and the North regions are always under 100, those of the South and the Southwest are always over this value. The Center-West oscillates around 100, attaining 105 in the education and knowledge component, 103 in the SII and the information and communication component, and 97 in the employment and income component.

3.7   REGIONAL INEQUALITIES (II): THE SUBCOMPONENTS

The regional inequalities measured according to the 12 subcomponents of the SII are presented, for 2001 and 2009, in Table 3.4. A few remarks may be useful regarding each SII subcomponent.

3.7.1   Employment and Income

The rate of occupation in Brazil increased slowly during the period 2001–09. Reflecting adverse economic conditions, it was 90.7 percent

Table 3.4 Brazil: regional inequalities measured by the SII's subcomponents, 2001 and 2009 (values and Brazil = 100)

SII's subcomponents	Brazil		North		Northeast		Southeast		South		Center-West	
	2001	2009	2001	2009	2001	2009	2001	2009	2001	2009	2001	2009
Component: employment and income												
Occupation rate, %	90.7	91.7	90.4	91.4	91.3	91.1	89.2	91.1	93.5	94.0	91.1	92.1
Rate of employment formalization, %	56.5	62.6	41.4	46.6	39.6	45.8	63.7	70.2	65.5	70.3	48.7	60.3
Proportion of non poor in population, %	64.9	78.2	58.9	74.7	49.3	66.4	70.6	82.1	82.1	92.3	62.2	77.8
Coefficient of equality	4.12	4.63	4.38	4.77	4.04	4.44	4.42	4.96	4.58	5.15	4.10	4.47
Component: education and knowledge												
Rate of litteracy, %	87.6	90.3	88.8	89.4	75.8	81.3	92.5	94.3	92.9	94.5	89.8	92.0
Persons with 4 or more years of schooling, %	58.8	68.8	62.3	67.4	45.8	59.6	64.5	72.9	62.7	72.4	61.2	72.2
Persons with 9 or more years of schooling, %	31.8	45.0	33.5	42.8	23.6	36.5	36.2	50.0	31.6	45.0	33.1	47.4
Persons with 12 or more years of schooling, %	10.2	14.8	6.7	11.1	5.6	9.3	12.8	17.7	11.3	16.9	10.5	16.8
Component: information and communication												
Households with microcomputers, %	12.6	34.7	6.5	20.3	5.2	18.5	17.3	43.7	13.9	42.6	10.6	35.7

Table 3.4 (continued)

SII's subcomponents	Brazil		North		Northeast		Southeast		South		Center-West	
	2001	2009	2001	2009	2001	2009	2001	2009	2001	2009	2001	2009
Component: information and communication												
Households with access to the internet, %	8.5	27.4	4.0	13.2	3.5	14.4	12.0	35.4	8.7	32.8	7.4	28.2
Households with television sets, %	89.1	95.7	86.1	90.8	78.4	92.5	94.4	97.9	92.3	96.9	88.5	95.7
Households with a telephone set, fixed or mobile, %	58.9	84.3	51.6	72.4	35.9	66.8	70.6	88.9	64.8	89.8	59.9	87.9
Component: employment and income												
Occupation rate, %	100	100	100	100	101	99	98	99	103	103	101	100
Rate of employment formalization, %	100	100	73	74	70	73	113	112	116	112	86	96
Proportion of non poor in population, %	100	100	91	96	76	85	109	105	127	118	96	100
Coefficient of equality	100	100	106	103	98	96	107	107	111	111	100	97

38

Component: education and knowledge											
Rate of literacy, %	100	101	99	86	90	106	104	106	105	102	102
Persons with 4 or more years of schooling, %	100	106	98	78	87	110	106	107	105	104	105
Persons with 9 or more years of schooling, %	100	105	95	74	81	114	111	99	100	104	105
Persons with 12 or more years of schooling, %	100	65	74	55	63	125	119	111	114	103	113
Component: information and communication											
Households with microcomputers, %	100	52	58	42	53	138	126	110	123	85	103
Households with access to the internet, %	100	47	48	42	53	141	129	102	120	86	103
Households with television sets, %	100	97	95	88	97	106	102	104	101	99	100
Households with a telephone set, fixed or mobile, %	100	88	86	61	79	120	105	110	107	102	104

Sources: IBGE's PNADs (2001, 2009) (special tabulations from micro data).

in 2001 (corresponding to an unemployment rate of 9.3 percent). In spite of the negative impact of the 2008–09 world recession on Brazilian economic growth, in 2009 it attained 91.7 percent (unemployment was 8.3 percent). The Southeast and the Northeast were responsible for the lower regional rates in 2009 (91.1 percent, or unemployment of 8.9 percent in both cases). In the other regions, discrete variations around Brazil's average occurred, due to local contingencies affecting the productive activities. The South had the best performance in this subcomponent.[19]

The percentage of formally contracted employees evolved in Brazil as a whole from 57 percent in 2001 to 63 percent in 2009, growing 10.4 percent in this period (1.3 percent per year). This formalization rate was low in the Northeast, in spite of jumping from 40 percent in 2001 to 46 percent in 2009, that is, advancing 13.4 percent; and in the North, where it progressed from 41 percent to 47 percent, that is, 14.7 percent. The South maintained pole position in this indicator: it was 66 percent in 2001 and 70 percent in 2009.

The proportion of non-poor in the population increased in Brazil from 65 percent in 2001 to 78 percent in 2009 (poverty reduction from 35 percent to 22 percent, a fall of 13 percent). At one extreme, the Northeast, the percentages were, respectively, 49 percent and 66 percent (poverty reduction from 51 percent to 34 percent, a drop of 17.1 percent). At the other, the South, they were 82 percent and 92 percent (poverty reduction from 18 percent to 8 percent, dropping 10 percent).

The coefficient (or rate) of equality (the complement to 1 of the Gini coefficient multiplied by 10) grew in all the regions, attaining in 2009, 5.15 in the South, 4.96 in the Southeast, 4.77 in the North, 4.47 in the Center-West and 4.44 in the Northeast (it was 4.63 in Brazil). These results follow a trend of slow but stable improvement in interpersonal disparities of income which was effective since 1997.

3.7.2 Education and Knowledge

The already small interregional differentiations observed in 2001 among the literacy rates in Brazil have been further reduced during 2000 to 2010. In 2009, the literacy rate for persons of 15 years and over was 81.3 percent in the Northeast, that is, 90 percent of the national rate of 90.3 percent. That of the North, 89.4 percent, corresponded to 99 percent of the national rate; the one of the Center-West, 92.0 percent, was 2 percent higher; and the rates of the South and the Southeast, 94.5 percent and 94.3 percent, respectively, were 5 percent and 4 percent higher than Brazil's rate.

In 2009, the percentage of persons with four years and more of schooling, being low in the Northeast (59.6 percent, equivalent to 86 percent of Brazil's rate, which was 68.8 percent), was 98 percent of the national rate in the North, 5 percent higher in the South and the Center-West and 6 percent higher in the Southeast.

The regional disparities are more important for the 2009 percentage of persons with 9 years and more of schooling: 81 percent of Brazil's rate in the Northeast, 95 percent in the North, 100 percent in the South, 105 percent in the Center-West and 111 percent in the Southeast. The larger disparities occur, as may be anticipated, for the percentage of persons with 12 years and more of schooling: 63 percent of Brazil's rate in the Northeast, 74 percent in the North, 113 percent in the Center-West, 114 percent in the South and 119 percent in the Southeast.

3.7.3   Information and Communication

The percentage of households equipped with digital inclusion tools (microcomputers, Internet, television and telephone sets) increased rapidly in Brazil during 2000 to 2010.

In 2001 the percentage of Brazil's households with microcomputers was 12.6 percent; with Internet, 8.5 percent; with television sets, 89.1 percent; and with telephone sets, fixed or mobile, 58.9 percent. In 2009 the percentages were, respectively, 34.7 percent, 27.4 percent, 95.7 percent and 84.3 percent.

The Brazilians have therefore experienced a true digital revolution. It encompasses, it is true, pronounced regional imbalances. In the Northeast, the percentage of households with computers in 2001 was only 5.2 percent, a mere 42 percent of Brazil's rate; the percentage of households with Internet was only 3.5 percent, 42 percent of Brazil's rate. These numbers grew significantly in 2009: to 18.5 percent for microcomputers (53 percent of Brazil's rate), 14.4 percent for Internet access (again 53 percent of Brazil's rate). But the inequalities between Brazil and its poorer region remained dramatically high.

It is to be noted that, in 2001, the percentage of households with television sets in the Northeast was already high: 78.4 percent, or 88 percent of Brazil's rate. These numbers increased quickly: to 92.5 percent and 97 percent in 2009, respectively. In this same region, the percentage of households with telephone sets exploded from 35.9 percent in 2001 to 66.8 percent in 2009, equivalent to 61 percent and 79 percent of the national values.

In 2009, the North surpassed the Northeast in the percentage of households with microcomputers (20.3 percent compared with 18.5 percent) and with telephone sets (72.4 percent, compared to 66.8 percent). That region lost to the Northeast in Internet access (13.2 percent compared to 14.4 percent) and television sets (90.8 percent against 92.5 percent).

In this contest for digital inclusion the Center-West surpassed Brazil as a whole in 2009, with the South following the Brazilian pace and the Southeast, well placed ahead, somehow reducing its relative speed.

3.8   METROPOLITAN, URBAN AND RURAL IMBALANCES

Table 3.5 presents the SII by rural, urban and metropolitan areas for Brazil and its regions in 2001 and 2009. Important disparities of levels of social inclusion appear both in Brazil as a whole as well as in each region. Their sizes tend to be large between rural and metropolitan areas, medium between rural and urban areas, and small between urban and metropolitan areas.

In 2001, for example, the SII for rural Brazil was 2.15, for urban Brazil was 4.60 and for metropolitan Brazil was 5.37. These values correspond to 48 percent, 103 percent and 121 percent of Brazil's SII for this same year, which was 4.46. In 2009, these disparities had diminished: the SII for rural Brazil was 4.10, urban Brazil was 6.68, metropolitan Brazil was 7.37. Yet they remained considerably elevated, corresponding, respectively, to 63 percent, 103 percent and 113 percent of the national SII (6.51).

Similar gaps occur within the regions. They were larger in 2001, smaller in 2009, a repetition, on the regional scale, of the phenomenon of convergence already verified among the regions. It also prevails, as shown below, among the states.

These trends may be examined, for Brazil and its regions – and by rural, urban and metropolitan areas – in Table 3.5, particularly in columns 4 to 7. They measure the variations, absolute and relative, as well as the growth rates of the different SIIs between 2001 and 2009.

For Brazil, for instance, the percentage variation of the rural SII was 91.2 percent in this period, that of the urban SII was 45.2 percent, and that of the metropolitan SII was 37.3 percent. The average annual growth rates were, respectively, 8.4 percent, 4.8 percent and 4.0 percent.

In 2001 as well in 2009, the gaps between the rural Northeast (SIIs of 1.78 and 3.27) and Brazil as a whole were very large, the regional figures being 40 percent and 50 percent, respectively, of the national ones in these two years. Large gaps existed in 2009 between the rural North and Brazil (60 percent) and, to some extent, between the rural Center-West and Brazil (77 percent).

Table 3.5   *Brazil and its regions: SIIs for rural, urban and metropolitan*
             areas, 2001 and 2009

Country, regions, areas	SII		Variation, % 2001–09	Growth, %* 2001–09	Brazil = 100	
	2001	2009			2001	2009
Brazil	**4.46**	**6.51**	**45.9**	**4.8**	**100**	**100**
Rural Brazil	2.15	4.10	91.2	8.4	48	63
Urban Brazil	4.60	6.68	45.2	4.8	103	103
Metropolitan Brazil	5.37	7.37	37.3	4.0	121	113
North	**3.88**	**5.45**	**40.4**	**4.3**	**87**	**84**
Rural North	. . .	3.92	. . .	. . .	. . .	60
Urban North	3.87	5.77	49.3	5.1	87	89
Metropolitan North	4.50	6.34	40.9	4.4	101	98
Northeast	**2.81**	**4.82**	**71.7**	**7.0**	**63**	**74**
Rural Northeast	1.78	3.27	84.2	7.9	40	50
Urban Northeast	3.17	5.13	62.0	6.2	71	79
Metropolitan Northeast	4.18	6.16	47.4	5.0	94	95
Southeast	**5.28**	**7.38**	**39.9**	**4.3**	**118**	**114**
Rural Southeast	2.97	5.15	73.4	7.1	67	79
Urban Southeast	5.34	7.50	40.6	4.3	120	115
Metropolitan Southeast	5.61	7.63	35.9	3.9	126	117
South	**5.48**	**7.63**	**39.1**	**4.2**	**123**	**117**
Rural South	3.78	5.79	53.0	5.5	85	89
Urban South	5.75	7.88	36.9	4.0	129	121
Metropolitan South	6.05	8.12	34.2	3.7	136	125
Center-West	**4.37**	**6.69**	**53.3**	**5.5**	**98**	**103**
Rural Center-West	2.80	5.03	80.0	7.6	63	77
Urban Center-West	4.45	6.73	51.4	5.3	100	104
Metropolitan Center-West	5.69	7.80	37.1	4.0	128	120

Note: * Average annual growth (%).

Sources: IBGE's PNADs (2001, 2009) (special tabulations from micro data).

Table 3.5 also indicates that the advantages of the metropolitan South, Southeast and Center-West were considerably attenuated between 2001 and 2009 and shows the advancement of their urban areas towards the levels of social inclusion achieved by their metropolitan counterparts.

Based on Table 3.5, the gaps in social inclusion among rural, urban and metropolitan areas presented in Table 3.6 cover Brazil as a whole and its five regions for 2001 and 2009. These gaps are of three kinds: urban–rural, metropolitan–urban and metropolitan–rural, and correspond to

Table 3.6   Brazil and regions: gaps of social inclusion, 2001 and 2009

Country, regions	2001	2009	Variação, %
Urban–rural			
Brazil	2.14	1.63	−24.02
North	. . .	1.47	. . .
Northeast	1.78	1.57	−12.04
Southeast	1.80	1.46	−18.92
South	1.52	1.36	−10.52
Center-west	1.59	1.34	−15.87
Metropolitan–urban			
Brazil	1.17	1.10	−5.49
North	1.16	1.10	−5.62
Northeast	1.32	1.20	−9.03
Southeast	1.05	1.02	−3.33
South	1.05	1.03	−2.02
Center-West	1.28	1.16	−9.47
Metropolitan–rural			
Brazil	2.50	1.80	−28.19
North	. . .	1.62	. . .
Northeast	2.35	1.88	−19.98
Southeast	1.89	1.48	−21.63
South	1.60	1.40	−12.33
Center-West	2.03	1.55	−23.83

Source: Table 3.5.

the quotients of the respective SIIs. As will be noted, in 2001 these gaps are systematically larger than those of 2009. This means that during this period there have been generalized reductions in the disparities of social inclusion.

For Brazil, the urban–rural gap in 2001, which was 2.14, fell to 1.63 in 2009 (that is, the gap between the SII for urban Brazil and the SII for rural Brazil was reduced by 24 percent between 2001 and 2009). Brazil's metropolitan–urban gap, which was 1.17 in 2001, fell to 1.10 in 2009, a reduction of 5.5 percent. And Brazil's metropolitan–urban gap, which was 2.50 in 2001, fell to 1.80 in 2009, a reduction of 28.2 percent in the period.

The reductions are of course larger in the case of the metropolitan–rural gaps, for Brazil as well as its regions, being smaller in the case of the metropolitan–urban gaps. These data are presented in the last column of Table 3.6, which measures the observed percentage reduction that occurred between 2001 and 2009.

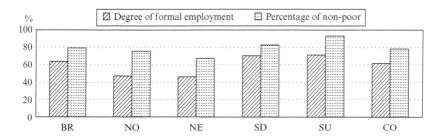

Figure 3.5 Brazil and its regions: SII subcomponents, 2009 (I)

For the Southeast, for instance, the reduction between 2001 and 2009 in the metropolitan–rural gap was 21.6 percent; that in the urban–rural gap was 18.9 percent; and that in the metropolitan–urban gap was 3.3 percent. For the Northeast, these gaps were, respectively, 20.0 percent, 12.0 percent and 9.0 percent.

The same pattern occurs, although attenuated, in the South, with a reduction of 12.3 percent in the metropolitan–rural gap, of 10.5 percent in the urban–rural gap and of 2.0 percent in the metropolitan–urban gap. It increases nonetheless in the Center-West, which shows reductions of 23.8 percent, 15.9 percent and 9.5 percent.

For the Northeast and the Center-West, note the reductions that occurred in the metropolitan–urban gaps: of 9.0 percent in the first case, 9.5 percent in the second. The urban network of the Northeast, formed by many small towns which exhibit almost the same economic and social characteristics and ways of living of the surrounding rural areas, explains this phenomenon. In the Center-West, it is explained by the large economic and social distance that increasingly prevailed, in the last decades, between its dense metropolitan center – Brasília, or the Federal District – and the thin and dispersed net of urban nuclei spread through Brazil's vast Central Plateau. Figure 3.5 shows these characteristics in the two observed years, 2001 and 2009, for Brazil, its regions and the three areas considered.

3.9 INEQUALITIES AMONG THE STATES: CONVERGENCE

The disparities of levels of social inclusion between states (the Federal District of Brasília included), organized by descending rank of SIIs for 2009, are presented in Table 3.7 and Figure 3.6.

Columns 6 and 7 of Table 3.7 present the states' SIIs, with Brazil equal to 100. The SIIs of Santa Catarina state were 36 percent and 25 percent

Table 3.7   Brazil: interstate imbalances measured by the SII, 2001 and 2009

States, ranked by the 2009 SII	IIS		Variation, % 2001–09	Brazil = 100	
	2001	2009		2001	2009
1 Santa Catarina	6.05	8.14	34.4	136	125
2 Federal District (Brasília)	5.69	7.80	37.1	128	120
3 São Paulo	5.71	7.78	36.3	128	120
4 Paraná	5.13	7.49	46.1	115	115
5 Rio Grande do Sul	5.52	7.48	35.5	124	115
6 Rio de Janeiro	5.42	7.40	36.6	122	114
7 Espírito Santo	4.51	6.86	52.2	101	105
8 Minas Gerais	4.46	6.66	49.4	100	102
9 Mato Grosso do Sul	4.50	6.62	46.9	101	102
10 Mato Grosso	3.99	6.51	63.4	89	100
11 Goiás	4.12	6.19	55.7	92	95
12 Rondônia	4.29	6.17	43.9	96	95
13 Roraima	3.94	6.14	56.0	88	94
14 Acre	4.32	5.97	38.4	97	92
15 Amapá	5.01	5.86	16.9	113	90
16 Amazonas	4.47	5.78	29.3	100	89
17 Tocantins	2.75	5.74	108.5	62	88
18 Sergipe	3.38	5.23	54.6	76	80
19 Rio Grande do Norte	3.55	5.22	47.2	80	80
20 Ceará	2.85	5.02	76.2	64	77
21 Pará	3.68	5.01	36.1	83	77
22 Pernambuco	3.09	4.88	58.2	69	75
23 Bahia	2.67	4.86	82.1	60	75
24 Paraíba	3.12	4.81	54.1	70	74
25 Piauí	2.45	4.51	84.1	55	69
26 Alagoas	2.35	4.41	87.9	53	68
27 Maranhão	2.34	4.40	87.8	53	68

Sources: IBGE's PNADs (2001, 2009) (special tabulations from micro data).

superior to the Brazilian SIIs for 2001 and 2009; the SIIs of Alagoas and Maranhão states were only 53 percent and 68 percent, respectively, of Brazil's.

The coefficients of variation, V, for the 2001 and 2009 SIIs (columns 3 and 4), 27.6 percent in the first case and 18.9 percent in the second, indicate the significant reduction in interstate disparities of social inclusion which occurred in the last decade.

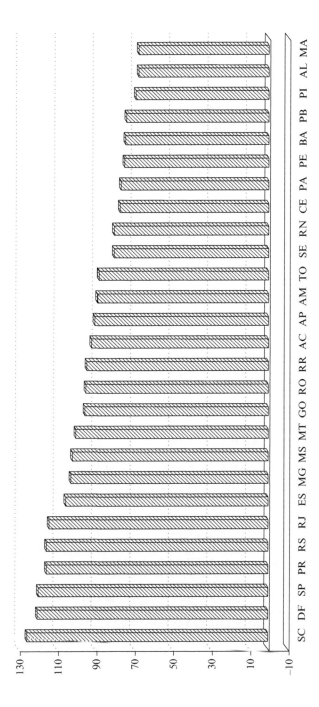

Figure 3.6   Interstate imbalances, measured through the SII 2009 (SII Brazil = 100)

It is worthwhile to observe the inverse correspondence among the SII grades for 2009 (column 4 of Table 3.7) and percentage variations verified for 2001–09 (column 5): they show a tendency to be smaller for the higher SIIs and larger for the lower ones.

The first six states of Table 3.7, with SIIs medium-high in 2009 (grades over 7.00) had percentage variations in their SIIs between 46.1 percent and 34.4 percent in 2001–09. But for the six states with grades inferior to 5.00 – that is, with low social inclusion – the same variations were higher, going from 54.1 percent to 87.9 percent.

This trend is also captured by a coefficient of correlation, R, between the two variables of −0.572 (and a coefficient of determination, R^2, of 0.327), thus reinforcing the evidence of convergence over time of the Brazilian states' levels of social inclusion, when measured by the SII.

NOTES

1. "Lorsque, dans la république, le peuple en corps a la souveraine puissance, c'est une démocratie" (Montesquieu (1748), V. 1, Part I, Book II, Chapter 2, p. 39).
2. See, for example, *The Federalist* (1787–88), n. 10 (Madison), p. 51; n. 9 (Hamilton), p. 47.
3. Mill (1861 [1952]), p. 341.
4. Mill (1861 [1952]), p. 382.
5. See Tucídides (1952), Book 2, p. 396.
6. This is Attica's estimated population in Pericles' time. See on this subject Hignett (1967).
7. *The Federalist* (1787–88), n. 79 (Hamilton), p. 233.
8. Kant (1797 [1952]), p. 436.
9. See Adler and Gorman (1952), V. 1, pp. 303–10.
10. See Adler and Gorman (1952), V.1, p. 224.
11. Mill (1861 [1952]), pp. 330, 339, 381.
12. For a more detailed review of the principles of modern democracy, see Albuquerque (2009).
13. For details on the calculus of the SII, see the Appendix. The SII and its components vary hypothetically from 0.00 to 10.00.
14. See IBGE (2002, 2009).
15. According to this classification, in 2009 an SII equal or higher than 8.50 would have a grade of social inclusion considered high.
16. This means that in this period, for an average annual growth of 1 percent GDP per capita there was an increase in the SII of 2.3 percent.
17. The correlation coefficient, R, between the SII grades and their average annual growth rate in 2001–09 was −0.694, R^2 being 0.482.
18. As mentioned in the Appendix, the 2001 data for the North exclude the rural population. Therefore, they are not strictly comparable with the 2009 data.
19. Brazil's "Pesquisa Mensal de Emprego", conducted by IBGE in the metropolitan regions, revealed that, in 2010, a year of high economic growth (over 7 percent) the unemployment rate was reduced to 6 percent.

REFERENCES

Adler, Mortimer J. and William Gorman (eds) (1952), *The Great Ideas: A Syntopicon of Great Books of the Western World*, 2 vols, Chicago, IL: Britannica.

Albuquerque, Roberto Cavalcanti de (2009), "Proteção social e geração de oportunidades", in José Celso Cardoso Jr (ed.), *Desafios ao desenvolvimento brasileiro: contribuições do Conselho de Orientação do Ipea*, Brasília: Ipea, pp. 153–88.

Hamilton, Alexander, James Madison and John Jay (1952), *The Federalist*, Great books of the western world No. 43, Chicago: Encyclopedia Britannica.

Hignett, Charles (1967), *A History of the Athenian Constitution to the End of the Fifth Century BC,* London and Oxford: Clarendon Press.

Instituto Brasileiro de Geografia e Estatística (IBGE) (2001, 2008 and 2009), *PNADs (Pesquisas Nacionais por Amostra de Domicílios)*, Rio de Janeiro: Instituto Brasileiro de Geografia e Estatística.

Kant, Immanuel (1797 [1952]), *The Science of Right*, trans. W. Hastie, Great Books 42, Chicago, IL: Britannica.

Mill, John Stuart (1861 [1952]), *Representative Government*, Great Books 43, Chicago, IL: Britannica.

Montesquieu, Charles-Louis de Secondat, baron de La Brède et de (1748), *De l'esprit des lois*, Paris, Gallimard, 1995 (texte de 1758), 2 v., partie I, livre II, chapitre 2.

Tucídides (1952), *The History of the Peloponnesian War*, trans. Richard Crawley, Great Books, Chicago, IL: Britannica.

APPENDIX: METHODOLOGICAL ANNEX

The Social Inclusion Index (SII), is a synthetic indicator conceived with the purpose of measuring the relative levels of social inclusion in selected years. The SII aggregates, in a unique relative measure unit, 12 different indicators of social and economic inclusiveness, put together according to a methodology that follows three phases.

In the first phase, a measure of the evolution of a specific variable of social inclusion, I_{ij}, is calculated for each of the 12 indicators, I_i, also called subcomponents, and for each social situation (Brazil as a whole, its regions, areas and states), j, defined as:

$$I_{ij} = 1 - \frac{\max_j I_{ij} - I_{ij}}{\max_j I_{ij} - \min_j I_{ij}}$$

In the second phase, a measure of more complex social inclusion processes, Cij, is calculated, for each of the SII's three components, C_i, which is an aggregation of four indicators or subcomponents, and for each social situation, j, which are expressed by simple or weighted averages of the I_{ijs}:

$$C_{ij} = \frac{1}{n} \sum_{j=1}^{n} I_{ij}.$$

In the third phase, the SIIs are calculated as a simple average of their three components:

$$SII_{ij} = \frac{1}{n} \sum_{i=1}^{n} C_{ij}.$$

The SIIs and their three components must be viewed as relative measures of the levels of social inclusion produced by the 12 indicators in a given year. This is particularly important because these indicators are normalized, thus expressing a value which only makes sense within the adopted scale of reference. As relative measures, the SIIs and their components are expressed by a grade that hypothetically varies between 0 and 10 and has three significant figures (for example: 7.45, 8.00, 6.38 and so on).

The SII was calculated for Brazil as whole; its five regions; the metropolitan, urban and rural areas; and the 27 states (the Federal District, Brasília, included) for the years 2001, 2008 and 2009 (the SIIs for 2010 were estimated by projections of the observed tendencies). The three components and 12 subcomponents are the following.

The first component, employment and income, corresponds to the Economic Inclusiveness Index. It is formed by four subcomponents or indicators: (1) the occupation rate, that is, the percentage of the economically active population (EAP), which is employed (weight of 0.3); (2) the rate of employment formalization, that is, the percentage of remunerated employees formally contracted and socially protected by the national security system (weight of 0.2); (3) the proportion of non-poor in the population (weight of 0.3); and (4) the coefficient of equality, that is, the complement to one of the Gini coefficient (weight of 0.2).

The second component, education and knowledge, corresponds to the Educational Inclusiveness Index. It is also formed by four indicators: (1) the rate of literacy of the population 15 years old or more (weight of 0.1); (2) the percentage of persons 15 years old or more and with four years and more of schooling (weight of 0.2); (3) the percentage of persons 20 years old or more and with nine years and more of schooling (weight of 0.3); and (4) the percentage of persons 24 years old or more and with 12 years and more of schooling (weight of 0.4).

The third and last component, information and communication, corresponds to the Digital Inclusion Index. It is formed by four other indicators: the percentage of households with: (1) a microcomputer (weight of

0.3); (2) access to the Internet (weight of 0.3); (3) at least one television set (weight of 0.2); and (4) a telephone set, fixed or mobile (weight of 0.2).

The three components of the SII have equal weights. In the process of normalization of the values observed for each indicator or subcomponent, the lower values were minimally adjusted in order to avoid zeros in the calculations of the three components of the SII.

The database of the SII was made possible by special tabulations which have aggregated, according to desired spatial as well as conceptual categories, the micro data of the Pesquisas Nacionais por Amostra de Domicílios, PNADs,[1] for 2001, 2008 and 2009. The Pnad of 2001 did not cover the rural populations of the following states of the North region: Rondônia, Amazonas, Roraima, Pará and Amapá.[2]

In this chapter the metropolitan North corresponds to the metropolitan area of Belém, in the state of Pará; the metropolitan Northeast, to the metropolitan areas of Fortaleza, Ceará; Recife, Pernambuco; and Salvador, Bahia. The metropolitan Southeast corresponds to the metropolitan areas of Belo Horizonte, Minas Gerais; Rio de Janeiro, state of Rio de Janeiro; and São Paulo; state of São Paulo. The metropolitan South corresponds to the metropolitan areas of Curitiba, Paraná; and Porto Alegre, Rio Grande do Sul. And the metropolitan Center-West corresponds to the Federal District (Brasília). See Figure 3.1, at the beginning of this chapter.

NOTES

1. Brazil's annual national household sample surveys.
2. Therefore, the data for 2001 for the North and its states are not strictly comparable to those of 2008 and 2009.

4. Social programs, industrial deconcentration and the recent decrease in regional income inequality in Brazil

Raul da Mota Silveira-Neto and Carlos Roberto Azzoni

4.1   INTRODUCTION

As pointed out in a series of studies, personal income inequality in Brazil has presented a quite auspicious trend in this century, at least in comparison to the long-lasting country standards (Barros et al., 2006; Ferreira et al., 2006; Hoffmann, 2006; Soares, 2006a, 2006b). Silveira-Neto and Azzoni (2011) showed that such a new trajectory is also replicated in the indicators of regional income inequality among its states. It could be argued that this reduction in regional inequality reflects the convergence of labor productivity predicted by the neoclassical growth model. There are good reasons, however, suggesting that such an argument is insufficient to capture the nature of the recent reduction of regional income inequality in Brazil. First, the intensive income transfer programs carried out by the federal government (Bolsa Família and Benefícios de Prestação Continuada) present regional repercussions. Second, credit policy targeted at specific sectors (mainly manufacturing) seems to have some power in promoting sectoral development in the country's poorest states. This is the conclusion of Silva et al. (2009) in their analysis of investment projects financed with resources from the Constitutional Development Funds (National Fund for the Development of the Northeast Region, FNE; National Fund for the Development of the North Region, FNO; and National Fund for the Development of the Center-West Region, FCO). Third, a regional deconcentration of manufacturing production is observed in recent years, creating a more qualified demand for labor in poorer states. This could be a response to incentives, to the enlargement of peripheral markets, or merely the effect of new comparative advantages in the context of greater competition.

Based on a decomposition of the Gini index of regional per capita income inequality, Silveira-Neto and Azzoni (2011) have already shown the important role of social policies of income transfers in reducing inequality since 1995. This work extends our previous efforts towards the identification of the sources of regional inequality reduction between 1995 and 2006 in three directions. This study considers not only the the the Bolsa Familia program (BF), but also the Benefícios de Prestação Continuada program (BPC). Additionally, we consider labor income originated in different economic sectors (agriculture, industry, services and public administration). This enables us to assess the role of industrial deconcentration in reducing regional income disparities. Finally, by applying a decomposition of the Gini index, we provide a quantitative measure (elasticity) of the reaction of regional inequality of per capita income with respect to variations in the various components of income. This is valuable information for the establishment and evaluation of alternative policies to tackle regional disparities.

In addition to this introduction, this chapter presents four more sections. Section 4.2 describes the breakdown of per capita income by state into different sources. It also presents the important spatial dimensions of cash transfer programs and characterizes the industrial deconcentration between 1995 and 2006. Section 4.3 presents the importance of each income source in explaining the reduction in regional income inequality and the estimated elasticities of inequality relative to changes in each source of income. In section 4.4 we present the conclusions and policy implications of the work.

4.2 INCOME SOURCES, SPATIAL DIMENSION OF SOCIAL PROGRAMS AND REGIONAL INDUSTRIAL CONCENTRATION

4.2.1 Income Sources

In this section we present some evidence on the spatially differentiated destination of the resources from two important social policies recently implemented: the Bolsa Familia program (BF) and the Benefícios de Prestação Continuada program (BPC). Although these programs do not have a spatial interest, since they focus on individuals or families, they clearly have differentiated regional impacts, benefiting the poorer regions relatively more. Such impacts occur, moreover, in a context of spatial deconcentration of employment and labor income in the industrial sector. Given the employment profile of this sector, this is an additional factor

Table 4.1   Shares in total income, by region, 2006 (%)

	North	North-east	South-east	South	Center-West
Labor in agriculture	4.5	6.9	4.2	7.4	9.9
Labor in manufacturing	14.8	12.3	17.8	18.3	12.1
Labor in the tertiary	46.2	42.1	45.5	44.3	46.0
Labor in the public administration	17.5	10.0	7.0	6.1	12.7
Labor income	83.00	71.30	74.50	76.10	80.70
Retirement and pensions	11.6	22.5	21.3	19.0	14.1
Rents and donations	0.6	0.7	1.0	1.4	0.7
Income from Capital	2.5	2.1	2.4	2.8	2.9
Other income	14.70	25.30	24.70	23.20	17.70
Bolsa Família	1.2	2.1	0.4	0.3	0.7
BPC	1.0	1.2	0.3	0.2	0.7
Social programs	2.20	3.30	0.70	0.50	1.40

Source: authors' estimates from micro-data, PNAD, IBGE.

in the reduction of regional inequality of income in Brazil in the recent period.

Total (all sources) income in state e, ($e = 1, \ldots, 27$), is the sum of: labor income in agriculture; labor income in manufacturing; labor income in the tertiary sector; labor income in public administration; retirement income; income from rents and donations; income from capital (interests, dividends, and so on); transferences from the BF; and transferences from the BPC. Information is aggregated from micro data from PNAD – Pesquisa Nacional por Amostras de Domicílios (National Survey on Samples of Households), from the IBGE, the national statistics office. The usual caveats relating to the quality of self-declaratory data on capital income applies. For estimating income coming from social programs, we adopted the methodology proposed by Soares et al. (2006). We have assigned all labor income for each individual to their most important economic activity.

Table 4.1 presents the shares of the nine income sources in total income in the five macro regions in Brazil. It shows that social programs are more important in the Northeast and North regions (3.2 and 2.2 percent of total income, respectively). On the other hand, labor income from manufacturing is more important for the Southeast and South regions. The richest region, the Southeast, has also the lowest share of labor income in agriculture.

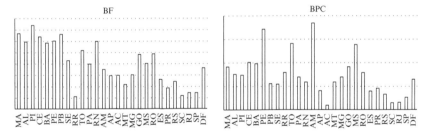

Source: authors' calculations from micro-data from PNAD 2006.

Figure 4.1   Monthly per capita value (R$) by state, 2006 (states in increasing level of per capita income of 1995)

4.2.2   The Spatial Dimension of Social Programs

The Bolsa Familia program is the most important social program of income transfer carried out by the federal government. It consists of cash transferences to families below the official indigence or poverty lines. In 2006 the value transferred monthly to each family was R$100 or R$50 (poverty and indigence lines, respectively), plus R$15 per child under the age of 14 (limited to three), conditional on some obligations related to child education and health. The per capita value received in 2006 by families in the ten poorest states was almost double the amount received by those in the ten richest states. The per capita monthly value received by all families in the poor state of Maranhão was R$6.70; for the state of São Paulo, it was only R$1.40. The (BPC) program provides an unconditional monthly transference equivalent to one minimum wage (R$350 in 2006) to elderly people or handicapped persons in families with per capita income levels below one-fourth of the minimum wage. In 2006, 12.6 percent of the population received money from the BPC: 26.7 percent in the poor Northeast region and only 5.9 percent in the rich Southeast region. Considering the entire population, the average per capita values for the two poorest states of Maranhão and Piauí were R$3.70 and R$3.00, respectively; for São Paulo and Santa Catarina states, the values were only R$1.10 and R$0.62, respectively.

Figure 4.1 presents the per capita value distributed to each state by BF and BPC in 2006. Since the states are displayed in increasing order of per capita income (poor states to the left, rich states to the right), the figure makes it clear that these programs have a pro-poor bias, in regional terms. This bias is more evident in BF, but is also present in BPC.

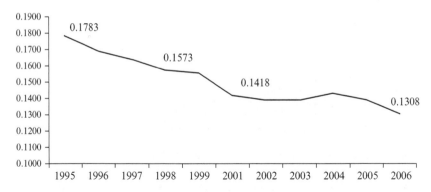

Source: authors' calculations from micro-data from PNAD.

Figure 4.2   Regional Gini for manufacturing employment

4.2.3   Regional Deconcentration in Manufacturing

The values in Table 4.1 have indicated that states in the Southeast and South regions had the largest shares of labor income in manufacturing in 2006. This snapshot does not inform us about the important recent movement of industrial deconcentration, both in employment and in labor income. The aggregated share in employment of the 13 poorest states increased from 21.6 percent in 2005 to 24.6 percent in 2006; the aggregated share of the states in the Northeast and North regions (except the state of Amazonas, home of an import tax-free area), increased from 21.7 percent to 24.8 percent.

Figure 4.2 presents the evolution of the Gini coefficient of the regional distribution of industrial employment among states. It measures inequality by comparing the cumulative distribution of total employment among states with the cumulative distribution of industrial employment. The decreasing trend is paramount, indicating that regional concentration in manufacturing employment has decreased. This could be related to aggressive attraction mechanisms implemented by the poorest states, or to specific actions of the federal government. It could, on the other hand, be simply the result of actions taken by companies to sustain competitiveness in a context of stronger foreign competition. It could also be a result of the reduction in schooling disparities and income growth in peripheral states (Krugman, 1991). The final fact is that the poorest states increased their shares both in labor income and in employment in manufacturing.

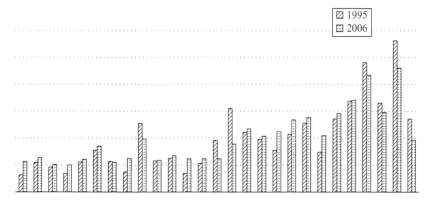

Source: authors' calculations from micro-data from PNAD.

Figure 4.3   Manufacturing relative to global per capita income (states in increasing level of per capita global income)

Such a reduction in the inequality of the distribution of industrial employment is accompanied, in addition, by a reduction in the inequality of manufacturing per capita income among states. This indicates that the redistribution of industrial employment was accompanied by improvements in the profile of labor demand by firms in the poorest states. Figure 4.3 shows per capita manufacturing labor income in the states in relation to the per capita income from all sources. As in the graphs in the previous figure, states are ordered in increasing order of per capita income values in 1995. The first thing to notice is that manufacturing labor income is lower than global per capita income in the poorest states (with the exception of the state of Roraima – RR). Manufacturing tends to pay more than the other sources in the richer states located on the right side of the figure, with the exception of the states of Espírito Santo and the Federal District, Brasília. Secondly, the ratio of manufacturing to global per capita income has increased in the poorest 13 states (with the exception of Paraíba – PB), and decreased in the four richest states. The Gini index for the regional distribution of per capita manufacturing labor income decreased from 0.3260 in 1995 to 0.2572 in 2006, a fall of 21.1 percent.

Figures 4.4 and 4.5 present maps with the regional distribution (by state) of per capita income values for all sources.

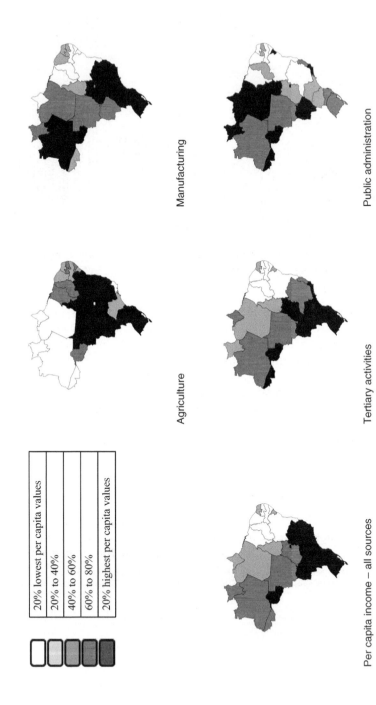

Manufacturing

Public administration

Agriculture

Tertiary activities

20% lowest per capita values

20% to 40%

40% to 60%

60% to 80%

20% highest per capita values

Per capita income – all sources

Figure 4.4   Regional distribution of labor income

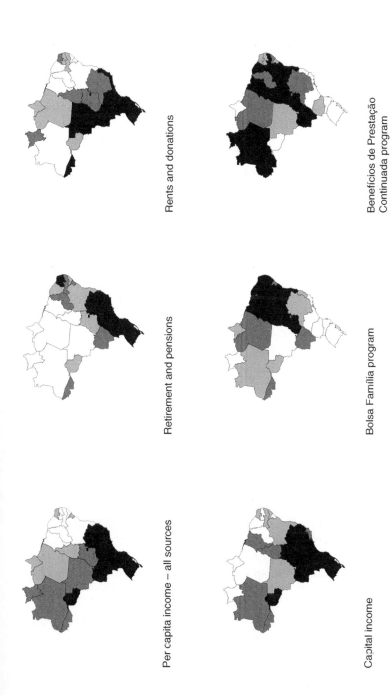

Rents and donations

Benefícios de Prestação
Continuada program

Retirement and pensions

Bolsa Família program

Per capita income – all sources

Capital income

Note: see Figure 4.4 for key.

Figure 4.5 Regional distribution of non-labor income

4.3   IDENTIFYING THE SOURCES OF CHANGES IN REGIONAL INEQUALITY

The Gini coefficient, as well as other measures of generalized entropy, can be decomposed to show the contributions of different sources to the level of inequality. Hoffman (2004, 2006) and Soares (2006a, 2006b) have studied the evolution of personal distribution of income; Silveira-Neto and Azzoni (2011) have dealt with the regional aspects of recent modifications in income inequality. The Gini index can be expressed as the sum of the coefficients of concentration multiplied by the respective weights of the different sources of income. It can be written as $G = \Sigma^{N}_{f=1}\alpha_f C_f$, where N is the number of income sources, a_f is the participation of income source f in per capita income, and C_f is the concentration coefficient for income source f. The latter is obtained from the concentration curve, which shows how the cumulative proportion of source f varies in relation to the cumulative proportion of population. With b_f being the area between the concentration curve for source f and the horizontal axis, then $C_f = 1 - 2.\beta_f$, with $-1 < C_f < 1$. Changes in time can be associated to changes in the shares of income sources in total income and to inequality changes within different sources. Formally:

$$\Delta G = \sum_{f=1}^{N} (\overline{C}_f - \overline{G})\Delta\alpha_f + \sum_{f=1}^{N} \overline{\alpha}_f \Delta C_f, \text{ with } \overline{G} = \frac{1}{2}(G_t + G_{t-1}) \quad (4.1)$$

The first member in ΔG is the participation effect. It shows that the increase (decrease) in the share of a particular income source with higher(lower)-than-average inequality will increase (decrease) global inequality. The second member is the concentration effect, showing the impact of variations in the concentration levels within the different income sources.

Table 4.2 presents the estimated participation and concentration coefficients of the different sources of income. It is clear that labor income in agriculture, manufacturing and the tertiary sectors lost importance: shares of 72 percent in 1995 and 65 percent in 2006. Labor income from public administration was the only labor source showing a slight increase, and the share of the overall labor income dropped from 83 percent to 77 percent. Retirements and pensions[1] increased in importance, moving from 13.7 percent to 17.8 percent, while the other non-labor sources, excluding the social programs, were practically stable. The social programs did not exist in 1995, and accounted for 1.7 percent of total income in 2006. As for the concentration levels within each income source in 1995, labor income in agriculture, and retirements and pensions, were less concentrated than

Table 4.2 *Concentration and participation of income sources: Gini Index, 2006*

	1995		2006	
	Coefficient of concentration	Participation (%)	Coefficient of Concentration	Participation (%)
Labor in agriculture	−0.0331	7.96	0.0932	5.98
Labor in manufacturing	0.2959	16.03	0.2290	14.62
Labor in the tertiary	0.2398	48.27	0.2089	44.88
Labor in public administration	0.2811	10.97	0.2048	11.71
Retirements and pensions	0.1645	13.66	0.1827	17.76
Rents and donations	0.2760	0.70	0.2887	0.85
Income from capital	0.2338	2.41	0.2162	2.53
BF	–	0.00	−0.1997	0.99
BPC	–	0.00	−0.1500	0.68
Total (Gini)	0.2214	100	0.1942	100

Source: authors' estimates from micro-data from PNAD, IBGE.

total income (concentration coefficients smaller than the Gini index); labor income from manufacturing, on the other hand, was the most concentrated. The social programs joined agriculture and retirements and pensions in 2006, as the less concentrated. However, there was an increase in their concentration levels, although they still remain below the average. On the other hand, labor income in manufacturing, in the tertiary sector and in public administration presented reductions in their concentration coefficients, a movement that was not enough to take them from above the average.

The indicators presented above give a good idea of the importance of the changes in the share and concentration of the different income sources in the changes in regional income inequality in the period. However, they do not inform us, for example, whether a 10 percent increase in the share of Bolsa Família will have the same effect as a 10 percent increase in the share of retirement and pensions. In order to come up with a solution to this problem, we apply to the Gini coefficient a decomposition procedure presented by Leman and Yitzhaki (1985).

Let y_e indicate the total income in a state, which is the sum of the N; F indicates the cumulative function of the distribution of such income, y_f is the amount of income originated in source f, and F_k is the cumulative function of income source k. The Gini coefficient can be obtained by:

$$G = \sum_{f=1}^{N} R_f G_f S_f \tag{4.2}$$

where: $R_f = \text{cov}(y_f, F)/\text{cov}(y_f, F_f)$; $S_f = \bar{y}_f \sqrt{y}$ is the ratio of the average income of source f to the average income from all sources, G_f is the Gini coefficient of income source f, $\text{cov}(y_f, F)$ is the covariance between the income from source f and the cumulative income function, and $\text{cov}(y_f, F_f)$ is the covariance between the income from source f and the cumulative function of the income from this source. A useful advantage of using the decomposition expressed in (4.2) is that it allows for the calculation of the elasticity of the global Gini relative to variations in income sources. Leman and Yitzhaki (1985) show that the percentage impact on the global Gini of a percentage change in income source f, e_f, is given by the difference between the share of the global Gini explained by that specific income source and its share in total income, that is:

$$\frac{\partial G/\partial e_f}{G} = \frac{(S_f G_f R_f)}{G} - S_f \tag{4.3}$$

Table 4.3 shows the estimated elasticities for the end years of the period. The negative signs for agriculture, retirement and pensions, and the government transfer programs indicate that they favor the reduction in inequality. In 2006, an increase of 10 percent in the labor income in agriculture was associated with a decrease of 0.31 percent in the regional inequality of per capita income. The same interpretation applies to the other sources. In terms of intensity, agriculture is the source with the largest contribution to the reduction of inequality, although its importance declined between the two years. Manufacturing was the income source with the largest contribution to inequality in 1995, followed by the tertiary sector; they changed positions in 2006, both with less intensity. Property rent, and interest and dividends, contributed to the concentration in both years, even more so in 2006, but the elasticity values were low as compared to the other sources. The government transfer programs combined beat agriculture in terms of elasticity (0.32): an increase of 10 percent in the Bolsa Família transfers alone, representing approximately 0.1 percent of total income, is associated with a decrease of 0.2 percent in the regional inequality of per capita income. In order to have a dimension of the importance of this variation, it corresponds to 16.6 percent of the annual variation in the Gini coefficient.

Table 4.3   Elasticities

Income source		Elasticity of regional inequality to income source	
		1995	2006
Labor	Agriculture	−0.092	−0.031
	Manufacturing	0.055	0.027
	Tertiary	0.041	0.034
	Government	0.029	0.006
Non-labor	Retirement + pensions	−0.036	−0.011
	Property rent + other	0.002	0.004
	Interests and dividends	0.001	0.003
	Social programs		
	Bolsa Família	–	−0.02
	BPC	–	−0.012

Source: calculated by the authors from PNAD micro data.

The final contribution of each income source to the change in inequality in the period is the combined result of changes in participation and changes in concentration. For example, manufacturing income lost importance, but at the same time it became less concentrated. On the other hand, retirement and pensions increased its share and became more concentrated. Equation (4.1) allows for assessing the importance of changes in the share and concentration of each income source in the changes in the Gini coefficient.

The results are shown in Table 4.4. They indicate that the concentration effect accounts for 86 percent of the total change, leaving only 14 percent for the participation effect. That means that the inequality change experienced in the period is more related to the way income is regionally distributed within each income source than to changes in the importance of these sources. This is exemplified by the fact that the largest concentration effects are observed in manufacturing and in the tertiary sector. The participation effect is also positive for these two sectors, reflecting their important role in explaining the changes in regional income inequality in the country in the period. However, their concentration profiles are more important that their changing shares, meaning that the changing regional distribution of these activities is the most relevant aspect to take into consideration.

Column C indicates that labor-related income sources account for 81 percent of the change in the geographical Gini coefficient (sum of the first

Table 4.4   Concentration and participation effects

Income source		Effects composing the change in regional inequality between 1995 and 2006 (%)		
		Concentration effect	Participation effect	Total
Labor	Agriculture	−32.3	−12.9	−45.2
	Manufacturing	37.6	2.8	40.4
	Tertiary	52.9	2.1	55.0
	Government	31.7	−1	30.8
Non-labor	Retirement + pensions	−10.5	5.1	−5.4
	Property rent + other	−0.4	−0.4	−0.8
	Interests and dividends	1.6	−0.1	1.5
	Social programs			
	Bolsa Família	3.6	11.2	14.8
	BPC	1.9	7	8.9
Global		86.1	13.9	100

Source: calculated by the authors from PNAD micro data.

four lines) in spite of the important negative contribution of agriculture, while non-labor-related sources explain only 19 percent, almost all of which is related to the two government income transference programs. Retirement and pensions, and property rent and other, contributed to decreasing the regional concentration. Adding up the role of the government as a sector (30.8 percent), in which payment to public servants dominates, and the two social programs (14.8 percent + 8.9 percent), the public sector contributes 54.5 percent to the total reduction in the geographical Gini coefficient. Considering only those sources that contributed to the reduction in inequality, the public sector accounted for 37.5 percent (54.5 percent over 145.2 percent). These numbers highlight the relevance of public policy in shaping the recent regional inequality changes in the country.

4.4   CONCLUSIONS

This study has concentrated on finding the sources behind the recent reduction in regional inequality in Brazil. Special emphasis was devoted to the spatial influences of social programs, expanding the focus of previous work developed by the authors (Silveira-Neto and Azzoni, 2011). One extension is the separation between labor and non-labor income, with the social programs receiving special attention. Additionally, the sectoral source of labor income was highlighted, allowing for the assessment of the influence of changes in the sectoral composition of income. As for the social programs, the Benefícios de Prestação Continuada program was included for the first time in a study of regional inequality. Computing elasticities indicating the sensitiveness of regional inequality to changes in the composition of income sources was a step forward in relation to the existing literature.

The results indicate that the largest share in the reduction of regional inequality in per capita income relates to labor income (81 percent). Within this source, changes in manufacturing and the tertiary sector favored reduction in inequality, while changes in agriculture contributed otherwise. Within non-labor income sources, changes in the concentration of retirements and pensions and rents and donations also contributed to reducing regional inequality. Finally, the social programs presented a clear pro-poor regional profile: the BF contributed 15 percent and the BPC 9.3 percent of the reduction in the regional Gini between 1995 and 2006. The contributions occurred in spite of these programs representing less than 3.5 percent of total income. As for the social programs which account for this small share of total income, the results indicate that the Bolsa Família program is more efficient in reducing regional income inequality than payments from retirements and pensions, with larger weights in total income.

The implications for the establishment of policies to combat regional per capita income inequality are clear. Although social programs are not explicit regional policies, they clearly have a pro-poor regional focus, since they concentrate on poor people, and poor regions tend to have a larger share of poor people. Therefore, non-spatial social programs are really regional programs. With respect to sectoral incentives, particularly with regard to manufacturing, it is not possible to say from the evidence obtained in this study that these have been effective. The mere increase in the share of manufacturing in total income brings about an increase in regional concentration, but the changes observed in income concentration within this sector has made it less concentrated in time.

NOTE

1. 'Retirements' refer to payments to retired workers during their lifespan. 'Pensions' are payments to spouses or other family members after the death of the worker, even if retired.

REFERENCES

Barros, R.P., M. Carvalho, S. Franco and R.S. Mendonca (2006), "Uma análise das principais causas da queda recente na desigualdade de renda brasileira", *Econômica (Niterói)*, **8**, 117–147.

Ferreira, F.H.G., P.G. Leite, J.A. Litchfield and G. Ulyssea (2006), "Ascensão e quedada desigualdade de renda no Brasil", *Econômica*, Rio de Janeiro, **8** (1), 147–171.

Hoffmann, R. (2004), "Decomposition of Mehran and Piesch inequality measures by factor components and their application to the distribution of per capita household income in Brazil", *Revista de Econometria*, **24** (1), 149–171.

Hoffman R. (2006), "Transferências de renda e a redução da desigualdade no Brasil e cinco regiões entre 1997 e 2004", *Econômica*, Rio de Janeiro, **8** (1), 55–81.

Leman, R.I. and S. Yitzhaki (1985), "Income inequality effects by income source: a new approach and applications to the United States", *Review of Economics and Statistics*, **67**, 151–156.

Neri, M.C. (2010), "The decade of falling income inequality and formal employment generation in Brazil", in OECD (ed.), *Tackling Inequalities in Brazil, China, India and South Africa: The Role of Labour Market and Social Policies*, Paris: OECD Publishing, pp. 57–107.

Silva, A.M.A., G.M. Resende and R.M. Silveira-Neto (2009), "Eficácia do gasto public: uma avaliação do FNE, FNO e FCO", *Estudos Econômicos*, **39** (1), 89–125.

Silveira-Neto, R. and C. Azzoni (2011), "Non-spatial government policies and regional income inequality in Brazil", *Regional Studies*, **45** (4), 453–454.

Soares, S. (2006a), "Distribuição de renda no Brasil de 1976 a 2004 com ênfase no período entre 2001 e 2004", Textos para discussão, No. 1166, Brasília: IPEA.

Soares, S. (2006b), "Análise de bem-estar e Decomposição por fatores da queda na desigualdade entre 1995 e 2004", *Econômica*, Rio de Janeiro, **8** (1), 83–115.

5. Labor policies in Brazil

**Márcia Azanha Ferraz Dias de Moraes,
Fabíola Cristina Ribeiro de Oliveira and
Camila Kraide Kretzmann**

5.1 INTRODUCTION

Despite modernization and rapid economic growth in many developing countries, including Brazil, unemployment remains a serious problem. Technological changes have altered the profile of the workers that a company needs. Employees with higher levels of schooling, and who are more capable of undertaking the required training courses for the improvement of their skills, are favored over low-skilled workers, who are excluded and subsequently find it more difficult to access the work market. This, in turn, leads to inequalities in terms of salaries and wages.

Policies in different sectors of the Brazilian economy are expected to diminish the problem. According to Moura and Marinho (2002), labor and employment policies can be split into two groups, namely, passive and active. Passive policies seek to reduce the number of people unemployed. This can be done either by workers retiring sooner or by delaying the entry of young people into the job market and encouraging them to stay longer at school. This type of policy has not been widely used in Brazil, given the country's fiscal situation.

Active policies seek to increase the actual number of jobs. This can be done by using incentives (creating public sector jobs; subsidizing employment for young people or the unemployed; supplying credit and support for small businesses; incentives for sectors that make intense use of labor), or by training and qualifying workers and intermediating between companies and job seekers. Therefore, the general aims of such policies are to increase the actual number of jobs, protect the unemployed and provide professional training to improve human resources.

Other authors highlight the importance of minimum wage policies, which have an impact on both the labor market and pensions. Ulyssea and Foguel (2006) summarized the main results of the effects of the minimum wage policies as follows:

(1) there is a consensus on the effect of reducing the inequalities of the distribution of the income of those in work; (2) there seems to be a negative, albeit lower, effect on employment; (3) the negative impacts appear to have a stronger effect on the informal economy, although the impact remains small; and (4) preliminary evidence suggests that the minimum wage has a significant effect on the probability of moving from formal to informal labor and, on a lower scale, to unemployment and inactivity.

This chapter seeks to present the different labor policies adopted in Brazil in recent years. Considering the importance of the minimum wage on the labor market, the chapter also seeks to examine the influence of the minimum wage on the income of employees from different sectors and regions in Brazil through an empirical application.

5.2   SOCIOECONOMIC CHARACTERISTICS OF EMPLOYEES

In this section, we analyze the main socioeconomic indicators of the workers by region of activity and sector. In the descriptive statistics and the estimated empirical model, the data of the National Household Sample Survey (PNAD), carried out by the Brazilian Institute for Geography and Statistics (IBGE) for workers in agriculture, industry, building, commerce and public administration between 2002 and 2009.[1]

Table 5.1 shows that between 2002 and 2009 the average wage of workers in almost all sectors rose, with the exception of public administration workers, whose earnings during this time fell 28.1 percent.[2] The average wage of workers increased by 36.9 percent in the agricultural sector (farming and livestock); by 8.8 percent in industry; by 17.9 percent in the building industry; by 9.4 percent in commerce; and by 14.5 percent in the service industry. The increase in the wages of agricultural workers came closest to matching the value of the variation of the minimum wage in real terms, which was 48.4 percent over the period 2002–09.

Although the biggest increase was in agricultural wages, the sector also features the lowest wages and levels of schooling. In 2009, agricultural wages corresponded to only 45 percent and 40 percent of the average wage paid to employees in the industrial sector and service industry, respectively. In 2009, the average length of schooling for agricultural workers was less than half that of the average schooling of the other sectors.

It is important to bear in mind that the farming and livestock sector is one of the only sectors in the Brazilian economy that continues to employ workers with extremely low levels of schooling, even going so far as to hire illiterate people (Oliveira, 2009, p. 72). The workforce of the building

Table 5.1 Socioeconomic indicator of workers, Brazil, 2002 and 2009

Year	Sector of activity	No. of people (1000s)	Registered employees %	Average schooling	Average age	Average income (R$)	Gini index
2002	Agriculture	4325.8	30.2	3.0	34.7	379.48	0.353
	Industry	8074.8	77.1	7.9	32.5	1066.36	0.484
	Building	2666.3	44.5	5.4	33.8	738.83	0.434
	Commerce	6971.8	65.6	8.6	29.6	786.47	0.422
	Public Administration*	1488.9	47.2	9.2	36.2	1808.75	0.523
	Services	14392.1	50.6	7.7	34.5	732.02	0.478
2009	Agriculture	4459.6	36.8	4.2	36.4	519.34	0.345
	Industry	9935.0	83.1	9.2	33.5	1159.84	0.417
	Building	3434.0	55.7	6.7	35.0	870.80	0.374
	Commerce	9612.1	73.4	9.6	30.8	860.59	0.347
	Public Administration*	1558.3	40.8	10.7	37.0	1301.43	0.470
	Services	17496.0	54.7	8.9	36.0	837.86	0.428

Note: * Exclusively statutory public sector and military staff.

Source: Prepared by the authors based on the micro data of the PNAD (2002–09).

industry also has a low educational level. This study found that for 2009, workers in this sector had spent on average only 6.7 years in school.

As for inequality in terms of income in all sectors, as measured by the Gini Index, the coefficients for 2009 were at lower levels than in 2002. But it is worth mentioning that the reduced inequality of incomes of rural workers is lower than the reductions seen in other sectors.

When we compare some socioeconomic indicators among the geographic Brazilian regions and also with the indicators of the state of São Paulo, we can observe that they are all better in the Southeast region, and even better for the state of São Paulo. In 2009, the average amount of schooling in São Paulo state was 9.2 years; in the Northeast, it was 7.4 years which was below the national average of 8.5 years.

Regarding the average wage, employees in the Northeast region earned only 55 percent of the wages of their counterparts in the state of São Paulo in 2009. Furthermore, the percentage of registered employees in the Northeast (45.2 percent) is also relatively lower when compared with the other regions (48.2 percent in the North region; 64.5 percent in the South-east region; 71.2 percent in the South region; 60.3 percent Center-West; and 62.5 percent in the country as a whole). The proportion of formal workers in the state of São Paulo is the highest (74.5 percent). Being formally registered ensures that basic rights for workers are recognized. These include a public retirement plan, remunerated annual vacation, annual extra-salary and guaranteed protection from unemployment.

5.3   LABOR POLICIES IN BRAZIL

Cardoso et al. (2009) reviewed recent public policies concerning employment in Brazil. According to these authors, the Constitution of 1988 and Law no. 7.998 of 1990[3] created the foundation of a national strategy for employment, labor, and income.

The authors claim that a set of government programs is being built up in Brazil to help the national labor market. The aims of the programs are: (1) to combat the effects of unemployment using monetary measures, such as unemployment benefits; (2) to retrain workers and include them in the market through professional training, qualification programs, and intermediation between companies and job seekers; and (3) to encourage or stimulate new jobs through facilitated access to credit for companies and/or freelance workers. The main policies of the Public System of Labor, Employment and Income implemented in Brazil are presented next.

5.3.1 National Employment System (SINE)

The National Employment System (SINE) was implemented in 1975. The main goal of this system is to help place workers in jobs nationwide by setting up job agencies. To achieve this goal, it was necessary to organize a system of information for the labor market, identifying workers and their profiles to create a database.[4] The SINE is currently coordinated by the Ministry of Labor and Employment through the Secretariat of Labor Policies and Salaries. It has been decentralized and each state has its own secretariat.

The resources required by the SINE are provided by the Worker's Aid Fund (FAT).[5] The allocation of resources for each state unit and each operational unit follow the performance criteria, rewarding the state and operational units with the highest number of workers placed in jobs, especially those workers who are at a disadvantage in the labor market (Cacciamali, 2005). Saboia and Falvo (2010) see the SINE as the main public program for helping workers in Brazil. These authors view it as operating in a way that is integrated with the payment of unemployment benefits. The main instruments used to operationalize the services provided by the SINE are: (1) the database of workers seeking employment; (2) company registration; and (3) the classification of jobs according to the CBO (Brazilian Job Classification System).

However, the structure of the system is limited since the SINE has service stations in only one-fifth of Brazilian towns and districts, and only 70 percent of its 1100 service stations are computerized. Furthermore, the program "competes" not only with other public and private agencies that seek to place workers in employment, but also with advertisements in newspapers and magazines, websites and relationship networks (Saboia and Falvo, 2010, p. 321). According to the authors, the SINE is an accurate reflection of demand in the job market, although its image is mostly one of an agency that seeks unskilled workers. They also point out that the current challenge of the system is to improve the profile of the jobs it has on offer and the candidates on their files. They also have to improve their mechanisms for contact with workers.

According to data of the Brazilian Ministry of Labor and Employment, there is a growing trend for all the indicators in the 2000–2008 period. The number of people registered by the SINE was 4 805 433 in 2000, and increased to 5 987 808 in 2008, an increase of 24.6 percent. The number of jobs offered increased from 1 281 220 to 2 526 628, indicating an increase of 97.2 percent.

As for positions filled – that is, the ratio of jobs offered to jobs taken – this oscillates during the period and appears to have dropped in recent years (45.4 percent in 2000 and 42.3 percent in 2008). Saboia and Falvo

(2010) point out that there are significant differences in the regional performance of intermediation between companies and job seekers. This is a confirmation of the uneven structure of the institution and the different dynamic of the job markets in different regions of the country.

The number of jobs offered is systematically higher in the more developed states due to the higher number of companies present in these regions. In 2008, jobs on offer in the Southeast accounted for approximately 50 percent of all jobs. If the South is included, this number rises to 72 percent. As for the variation of job offers, the percentage growth in the Center-West deserves to be mentioned.

However, when it comes to the program's success rate (the ratio of jobs offered to positions filled), the North and Northeast have the highest indicators. Saboia and Falvo (2010) point out that, according to the Ministry of Labor and Employment, the different indicators of the SINE from one region to another can be accounted for by the size of the job market, with the more developed states (Southeast and South) having other means of helping workers find jobs, thereby competing with the SINE. This would explain the lower success rate in these regions in terms of filling vacancies.

As for the profile of jobs offered and filled, the authors emphasize that most are in the fields of commerce and discrete manufacturing, which require lower skills. The number of vacancies offered and filled in administrative services is also relatively high.

Moretto (2010) points out that private companies seek workers with greater chances of being absorbed. Public intermediation service is sought by less skilled workers with lower levels of schooling who, therefore, have greater difficulty in finding a job. These workers end up being chosen for temporary work, in jobs where workers are easily substituted.

The author warns that in order to improve its performance the public service will have to make considerable efforts to attract workers with better qualifications and more schooling, meaning that they are more likely to be hired. The service should also improve how it deals with workers who have more difficulty in entering the work market.

The conclusion is that over time the SINE has improved its performance in terms of the number of vacancies offered and filled, but there are significant regional differences, especially its effectiveness in the less dynamic markets of the North and Northeast. An analysis of the profile of the vacancies on offer shows that most require low levels of skill.

5.3.2   Unemployment Benefits and Bonus Salaries

The Federal Constitution of 1988 created the Unemployment Benefit Program (later regulated by Law no. 7.998/1990), which ensures the payment of unemployment benefits to provide temporary aid to the unemployed who worked in the formal market. Law no. 8.019/1990 (which modified Law no. 7.998/90) states that the program would be put into practice in conjunction with the states and local government through the SINE, strengthening the decentralization of both programs.

Therefore, with the creation of the Unemployment Benefit Program, the SINE and the network through which this program is operated became integrated, including intermediation between companies and job seekers, generating information about the work market and operational aid to the Program for the Generation of Employment and Income (http://www. mte.gov.br/sine/oquee.asp).

The Unemployment Benefit Program became the main instrument for ensuring that income was paid to dismissed workers. It is believed that during periods of low economic dynamism or recession, the number of beneficiaries and the volume of payouts tend to rise, while the opposite occurs in times of increased production.

Cardoso et al. (2009) point out that the main source of financing for this program is companies' turnover. It was established that the payment of unemployment insurance would be required for eligibility. This was done for a number of reasons, not only to encourage formal labor but also to improve the monitoring of the program and limit coverage, given the limited potential for financing.

Therefore, the program only provides coverage to those who pay into it, which is in accordance with the legal and institutional framework to provide temporary aid to the unemployed who work in the formal market. However, it is not so effective when it comes to dealing with the problem of unemployment on a wider scale.

As for the evolution of the number of beneficiaries regionally, it was observed that between 2001 and 2009 there was a growing trend in the number of people applying for unemployment benefits in all the large regions of the country. Over half of them were in the Southeast.

There are signs that, given the specifics of the Brazilian labor market, the number of beneficiaries of the unemployment benefit program is linked to the growing number of people in formal employment, which has been the case since 2005 (Moretto, 2010, p. 348). According to Moretto, the Unemployment Benefit Program is stable in its rate of coverage, providing benefits for two-thirds of the dismissed workers. However, contrary to expectations, at the same time that there was dynamism in the Brazilian economy, this proportion grew, especially after 2005, providing coverage to around 80 percent of redundant workers.

5.3.3   Training and Qualification Programs

Training policies should consider that companies require workers who know how to deal with the latest technologies. This new competitive environment tends to exclude those who are not prepared to undertake the necessary training programs, meaning that special attention should be paid to those who are at a disadvantage in the job market. Nevertheless, as reported by Cacciamali (2005), many of the steps taken to help these people have aimed to bridge the gaps in the school system (elementary and high school education).

Training and development of skills nationwide are mainly provided by employers. Employers' learning services are known as the National Learning Service and are run by their respective federations all over the country. Several specific sectors of the National Learning Services deserve to be mentioned: Industry (Senai), Commercial (Senac), Transport (Senat), and Agriculture (Senar). These are collectively known as System S.

If this system is efficient at training and teaching skills to employees and improving a company's competitiveness, it does not meet the needs of those at a disadvantage. Nor does it include the unemployed.

The financing of these programs comes from two main sources, originating in the taxation system. In the first case there is a deduction in the income tax of the expenditure of companies with training programs for their workers, in order to give an incentive to companies to invest in training programs. In the second case, companies pay a contribution (proportion of the payroll), which is transferred to public funds that are used for training and teaching skills.

The National Training Plan, which replaced the National Plan for Training Workers (also known as Planfor) aims to provide training and permanent professional education to reduce unemployment, combat poverty and social inequality, and increase productivity and competitiveness in the productive sector. Its global aim is to provide more professional training in the mid-to long term for at least 20 percent of the Economically Active Population every year.

In accordance with Cardoso et al. (2009), some indicators show that there have been positive advances in the quality of this program, which can be seen mainly through the increased duration of courses, which are now approaching 200 hours instead of the 60-hour durations of 2002. They also point out that there appear to have been articulations with other programs. Three-quarters of the pupils are also beneficiaries of other social inclusion policies or policies of work and income.

It is interesting to note the differences in expenditure for the Public Employment and Income System programs. According to Cardoso et al.

(2009), whereas the income guarantee programs (Unemployment Benefit and Bonus Wages) were R$12 billion and R$5 billion, respectively, expenditure on intermediation, training, and health and safety in the workplace did not even reach R$1 billion. Although not the only source of revenue, the FAT is the main source of financing for the programs mentioned above.

5.3.4 Minimum Wage Policies

Ulyssea and Foguel (2006) provide a wide-ranging discussion on the main research in both the Brazilian and the international literature concerning the impacts of the minimum wage on the work market. The authors identify and concentrate on two main trends found in the literature: the impact of the minimum wage on the distribution of salaries, and on employment.

Given the methodological differences that were found, the authors first discuss and then present the results of the works that they analyzed. The works they analyzed used two types of data, namely, time series and panel data.

They point out that irrespective of the approach used, the works seek to identify and quantify the impact of variations in the minimum wage on employment and the inequality of salaries and wages, keeping the other factors that could affect these variables constant. Therefore, it was necessary to use techniques that made it possible to isolate the impact of the minimum wage. To achieve this goal, the ideal procedure would be to have a treatment group that is affected by the policy and a control group that is not affected; that is, to identify two groups of workers that have the same observable characteristics, one being directly affected by the minimum wage policy and the other not, so that an estimate of the impact is made by comparing them both.

Therefore, according to Ulyssea and Foguel (2006), both groups should be identical to each other in every aspect except that one is subjected to the policy and the other is not. Any difference observed would then be attributed to the revision of the minimum wage.

Despite the difficulty of identifying the two groups with such characteristics with the available secondary data, the authors point out that some procedures are commonplace in the literature and that they enable an estimate of the impact of the minimum wage on different variables of the labor market, particularly on jobs.[6]

Ulyssea and Foguel (2006) reveal a second methodology that is widely diffused in Brazilian and international literature, in which the job variables are regressed against the minimum wage variable in order to obtain job elasticities in relation to the minimum wage, utilizing time series data. However, the authors argue that there are some disadvantages to using time series, most importantly that the counterfactual analysis is not defined. In other words, there is no group for adequate comparison, as discussed above.[7]

When it comes to using panel data, Ulyssea and Foguel (2006) emphasize that although there are advantages over time series analysis, the panel data model remains limited because there is no control group (which makes it difficult to identify the specific effect of the minimum wage on the variables of interest). They also point out that for this specification to be more adequate, it would be necessary to restrict the analysis to the group of workers whose wages are more directly affected by the value of the minimum wage.[8]

Ulyssea and Foguel (2006) classify the works of the authors they study into two major groups, the first dealing with the impacts of the minimum wage on the distribution of wages, and the second dealing with the impacts on employment. Regarding the first group, the authors point out an apparent consensus in the literature that the minimum wage has the effect of constricting the distribution of wages and, therefore, reduces inequality of wages for those who remain employed after the minimum is raised.

Concerning the impacts of the minimum wage on employment, the results are controversial. This can be explained to a certain extent by the different methodologies used, including those that do not utilize control groups.

Although they claim that it is difficult to arrive at a conclusion concerning the impacts of the minimum wage on employment, the results of the analyzed studies appear to point towards a small but nonetheless negative effect by the minimum wage on employment. The negative impacts appear to have greater effect on the formal sector (although still of a low magnitude), appearing to affect significantly the likelihood of a person moving from formal to informal employment and, on a smaller scale, to unemployment and inactivity.

Considering the two main trends of studies in the literature, Ulyssea and Foguel (2006) point out that the minimum wage constricts wage distribution. Consequently, wage inequality does not mean that the policy is successful in reducing poverty or in leading to more equal income distribution (measured as per capita family income), since reducing wage inequality does not mean reducing inequality in terms of income, although the concepts of wages and income are linked.

Ulyssea and Foguel (2006) also emphasize that poverty is a phenomenon of the family rather than one of individual workers. If the impact of the minimum wage is higher in groups of workers who are not necessarily from poor families, such as young workers, increasing the minimum wage reduces wage inequality but has no effect on poverty or inequality of income. Even if there are householders receiving a minimum wage, the policy of increasing it can have adverse effects on employment, especially the employment of those located at the bottom end (Ulyssea and Foguel, 2006).

The authors conclude that raising the minimum wage will benefit individuals from poor families who remain employed, but will be extremely harmful to those who lose their jobs or are forced into more precarious occupations with lower wages.

Cunha (2008) studied the wage differentials in the Brazilian agricultural sector over the period 1981–2005, based on the information from the PNAD. The author uses the Heckman procedure, in addition to the Oaxaca–Blinder decomposition, to analyze wage differentials between 1981 and 2005. Her findings suggest that wage differentials had been reduced, especially at the end of the period under study, and that the education, age and formal employment variables helped reduce wage differentials during that time; on the other hand, the gender, geographical region and weekly workload helped increase them. The author found that the minimum wage – and the gross domestic product (GDP) – reflected positively on wages.

5.4 REGRESSION EQUATION MODEL AND ECONOMETRIC METHODOLOGY

The earning equation for employees in agriculture, industry, the service sector, commerce, building and public administration will be adjusted by the ordinary least squares method, using the Heckman (1979) procedure. The model adopts as a dependent variable (Y) the Neperian logarithm of the income from the main source of work of employed people, with the following explanatory variables being considered:

- A binary variable for sex, which assumes a value of 1 for females and 0 for males.
- Five binary variables to distinguish six educational levels: illiterate or under a year of study (base), 1–3 years of study, 4–7 years of study, 8–10 years of study, 11–14 years of study, and 15 years or more of study.
- To distinguish the different salaries according to weekly workload, three binary variables were used: 15–39 hours (base), 40–44 hours, 45–48 hours and 49 hours or more.
- One variable to distinguish formal (base) and informal workers.

- Three binaries to distinguish color or race: white (base), black or brown, yellow, and indigenous.
- Five binaries for regions: North, Northeast (base), South, Southeast without São Paulo, Center-West and São Paulo state.
- Binaries will be introduced to distinguish different sectors of activity.
- Binaries to assess the effect of institutional factors on wages using the real value of the minimum wage.
- Binary variables will also be included to capture the effect of interaction between the minimum wage and position (registered or unregistered worker); between the minimum wage and sector; and between the minimum wage and region.
- Person's age, measured in decades.
- The square of the age variable (I^2), since income does not vary linearly with age.
- Some variables were added to the selection equation that represent certain personal and family features that affect the likelihood of an individual being in work but do not directly affect the income of those who do work. They are:
- Marital status, value of 1 if married, value of 0 if not.
- A binary was included to distinguish whether a person has children or not (base).
- A binary to distinguish position in the family: householder or other.
- Other sources of income besides main activity, in which the dummy variable has a value of 1 if there is another source of income and 0 if there is not.

Note that to evaluate the dynamic of the labor market and its interaction with inequalities and pre-existing social stratifications, the variables included must capture the effect of training and experience of individuals (schooling and age); of discriminatory practices that result in different salaries for equally productive workers with different non-productive attributes (color and gender); of the heterogeneity of workers concerning their productive potential (specialization of occupation); and of segmenting (region or sector of activity), which is translated into different wages for workers without any clear or tangible criteria (Ramos and Vieira, 2001, p. 2; Ramos, 2007, p. 290).

These variables obviously capture differences in the make-up of individual income from work, but are far from explaining all income variations of people in the work market in Brazil. Hoffmann (2000), for instance, warns that when adjusting an earning equation one must recognize that the coefficients obtained introduce some bias due to the exclusion of relevant explanatory variables.

The procedure proposed by Heckman (1979) was adopted to correct the possible problem of sample selectivity. The procedure consists of estimating two equations: the first determines the decision of the individual to enter the work market, through a probit equation using the maximum likelihood method to obtain the estimate of the inverse Mills ratio (Greene, 2003).

As highlighted by Sachsida et al. (2004), the basic idea of this procedure is based on the fact that the economic agent has a reservation wage, and will not enter the labor market for less. Thus, the choice to enter the market is governed by a decision rule that leads the agent to accept or decline the offered wage. The decision rule is defined thus: the individual enters the workforce whenever the wage exceeds his or her reservation wage (Scorzafave and Menezes-Filho, 2001, p. 443).

If the wage depends only on the offer of work, and excludes the role of seeking employment, the sample may be polluted by sample bias. However, when adopting the Heckit estimator, the wage equation appears to be linked to the selection equation, which in turn defines the decision to join the workforce.

Considering employed individuals who are part of the economically active population but who were unemployed between 2002 and 2009, in this sample there are 857 090 individuals, of whom 83 percent were employed. Thus, the fact that the sample is made up of a high percentage of workers with incomes suggests that the sample selectivity bias may not be a problem in this study, which enables the salary equations to be estimated using classic regression methods. Nevertheless, the maximum likelihood ratio test for the rho statistic, which measures the correlation between the selection equation and the determination of wages, indicates bias of the model's sample selection, implying that the procedure proposed by Heckman (1979) is preferable to the uncorrected ordinary least squares estimator.

Table 5.2 shows the results of the estimates obtained for the earnings equation, taking the Heckman procedure into account in two stages. The results for almost every coefficient in the model are significant to 1 percent, including the estimate of the inverse Mills ratio (λ). Only the indigenous race, the term of interaction of the minimum wage, and the field of activity of the building are significant to 5 percent; and the term of interaction of the minimum wage in the Southeast (excluding São Paulo) was not significant.

Differences are found between genders (captured by the negative sign of the coefficient of the sex variable): a lower salary is expected for females than for males. In terms of education, a higher salary is expected for those better educated. The coefficients for skin color of wage earners in the

*Table 5.2   Estimated earning equation for employees in the Brazilian
                economy, 2002–09*

Variable	Coefficient	Marginal Effect[1]
Constant	4.47365	*
Female person (Base: man)	−0.24650	−21.85*
Age		
Age / 10	0.30788	*
$(Age / 10)^2$	−0.02737	*
Schooling (Base: less than one year of study)		
1–3 years of study	0.10018	10.54*
4–7 years of study	0.24939	28.32*
8–10 years of study	0.40782	50.35*
11–14 years of study	0.65552	92.61*
15 years of study or more	1.44098	322.48*
Color (Base: white)		
Black or Brown	−0.06770	−6.55*
Yellow	0.11810	12.54*
Indigenous/Native	−0.03248	−3.20**
Region (Base: Northeast)		
North[2]	0.21255	23.68*
Southeast (excluding SP)	0.18309	20.09*
South	0.29134	33.82*
Center-West	0.40476	49.89*
São Paulo	0.64357	90.33*
Field of Activity (Base: agriculture)		
Industry	0.42182	52.47*
Building	0.26564	30.43*
Commerce	0.35543	42.68*
Public Administration	0.51061	66.63*
Services	0.39697	48.73*
Weekly workload (Base: 15–39 hours)		0.00
40-44 hours	0.26036	29.74*
45-48 hours	0.24809	28.16*
49 hours or more	0.32377	38.23*
Registered employees (Base: registered)	−0.43374	−35.19*
Real Minimum Wage – SMR/100	0.14224	15.29*
Real Minimum Wage and interactions		
(SMR/100)*(North)	−0.00898	−0.89*
(SMR/100)*(Southeast. excluding SP)	0.00106	0.11[ns]
(SMR/100)*(South)	−0.01289	−1.28*
(SMR/100)*(Center-West)	−0.02748	−2.71*
(SMR/100)*(São Paulo)	−0.06775	−6.55*
(SMR/100)*(Unregistered employee)	0.02615	2.65*
(SMR/100)*(Industry)	−0.03921	−3.84*

Table 5.2   (continued)

Variable	Coefficient	Marginal Effect[1]
(SMR/100)*(Building)	−0.01318	−1.31**
(SMR/100)*(Commerce)	−0.04266	−4.18*
(SMR/100)*(Services)	−0.02245	−2.22*
(SMR/100)*(Public Administration)	−0.05136	−5.01*
Lambda calculus	−0.69099	
Number of observations	857 090	

Notes:
* e ** indicate that the result is significant at the level of 1% and 5%, respectively ns = non-significant.
1. *b* is the coefficient, the percentage difference for each binary is é 100[exp(*b*) − 1]%.
2. Excluding the rural areas of RO, AC, AM, RR, PA and AP.

Source: Prepared by the authors based on PNAD micro data (2002–09).

Brazilian economy show that lower earnings are expected for people with black or brown skin compared to those with white.

The sector of activity may also result in substantial differences in expected income, because farming employees tend to earn less than those of other sectors. After considering the effects of other variables on the model, the differential associated with income in the sectors of this study in comparison with the average farming wage is: 66.6 percent higher in public administration, 52.5 percent higher in industry, 48.7 percent higher in services, 42.7 percent higher in commerce and 32.4 percent higher in building. This result is consistent with other works discussing the aspects of income distribution in Brazilian agriculture compared with other sectors, such as that of Hoffmann and Ney (2004) and Hoffmann and Oliveira (2008).

The effect of informality is captured because the unregistered employee earns less than a registered employee. Controlling the effects of the other variables in the equation, the unregistered worker tends to earn 35.19 percent less than a registered worker. It is important to emphasize that in addition to higher wages, formality ensures some basic rights for workers established in the legislation. These include a public pension plan, protection against unemployment in the form of unemployment benefits, and others.

The results of the estimated equation show that São Paulo state, considered separately in this analysis, tends to pay higher wages. In the other regions – the North (without the rural region of the states, except

Tocantins), Southeast (excluding São Paulo), South and Center-West –
workers also earn higher wages than employees in the Northeast.

Menezes et al. (2005) estimated and compared the wage determiners
between the metropolitan regions of São Paulo and Salvador using data
from the Employment and Unemployment Survey (PED) applying the
Heckman procedure and the Oaxaca decomposition. In brief, the authors
confirmed the existence of a differentiation of income between the regions,
especially due to the specifics of each region's economic condition.
Workers are paid more in São Paulo (which is corroborated in this study)
because they have better attributes for being included in the market, and
there are also higher levels of economic concentration.

Since the data utilized in this study cover eight different years, the equation also makes it possible to capture the effect of the real minimum wage
(SMR) on workers' wages. Note that the minimum wage was measured in
hundreds of reais (SMR/100) only so that the respective coefficient would
not be an inconveniently small number.

According to the estimated equation, an increase of R$100 in the
minimum wage is associated with an increase of little more than 15 percent
in the salaries of formally registered workers in the farming sector in the
Northeast.[9] For informal service workers in São Paulo state, an increase
of R$100 is expected to result in a rise of 8.1 percent for wage earners.[10]

5.5   FINAL CONSIDERATIONS

This chapter sought to present the most relevant policies of the Public
Employment, Labor and Income System, whose main source of financing
is the Worker's Aid Fund (FAT). The SINE Intermediation Program, the
Professional Training Program and the Unemployment Insurance and
Bonus Wage programs were also highlighted.

Considering the allocation of resources, more importance was given by
the authorities to the Unemployment Insurance and Bonus Wage policy,
which accounted for more expenditure over time. The analysis of the labor
policies indicates that in general there is a priorization of policies that
aim to improve the labor supply side, instead of the creation of jobs. For
instance, the main government programs aim to protect the unemployed,
to provide professional training and improve human resources, and to
intermediate between companies and job seekers.

Therefore, the general aim of such policies is to increase the number
of active workers, rather than to create jobs. Thus, considering the vast
heterogeneity of the Brazilian regions and labor market, these programs
can be quite ineffective in certain regions where there are no existent jobs.

Labor policies in Brazil should be strengthened to pursue the goals that have been pursued, that is, security, intermediation between companies and job seekers, and professional training and qualification. However, there is also a need for investment to create jobs, and this most often lies outside the responsibility of the Ministry of Labor and Employment. It is important to correlate labor policies with investment and local development policies.

There is a stable source of financing to carry out labor policies. There is also a trend of decentralization, which appears to make the policies more effective, but hinders the articulation of diverse programs.

It is important that the policies for the labor market be put into practice, which often does not occur because priority is given to social assistance programs, such as cash transfer programs, which pay higher political dividends.

An effort has been made, through empirical application, to explain the determinants of income for wage earners, and to examine the influence of the minimum wage as well as other variables commonly found in the literature, such as differences in the personal characteristics of individuals and regional heterogeneities.

One point to mention is that during the analysed period (2002–09) there is still discrimination against women in the labor market and that men continue to receive higher wages. Regarding levels of schooling, the longer a person stays in school, the higher their salary will be. Furthermore, another commonplace result confirmed by this study was that black and brown people earn lower wages than white people.

All the other large regions in Brazil had higher wages than those in the Northeast. However, São Paulo was the state with the highest salaries, possibly because of the better attributes and skills of its workers and greater economic agglomeration and concentration.

The lowest-paid economic activity is the agricultural sector. However, this sector is most sensitive to a real variation of the official minimum wage, meaning that the national minimum wage acts as a yardstick for agricultural wages.

There are signs that real increases in the minimum wage have directly impacted the Brazilian labor market. The interaction terms of the estimated regression, involving the national minimum wage, indicate that variations in the official national minimum wage influence positively and to a greater proportion the wages of the employees of the agricultural sector, compared to the employees of other sectors; as well as the wages of employees of the Northeast region. Moreover, it was possible to verify that workers who are formally registered also benefit more than those who are not.

NOTES

1. The information on wages refers to the value of earnings from workers' main source of income. Information from the PNADs from 2004 to 2009 concerning rural workers in the states of Rondônia, Acre, Amazonas, Roraima, Pará and Amapá (the old Northern region) are not considered due to the difficulty of accessing it because the PNAD did not begin collecting data in these rural areas until 2003. Also excluded are people whose weekly workload was less than 15 hours, people whose field of activity was classed as "Other", inaccurately defined activities and people under the age of 15. For each year, the latest version available up to 2010 was taken into account for the factors of expansion associated with each observation of the sample as supplied by the IBGE.

2. To make a comparison of incomes from different years, they will be expressed as the value in Brazilian reais as of August 2010, using the National Consumer Price Index (INPC) as an inflator, as proposed by Corseuil and Foguel (2002).

3. The Constitution of 1988, through Articles 7, 22 and 239, established unemployment benefit as a social security right and established the PIS/PASEP as its source of financing, while Law 7.998 of January 1990 regulated this constitutional article and broadened the attributions of the Worker's Aid Fund (FAT) (Cardoso et al., 2009, p. 136). The PIS (Programa de Integração Social – Social Integration Program) and PASEP (Programa de Formação do Patrimônio do Servidor Público – Program of the Civil Servants' Assets), better known by the acronym PIS/PASEP, are a social contribution tax, payable by legal entities, in order to finance the payment of unemployment insurance, bonus and participation in revenues of agencies and entities for public and private workers.

4. See http://www.mte.gov.br/sine/oquee.asp.

5. Law number 7.998/1990 regulated the Unemployment Benefit Program (created from the Federal Constitution of 1988), and also established the FAT.

6. Such as the differences-in-differences, propensity score matching or regression discontinuity.

7. For further details, see Ulyssea and Foguel (2006).

8. The authors cite that in the international literature, especially the North American literature, studies are concentrated on teenagers and young people because for these groups there is a perceived higher correlation with the minimum wage with the salaries of this group. Thus, the estimate of the coefficient for the minimum wage may supply an adequate approximation of the impact of the minimum wage on employment.

9. The result for the registered employee in the agriculture sector in the Northeast is obtained directly by calculating the percentage difference corresponding to the coefficient of the minimum wage.

10. To arrive at this value it is necessary to add the coefficient of the minimum wage (SMR/100) and the interaction coefficient of the employee in São Paulo State $c = (0.14224 + 0.026152 - 0.06775 - 0.02245)$ and then obtain the rate of return using the formula $100[\exp(b) - 1]\%$.

REFERENCES

Cacciamali, M.C. (2005), "As políticas ativas de mercado de trabalho no Mercosul", *Estudos Avançados*, **19** (55), 85–104.

Cardoso Jr., J.C., R. Gonzalez and F. de Matos (2009), "Políticas públicas de emprego em contexto de baixo crescimento econômico: a experiência brasileira recente", in J. Macambira and L.M. da F. Carleial (eds), *Emprego, trabalho e políticas públicas*, Fortaleza: Banco do Nordeste do Brasil, Centro de Estudos Sindicais e de Economia do Trabalho, pp. 123–179.

Corseuil, C.H. and M.N. Foguel (2002), "Uma sugestão de deflatores para rendas obtidas a partir de algumas pesquisas domiciliares do IBGE", IPEA Texto para Discussão, 897, Rio de Janeiro: IPEA, jul.

Cunha, M.S. da. (2008), "Os empregados da agricultura brasileira: diferenciais e determinantes salariais", *Revista de Economia e Sociologia Rural*, Brasília, **46** (3), 597–621.

Greene, W.H. (2003), *Econometrics Analysis*, 5th edn, Upper Saddle River, NJ: Prentice-Hall.

Heckman, J. (1979), "Sample selection bias as a specification error", *Econometrica*, **47**, 679–694.

Hoffmann, R. (2000), "Mensuração da desigualdade e da pobreza no Brasil", in R. Henriques (ed.), *Desigualdade e pobreza no Brasil*, Rio de Janeiro: IPEA, pp. 81–107.

Hoffmann, R. and M.G. Ney (2004), "Desigualdade, escolaridade e rendimentos na agricultura, indústria e serviços, de 1992 a 2002", *Economia e Sociedade*, Campinas, **13** (2), 51–79.

Hoffmann, R. and F.C.R. de Oliveira (2008), "Remuneração e características das pessoas ocupadas na agroindústria canavieira no Brasil, de 2002 a 2006", in *Congresso Brasileiro de Economia e Sociologia Rural*, Rio Branco, Brasília: SOBER.

Menezes, W.F., J. Carrera-Fernandez and C. Dedecca (2005), "Diferenciações regionais de rendimentos do trabalho: uma análise das regiões metropolitanas de São Paulo e Salvador", *Estudos Econômicos*, São Paulo, **35** (2), 271–296.

Moretto, A. (2010), "As políticas de mercado de trabalho e a crise de 2008", in A. Moretto, J.D. Krein, M. Pochmann and J. Macambira (eds), *Economia, desenvolvimento regional e mercado de trabalho*, Fortaleza: Banco do Nordeste do Brasil, Centro de Estudos Sindicais e de Economia do Trabalho, pp. 345–361.

Moura, E.S. de and D.N.C. Marinho (2002), "As políticas de trabalho no Brasil: uma perspectiva do trabalhador", *Mercado de trabalho: conjuntura e análise*, **20**, 15–18.

Oliveira, F.C.R. de (2009), "Ocupação, emprego e remuneração na cana-de-açúcar e em outras atividades agropecuárias no Brasil, de 1992 a 2007", Dissertação (Mestrado em Economia Aplicada) – Escola Superior de Agricultura "Luiz de Queiroz", Universidade de São Paulo, Piracicaba.

Pesquisa Nacional por Amostra de Domicilios (PNAD) (2002–09), CD-Rom, Rio de Janeiro.

Ramos, L. (2007), "A desigualdade de rendimentos do trabalho no período pós-Real: o papel da escolaridade e do desemprego", *Economia Aplicada*, São Paulo, **11** (2), 281–301.

Ramos, L. and M.L. Vieira (2001), "Desigualdade de rendimentos no Brasil nas décadas de 80 e 90: evolução e principais determinantes", IPEA Texto para Discussão, 803, Rio de Janeiro: IPEA, jun.

Saboia, J. and J.F. Falvo (2010), "O papel do Sine na intermediação de mão de obra no Brasil – Nordeste e Sudeste", in A. Moretto, J.D. Krein, M. Pochmann and J. Macambira (eds), *Economia, desenvolvimento regional e mercado de trabalho*, Fortaleza: Banco do Nordeste do Brasil, Centro de Estudos Sindicais e de Economia do Trabalho, pp. 321–344.

Sachsida, A., P.R.A. Loureiro and M.J.C. de Mendon (2004), "Um Estudo Sobre Retorno em Escolaridade no Brasil", *Revista Brasileira de Economia*, Rio de Janeiro, **58** (2), 249–265.

Scorzafave, L.G. and N.A. Menezes-Filho (2001), "Participação feminina no mercado de trabalho brasileiro: evolução e determinantes", *Pesquisa e Planejamento Econômico*, Rio de Janeiro, **31** (3), 441–478.

Ulyssea, G. and M.N. Foguel (2006), "Efeito do salário mínimo sobre o mercado de trabalho brasileiro", IPEA Texto para Discussão, 1168, Rio de Janeiro: IPEA.

6. The impact of privatization on Brazil's regions

Edmund Amann and Werner Baer

6.1 INTRODUCTION

The regional concentration of economic activities has been a constant in Brazil's economic history. The first great export cycle was concentrated in the Northeast; this was followed by the gold export boom which moved major economic activities to the Center-South (especially Minas Gerais); and the coffee export cycle, which began in the nineteenth century, concentrated economic activities at first in Rio de Janeiro and surroundings, moving to the state of São Paulo in the middle of the nineteenth century, where the concentration remained, though spreading to some of the areas close to São Paulo.[1]

The regional concentration established during the coffee export cycle would remain as the country began a process of industrial growth based on immigrant labor demand. By the mid-twentieth century, as the country switched from an open to a closed economy, pursuing a policy of import substitution industrialization (ISI), the geographical concentration of economic activity centered still further on the South and Southeast where much of the Brazil's productive capacity and wealth were located.

In the twentieth century the dynamics of market forces tended to reinforce this regional concentration, as both domestic and foreign investors were interested in locating their activities in the region with the highest per capita income, the best infrastructure, the best human capital, and so on. Only special government actions through incentives, various types of transfer payments, and investments of state enterprises were able to bring about some reverse flow of investments.[2] Until the 1990s the relative weight of private domestic and foreign investment in Brazil was limited mostly to the Center-South, as the greatest attractions of a large protected market were to be found in the richer areas of the country. Thus, to compensate the backward regions for this uneven development process the state gradually entered the picture by transferring resources to peripheral regions through dedicated institutions such as SUDENE and SUDAM and special credits funneled through the Banco do Nordeste and the Banco do Brasil.

Since the early 1990s Brazil has adopted a series of neoliberal policy measures, the most important of which have been the opening of the economy (substantial reduction of tariff and other barriers to imports) and the privatization of state enterprises.[3] Our principal concern in this chapter is the regional impact of privatization.

6.2   THE UNFOLDING OF THE PRIVATIZATION PROCESS

Existing data from the Brazilian Development Bank (BNDES), which was the institution supervising the process of privatization, indicate that the bulk of privatizations occurred in the Center-South of the country. As will be noted in Table 6.1, only 0.2 percent of steel privatization occurred in the North and Northeast of the country; the biggest proportionate share of privatization to occur in this region was in petrochemicals (38.4 percent mostly located in the state of Bahia). In such sectors as fertilizers and electrical energy no privatization of federal enterprises occurred; while in mining, CVRD (now known as Vale), a Rio de Janeiro-based enterprise with extensive activities in the Northeast, was privatized in 1997.

In the privatization of railroads[4] the Northeast accounted for only 0.9 percent of the total, while for ports[5] the figure was 5 percent and for financial institutions it was 8.9 percent. At the state level (enterprises which had belonged to individual states) 34 percent of privatizations occurred in the electrical sector, 15 percent in the financial sector and 0 percent in gas, transportation and telecoms. In the entire country there occurred only one privatization in the sewage sector, that of the company serving the Amazonian city of Manaus. In the case of highway privatization (through the granting of concession contracts) this was exclusively limited to the states of São Paulo and Rio de Janeiro (Ribeiro et al., 2001). For the more peripheral states, low prospective toll revenues have rendered private provision of highway infrastructure unfeasible. This evidence seems to confirm the fact that, despite one or two stand-out cases, the bulk of the country's privatization took place mainly in the Center-South region of the country.

6.3   THE LOCATION OF STATE-OWNED ENTERPRISES

Why were there so many privatized enterprises located in the South and South East? This was for the simple reason that nationalized enterprises

Table 6.1   Brazil: the regional impact of privatization

a. Federal privatizations by sector: 1990–2006 (%)	
Electric Energy	30
Telecoms	32
Mining	8
Transportation	2
Petroleum & gas	7
Finance	6
Steel	8
Petrochemicals	4
Other	3
Total	100

b. The share of the Northeast and North in state-level privatization (%)	
Steel	0.2
Petrochemicals	38.4
Fertilizers	0.0
Electrical Sector	0.00
Railroads	0.9
Mining	0.0
Ports	0.5
Finance	8.9
Fixed telephone lines and long-distance services	24.6
Other sectors	0.0

c. State-level government privatizations (%)	
Electricity	74
Gas and sewage	10
Telecommunications	6
Banking and finance	8
Transport	2

d. The share of the Northeast and North (%)	
Electricity	34.1
Gas and sewage	0.0
Transport	0.0
Finance	15.4
Sewage	100.0 (Manaus)
Telecommunications	0.0

Source: Calculated from data supplied by the BNDES.

had sprung up in the public utilities and process industries to serve the growing private sector industries and their consumers. In the poorer regions of Brazil, the state was also active, but the dimension of the involvement was much smaller and more confined to the public utilities sectors. The enterprises concerned here tended to exist on a much smaller scale than their counterparts in the Center South.

One notable area of extensive state involvement in the peripheral regions prior to the privatization drive was that of finance. Here, special publicly owned federal and state banks had sprung up in an attempt to kick start investment and so address ingrained inter-regional income disparities. Among the most notable of these institutions is the Banco do Nordeste and the rural arm of the Banco do Brasil. Privatization of state banks took off in the 1990s but, again, due to the relatively small scale of these institutions outside of the Center South, the share of the North East and North in the privatization of state banks amounted to only 15.4 percent.

6.4   THE ROLE OF THE BNDES

The Brazilian Development Bank, the BNDES, has been and still is the major source of long-term finance in Brazil. Historically it was the major force behind the development of the steel industry, petrochemicals, ship-building and capital goods, all of which tended to be concentrated in the Center-South. The BNDES was an important factor in the country's privatization process, in which many newly privatized firms have been receiving a substantial amount of financial support from this institution. It can thus be said that accompanying privatization, the supporting role of BNDES has favored the richer regions, though the data reveal that the degree to which this is true has been diminishing. Table 6.2 shows how markedly BNDES financing has been skewed towards the Southeast: in 1997 the region accounted for 56.2 percent of all BNDES lending. By 2009 this figure had dropped to 52.6 percent. By contrast, the North and Northeast combined accounted for 15.5 percent in 1997 and 24.4 percent

Table 6.2   Regional allocation of BNDES loans (%)

	North	Northeast	Southeast	South	Center
1997	1.9	13.6	56.2	20	8.4
2009	8.2	16.2	52.6	15.2	7.9

Source: Calculated from BNDES.

Table 6.3   BNDES loans by sector (%)

	2000	2009
Agriculture	8.27	5.02
Oil and mining	0.52	2.36
Manufacturing of which:	44.55	44.22
Cellulose & paper	1.39	2.62
Metal products	7.35	3.29
Vehicles	6.75	4.34
Other transportation equipment	11.70	2.12
Commerce, public utilities and services of which:	46.64	48.09
Electricity & gas	6.27	10.79
Ground transportation services	5.22	17.40
Telecommunications	2.05	2.81
Public administration	0.29	3.04
Total	100	100

Source: Calculated from BNDES (2010).

in 2009. In terms of BNDES loans relating to the PAC (Accelerated Growth Program), 52 percent were focused on the South and Southeast as opposed to 31 percent for the less developed North and Northeast (BNDES, 2008, p. 57).

The relative concentration of BNDES lending in the Southeast is reflected in the sectoral pattern of the bank's activities. As Table 6.3 shows, BNDES lending is heavily biased in favor of sectors such as manufacturing and services. Within manufacturing, one notes a strong emphasis on financing activities in fuels, coke and automobiles. In the general services sector, lending is quite heavily concentrated in ground transportation and electricity. With respect to all these sectors, their relative preponderance in state gross domestic product (GDP) composition is relatively higher in the metropolitan Southeast than in the North and Northeast. This pattern of financing to some extent reflects the path of privatization, which had a heavy emphasis in petrochemicals, process industries and public utilities. The BNDES strategically prioritized the financing of privatized enterprise and, as stated, these tended to be geographically concentrated in the South and Southeast. Even in the BNDES program to support small and medium-sized enterprises (SMEs), about 75 percent of funds in 2008 were dispersed in the South and Southeast of the country; for the Northeast the figure was 9.5 percent (BNDES, 2009).

Given the marginal incidence of privatization outside the Center-South, it follows that any positive impacts stemming from privatization (such as efficiency gains or improved service provision) could only have been more modest in the peripheral regions. How could persistent regional inequalities be addressed, given the necessarily limited role of privatization in such regions? The answer here appears to be linked to the substantial amount of fiscal transfers to less favored regions which have been developed over a long period of time, not least in the post-privatization period.

Since the constitution of 1988, these transfers have accelerated thanks to more generous funding of state and municipal government activities by the federal government. Picking up the initiative of the government of Fernando Henrique Cardoso, the Lula administration has notably increased the scope of such interregional transfers through the expansion of the Bolsa Família, a conditional cash transfer program. In fact, the relative importance to the poorer states' finances of resources received from the federal government through social security and fiscal transfers far outstrips the importance of dedicated regional development initiatives such as SUDENE and SUDAM (Gomes, 2002, p. 21).

Further evidence to support this argument may be inferred from Table 6.4. It will be clear that the relative importance of sectors where the state plays an important role is greater in many Northeastern states compared with those of the Center-South. For example, Table 6.4 shows that the dependence of the poorer states on government expenditures (administration, health services, social security and so on) is much greater than that of wealthier states. In 2007 such expenditure varied between 16 and 30.6 percent of state GDP among these states, whereas in the richer states the equivalent expenditures ranged from 8.9 percent (in São Paulo) to 13.6 percent (in Minas Gerais).

It is therefore not surprising that the Northeast accounted for 52 percent of transfers relating to the Bolsa Família (PNAD). In terms of per capita public income transference, the PNAD data reveal that the highest per capita receipts of Bolsa Família can be found in Northeastern states. For example, in Pernambuco state, average per capita Bolsa Família receipts attained R$65 in 2005, whereas in São Paulo state the equivalent figure was just R$14. However, the Bolsa Família represents just one aspect of regional transfers. There are many other sources. For example, the FPE (Fundo de Participação dos Estados – State Participation Fund) represents a mechanism whereby some federal income tax and industrial products tax receipts are earmarked and distributed for use by states in accordance with their needs. Maciel et al. (2006, p. 5) show that fully 52.46 percent of this fund is allocated to the poor Northeast of the country. The rich Southeastern region, by contrast, enjoys a participation rate of just 8.48 percent.

Table 6.4   Share of state value-added

	Administration, health, public education and social secuity		Production and distribution of electricity, gas, water, sewage and urban cleaning	
	2003	2007	2003	2007
Brazil	15.1	15.5	3.4	3.6
Rondonia	27.3	28.8	1.3	3.1
Acre	35.6	34.3	1.4	1.9
Amazonas	16.8	16.8	0.7	2.0
Roraima	43.2	48.4	1.1	1.7
Pará	18.8	18.4	5.1	5.5
Amapá	43.2	44.8	1.7	1.0
Tocantins	20.5	24.5	5.6	7.0
Maranhão	20.6	20.7	1.7	2.1
Piauí	27.0	30.2	3.4	3.8
Ceará	20.8	21.3	4.1	5.3
Rio Grd do N	26.1	27.5	3.0	2.3
Paraíba	28.3	30.6	6.5	6.5
Pernambuco	22.8	23.5	4.5	5.1
Alagoas	23.8	25.3	5.6	5.4
Sergipe	21.7	24.5	11.6	8.1
Bahia	16.1	16.6	5.2	5.4
Minas Gerais	13.7	13.6	4.3	4.8
Espirito Santo	15.1	14.0	1.1	1.0
Rio de Janeiro	18.8	18.1	2.5	2.8
São Paulo	8.8	8.9	3.3	2.9
Paraná	9.8	10.6	4.9	5.3
Santa Catarina	10.7	11.1	3.5	6.0
Rio Gr. Do Sul	12.9	13.4	2.2	2.5
Mat. Gr. D. Sul	15.7	20.0	2.3	2.3
Mato Grosso	12.6	14.3	2.9	3.4
Goiás	13.2	14.3	5.5	5.3
Distr. Federal	54.2	53.8	1.1	1.4

Source: IBGE.

Similar trends can be adduced from Table 6.5. This shows the composition of receipts for Brazil's state governments in 2006. The poorer states of Brazil's North and Northeast depend to a much larger extent on transfers from the federal government than others. In the Amazon region, they made up between 59 and 79 percent of total state government receipts; in Brazil's Northeast they made up between 34 and 55

*Table 6.5   Incidence of transfers from federal government to the states:
proportion of total receipts and per capita*

	Total transfers as a proportion of total receipts (%)	Current transfers per capita (R$)
Rondonia	48	788
Acre	77	1959
Amazonas	34	560
Roraima	79	2515
Pará	44	417
Amapá	77	2178
Tocantins	67	1319
Maranhão	56	455
Piauí	59	593
Ceará	43	382
Rio Grd do N	48	698
Paraíba	49	565
Pernambuco	40	422
Alagoas	55	559
Sergipe	51	854
Bahia	34	373
Minas Gerais	23	316
Espirito Santo	18	404
Rio de Janeiro	27	595
São Paulo	10	207
Paraná	26	362
Santa Catarina	31	345
Rio Gr. Do Sul	23	370
Mat. Gr. D. Sul	26	469
Mato Grosso	28	553
Goiás	27	369
Distr. Federal	56	3047

Source: Mendes et al. (2008, pp. 25, 58).

percent of total receipts; while in the Center-South and South of Brazil
they varied between 10 percent (São Paulo) and 27 percent (Rio de
Janeiro).

On a per capita basis, again, the figures illustrate the relative importance of transfers to state governments in peripheral regions. For
example, Table 6.5 shows that for states in the North and Northeast,
typically between 60 and 70 percent of their expenditures per capita were
financed through transfers. For the Southern states, the equivalent figures

were much lower: in the case of São Paulo, for example, only 3 percent of the state's expenditure per capita was financed through transfers.

6.5 BANK PRIVATIZATION, CONSOLIDATION AND REGIONAL CREDIT

One of the most important forces governing the recent evolution of regional disparities in Brazil centers on the related roles of bank privatization and bank consolidation. In the 1990s a combination of market liberalization and privatization led to a process of bank mergers and sector consolidation. As a result of this, the number of banks declined from 216 in 1990 to 164 in 2003 (Crocco et al., 2009, p. 17). One of the facets of this trend was a reduction in the number of banks headquartered outside the rich Southeast and Center-South of the country. Almeida and Jayme (2008, p. 169) summarize the results of their econometric study examining the implications of this for lending in Brazil's peripheral regions. In their words:

> It was clear that the presence of bank branches and head offices in the regions is positively related to lending. Accordingly, the relocation of branches in a country's most developed regions, together with a regional concentration of bank head offices reduces the per capita credit stock in the other regions. (ibid.)

Their findings are consistent with data presented in Table 6.6 which shows credit per capita in 2002 reaching just R$167.87 in the Northeast, compared with R$912.77 in the Southeast and R$1693.79 in the South.

Table 6.6 Banking indicators by region, 2002

Region	Average workforce	Branches per capita	Credit per capita (R$)	Financial operations tax receipts per capita	Average monthly wage (R$)
Northeast	4251	3.70	167.87	32.07	550.09
Southeast	12740	14.49	912.77	133.76	761.01
South	7882	22.43	1693.79	115.20	790.00
Center-West	5474	11.32	1570.81	107.88	723.52

Source: Crocco et al. (2009, p. 20).

6.6   CONCLUSIONS AND FUTURE PROSPECTS

We have shown in this chapter that the benefits from privatization have been concentrated in the richer areas of Brazil. This was due to the fact that state enterprises had a much greater degree of involvement in that region than either in the poor Northeast or the less populated Center-West and Amazon regions. It is ironic, however, that this result has not created the appearance of a purely market-orientated economy in the richer regions of the country. This is clear from the fact that the traditional and new private sectors of the richer regions depend heavily on the government development bank, the BNDES. Therefore, although the market plays a role in forcing many firms in the private sector to upgrade their production methods as they face foreign competition (due to trade liberalization and the appreciated exchange rate), it would seem that the state is dominant in directing the investment resources of the country.

As far as the poor regions of the country are concerned, especially the Northeast, the small benefits received from privatization have been compensated by a massive increase in resource transfers through the fiscal system. Although this has contributed to the growth of the Northeast region and to an increase in the welfare of the poor (especially via Bolsa Família) the privatization process has not delivered the region from its traditional dependence on resource transfers. A major survey of the recent resurgence of growth in Brazil points to the fact that a large proportion has been taking place in the Center-South of the country. The report states that the growth has been a consequence of a large increase in investment projects; by contrast such growth as has been realized in the North and Northeast is attributable to government transfers.[6] It might be argued that our generalization is contradicted by the substantial growth of the petrochemical sector in Bahia and the installation of a modern manufacturing complex which developed around the construction of the new Ford Motor Company plant in that state. The latter, however, was the result of special incentives provided to Ford to establish itself in the region. It would seem that the forward and backward linkages of these developments are limited, since most inputs stem from imports from the South (or abroad) and, indeed, the principal market lies outside the region. As far as the petrochemical complex is concerned, this is a very capital-intensive undertaking which also relies on many externally sourced inputs.

In sum, the evidence suggests that without more radical policy shifts, the culture of dependency of Brazil's poorer regions will be perpetuated.

NOTES

1. Baer (2008), Ch. 2.
2. Baer (2008), Ch. 11.
3. Amann and Baer (2002).
4. For more detail on the concession contracts applied to the rail sector – and their concentration in the South and Southeast – see Campos Neto et al. (2010).
5. For more detail on the concession contracts applied to the ports sector – and their concentration in the South and Southeast – see IPEA (2009).
6. Report by MB Associados, *O Estado de São Paulo*, 20 June 2010, p. B1.

REFERENCES

Almeida, D. and F. Jayme Jr (2008), "Bank consolidation and credit concentration in Brazil (1995–2004)", *CEPAL Review*, August, 155–171.

Amann, Edmund and Werner Baer (2002), "Neoliberalism and its consequences in Brazil", *Journal of Latin American Studies*, **34**, 945–959.

Baer, Werner (2008), *The Brazilian Economy: Growth and Development*, 6th edn, Boulder, CO: Lynne Rienner Publishers.

BNDES (2008), *Relatório Annual 2008*, Rio de Janeiro: BNDES.

BNDES (2009), *Privatizações no Brasil*, Rio de Janeiro: BNDES.

BNDES (2010), *BNDES Trimestral*, 14 April, No. 11.

Campos Neto, C., B. Pêgo Filho, A. Romminger, I. Ferreira and L. Vasconcelos (2010), "Gargalos e demandas da infraestrutura ferroviária e os investimentos do PAC: mapeamento IPEA de obras ferroviárias", IPEA Texto Para Discussão, No. 1465, January.

Crocco, M., F. Santos and P. Amaral (2009), "The spatial structure of financial development in Brazil", paper presented at the Annual International Conference of the Regional Studies Association, Leuven, Belgium, April.

Gomes, G. (2002), "Regional development strategies in Brazil", paper written for the OECD and Ceará State Government International Conference on Regional Development and Foreign Direct Investment, 12–13 December.

IPEA (2009), "Analise do setor portuário Brasileiro no contexto do programa de aceleração do crescimento", in IPEA (ed.), *Brasil en Desenvolvimento: Estado, Planejamento e Políticas Públicas*, Brasília: IPEA, pp. 321–348.

Maciel, P., J. Andrade and V. Teles (2006), "Transferências fiscais e convergência regional no Brasil", mimeo.

Mendes, M., R. Miranda and F. Cosio (2008), "Transferências intergovernmentais no Brasil: diagnóstico e proposta de reforma", Consultoria Leglislativa do Senado Federal, Texto para discussão, No. 40.

Ribeiro, K., A. Dantas and K. Yamamoto (2001), "The Brazilian experience in road concessions: past, present and future", conference paper, University of Canterbury, New Zealand.

7. Science, technology and innovation policies in the regional development of Brazil

Luiz Ricardo Cavalcante and Simone Uderman

7.1 INTRODUCTION

Innovation is central to economic development, especially to the growth of output and productivity. The central role played by innovation in the progress of capitalism has been emphasized by authors like Schumpeter, who argued that: "the fundamental impulse that sets and keeps the capitalist engine in motion comes from the new consumers' goods, the new methods of production or transportation, the new markets, the new forms of industrial organization that the capitalist enterprise creates" (Schumpeter, 1950 [1942], p. 83).

Based upon this perception, several countries have been adopting science, technology and innovation (ST&I) public policies. These countries have been focusing on building ST&I policymaking capabilities, strengthening technological institutions, funding innovative projects, and forging ties between industry and the academic community. In Brazil, ST&I policies have been increasingly considered by the federal government when adopting industrial policies. Indeed, the main industrial policies implemented in Brazil during the 2000s – the Industrial, Technological and Foreign Trade Policy (PITCE) and the Productive Development Policy (PDP) – strongly emphasized the role of innovation in economic development. These policies are concerned with promoting structural changes in the Brazilian economy, and are only marginally directed to regional development issues.

On the other hand, regional development policies seem not to emphasize innovation as a way of reducing the high levels of inequalities that have historically marked Brazilian regions. The National Policy for Regional Development is essentially based on the traditional funding instruments to attract ordinary investments to the less developed regions.[1] On the state level, although the rhetoric of the development policies focuses on local development initiatives (such as so-called "local productive arrangements"), the heart of regional economic growth policies remains, in practice, uncoordinated investment attraction through tax breaks and financial incentives.

As a result, the high level of regional inequalities traditionally observed in Brazil tends to amplified when ST&I data are considered. This may have a negative impact on regional inequalities in the medium and long run.

7.2 LITERATURE REVIEW: ST&I AND REGIONAL DEVELOPMENT

It is quite clear that the effects of scientific and technological progress are widespread, and are responsible for inducing major changes in the economy and society from local to national spheres. Governments are increasingly undertaking the task of promoting, regulating, and articulating innovation activities. The impacts of ST&I policies are noteworthy in development. Developed countries typically invest more in research and development (R&D), as shown in Table 7.1.

The numbers above not only confirm that more developed countries invest more resources in R&D but also suggest some sort of "red queen effect" for the increasing Brazilian expenditures on R&D.[2] In fact, the slight increase between 2000 and 2008 (1.02 to 1.09 percent) is not to be

Table 7.1   Gross expenditures in R&D / GDP, selected countries, 2000–2008 (%)

	2000	2001	2002	2003	2004	2005	2006	2007	2008
Japan	3.04	3.12	3.17	3.20	3.17	3.32	3.40	3.44	3.42
United States	2.71	2.72	2.62	2.61	2.54	2.57	2.61	2.66	2.77
Germany	2.45	2.46	2.49	2.52	2.49	2.49	2.53	2.53	2.64
South Korea	2.30	2.47	2.40	2.49	2.68	2.79	3.01	3.21	3.37
Argentina	0.44	0.42	0.39	0.41	0.44	0.46	0.49	0.51	
Mexico	0.34	0.36	0.40	0.40	0.40	0.41	0.39	0.37	
Brazil	1.02	1.04	0.98	0.96	0.90	0.97	1.00	1.07	1.09
Russian Federation	1.05	1.18	1.25	1.28	1.15	1.07	1.07	1.12	1.03
India	0.82	0.85	0.82	0.80	0.78				
China	0.90	0.95	1.07	1.13	1.23	1.34	1.42	1.44	1.54

Source: OECD / Brazilian Ministry of Science and Technology (MCT, 2010) / Industrial R&D in India: Broad Indications.

compared to the path this indicator followed in countries like South Korea and China, where expenditures on R&D jumped from 2.30 to 3.37 percent and from 0.90 to 1.54 percent of national GDP, respectively.

Countries marked by high levels of R&D expenditures have room to improve the efficiency of their innovation policies in order to drive long-term economic growth. According to Pilat and Wyckoff (2010), success relies on enhancing the performance of the system as a whole, encouraging links between universities, public research institutions, and entrepreneurs eager to benefit from an environment which encourages innovation. An efficient financial structure, an accurate regulatory frame and a high-quality educational system add relevant support to the promotion of innovative activities. Considering the complexity and costs associated with these arrangements, and the requirement of legitimate coordination, it is recognized that the government's key role is to provide a solid foundation for new business areas.

As governments look at the potential of innovation and entrepreneurial solutions to boost growth and employment levels, ST&I policies have increasingly focused on "innovation" as opposed to "science and technology" (Kraemer-Mbula and Wamac, 2010). A variety of incentive mechanisms to increase the innovative capacity of societies have been implemented in various countries.

Some approaches outline the innovation process logic in an attempt to identify the most effective policies. In this chapter, these approaches are classified into three groups: the linear model, the chain-linked model and the innovation system (or systemic) approach.

In the early linear model, technology advances were assumed to rely on basic research, thought to be "the pacemaker of technological progress" (Bush, 1945; Viotti, 2004, p.24). As results in science are the basis for applied research, invention and technological findings, innovation emerges through a series of sequential stages. Diffusion of innovation is the last phase in this sequence.

Considering that innovation often stimulates science, and that feedbacks are missing in the simple linear model, many authors highlight the necessity to understand the complexity of the system. Kline and Rosemberg (1986, p.293) argue that the idea that science plays the central initiating role "is far too simple and is bound to inhibit and distort our thinking about the nature and use of processes of innovation". The chain-linked model points out that market opportunities often lead to a research path, pushing new science knowledge through feedback links. Science and development processes, therefore, go hand in hand. Strong emphasis on the crucial role played by the demand side in innovation processes leads to the conclusion that the first step in most innovations is not research, but design. Hence, market demands, innovation activities and commercial success are not only necessary ingredients, but frequently play a more important role than science in cost reduction and the improvement of system performance.[3]

During the 1990s, this conceptual framework expanded its perspective to include interactive linkages and multifaceted connections in the innovation system. Innovation occurs through an interactive process that takes place both within and among firms, organizations and institutions. This new approach falls under the label "national innovation systems" (NIS). The NIS approach claims that innovation activities are embedded within society, and emphasizes the interactions of firms and institutions throughout the system. According to Nelson (1993, p. 4), a national innovation system is a "set of institutions whose interactions determine the innovative performance of the national firms". Employing a broader definition, Lundvall (1992, p. 13) remarks that it includes the elements and relations which interact in the production, diffusion and use of new and economically useful knowledge.

A new policy perspective emerges from the chain-linked model and the systemic approach to innovation. Analyzing the chain-linked model, Edquist and Hommen (1999, p. 70) consider "complementary strengths of different types of firms, and effective co-ordination among these and other actors as essential to creation and development of viable 'innovation chains' for design, production, and marketing of new products". Consequently, public policies may focus on the building of this linkage structure. The NIS approach promotes links between firms, public laboratories and research centers. It suggests that public policies emphasize institutional aspects concerning financial support, regulatory issues and education.

However, even the Organisation for Economic Co-operation and Development (OECD) admits that there are concerns that the NIS approach "has too little operational value, and is difficult to implement" (OECD, 2002, p. 11). In fact, in spite of the theoretical upgrade, there is not much in the literature about the procedures to be used in order to build an innovative environment and achieve its main purposes. The persistence of policies that focus on science, rather than on technology and innovation, reflects the mismatch between the analytical categories used to support policies formulations and the performance of actions based upon less instrumental concepts (Cavalcante, 2009).

Regardless of its limitations, the linear model is not only "analytical", but also "instrumental". The implications of a policy emerge almost automatically from the sequence of phases and procedures within this framework. The systemic approach is chiefly "analytical", and barely "instrumental". Even if it can provide a more comprehensive understanding of the reality, it is hard to convert this knowledge into operational prescriptions to be implemented by governments.

The same restrictions apply to regional development policies, which face challenges associated to the incorporation of ST&I strategies. The concept of regional innovation system (RIS) emerged at the beginning of the 1990s. An RIS is characterized "by co-operation in innovation activity between firms and knowledge creating and diffusing organizations, such as universities, training organizations, R&D institutes, technology transfer agencies, and so forth, and the innovation supportive culture that enables both firms and systems to evolve over time" (Doloreux and Parto, 2004, p. 4). Extending the theoretical analysis and policy implications of the NIS to the regional level, it can be defined as a complex of innovation firms and institutions within a region, or as a subsystem of an NIS. By developing this complex, nations could prevent the geographical disequilibrium of regional technological and economic capacities, and develop the national economy as a whole (Chung, 2002).

To become attractive for companies, territories are supposed to set up specific policies to support their innovation strategies. Based upon Malecki (1980, 1987) and Luger and Goldstein (1991), it can be argued that location decisions for R&D-intensive investments usually consider aspects such as: (1) skilled labor availability; (2) urban infrastructure and amenities; (3) telecommunications infrastructure; (4) proximity to a major airport; and (5) a cooperation-friendly institutional environment. Cook and Memedovic (2003, p. 11) identify the key dimensions of a regionalized innovation system as: (1) the processes and policies supporting education and knowledge transfer; (2) arrangements for the governance of innovation; (3) the level of investment, especially in R&D; and (4) the type of firms and their degree of linkage and communication, in terms of networking, subcontracting, presence or absence of supply chains, and degree of co-makership between customers and suppliers.

Although regional economic theory has increasingly assimilated aspects related to the promotion and diffusion of innovation, the trend has hardly materialized in regional public policies. A review of the literature shows that, in the mid-twentieth century, growth poles (Perroux, 1955), cumulative causation (Myrdal, 1960 [1957]) and backward/forward linkages (Hirschman, 1958) were concepts that sustained regional development strategies. Most of the experiences centered on investment attraction, but had no specific focus on ST&I. In the late twentieth century, the perception that social capital (Putnam, 1993; Woocock, 1998) and local innovation systems (Storper, 1994; Breschi and Lissoni, 2001) are essential to broaden regional development perspectives disseminates a new vision.

However, the rhetoric seems to fail in its policy implications. The increasing importance of immaterial elements related to culture, social arrangements, institution environment, and the innovative use of knowledge and technologies require attention to cooperation and networking. The lack of instrumental prescriptions and the difficulties in implementing the proposals lead regional development policies to remain, in practice, focused on indistinct investment attraction.

In Brazil, most of the typical instruments employed to promote ST&I, such as grants to researchers and firms, financial and fiscal incentives aimed at innovative activities, and the construction of an environment conducive to innovation (quality universities, research centers and research parks), depends on national policies and resources. Brazilian Ministry of Science and Technology (MCT) data on the level of investments in R&D show that federal expenditures are more than double federal unit expenditures. As a result, ST&I strategies designed at the national level play an important role in defining the innovation capacity of each region.

The importance of federal intervention is also true for other countries, and some original initiatives are described in the literature. Baer and Miles (1999), for example, describe the experience of regional development policies in the Southeast of the United States. Deliberate national policies have radically transformed the potential development conditions of this area. Many proficient measures, including the establishment of military facilities, were used to push a sustainable growth cycle. A mix of growth pole and technology-based investments aided this region to catch up with the rest of the country and lower the income gap. Investment spillover effects assured sustainable roots and promoted a virtuous cycle of economic development which was not based on the traditional regional structure:

> defense activity had spillover effects on the local economies beyond the immediate job benefits of the installation itself. The activity required technically trained professionals, so local universities were given large grants to conduct the necessary research and development. Private technology companies would often open up branches near space and military installations to do contract work and this of course brought further positive externalities. (Baer and Miles, 1999, p. 184)

Such policies might be a way of overcoming what Oughton et al. (2002, p. 98) called the "regional innovation paradox". These authors highlighted that lagging regions tend to present a relatively lower capacity to absorb public funds directed to the promotion of innovation. The more innovation needed to increase the competitive position of firms in poorer regions, the more difficult it is to utilize public resources earmarked for innovation. According to the authors, solving the paradox requires policies that increase the capacity of regions to absorb investment funds for innovation-related activities, by working on both the demand and the supply side of the system. Luger (1994) points out that financial commitment and centralized policymaking are required to overcome the strong market forces that create ST&I disparities among and within regions.

7.3   ST&I POLICIES IN BRAZIL: AN OVERVIEW[4]

As shown in Table 7.1, Brazil invests approximately 1 percent of its gross domestic product (GDP) in R&D. Most of the resources come from government funds, which represented 54 percent of this amount in 2008 (MCT, 2010). Figure 7.1 shows the percentage of gross expenditures in R&D financed by governments in selected countries, and suggests that private R&D investments – considered more closely related to firm competitiveness – are still low compared not only to more developed countries, but also to developing countries such as China.

The Action Plan for 2007–10, conceived in 2006 and coordinated by the MCT, set priorities that guide the ST&I policies in Brazil (MCT, 2007).

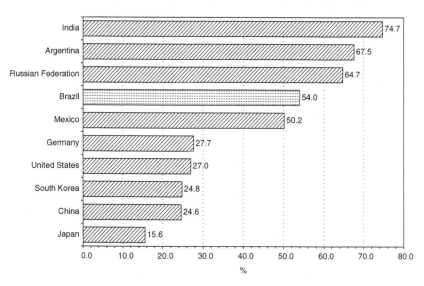

Source: OECD / Brazilian Ministry of Science and Technology (MCT, 2010) / Industrial R&D in India.

Figure 7.1   Percentage of the gross expenditures in R&D financed by the government, selected countries, last available year

Among these priorities, a national goal was established which has been replicated in the national industrial policy launched in 2008: to increase the ratio between private R&D expenditures and GDP from 0.51 to 0.65 percent by 2010. Embracing a more offensive strategy approach, the strategy to reach this goal is based on the use of different integrated instruments to support innovation and technological progress. A broad concept of industrial policy emerges and is associated with the NIS assumptions.

As a result, the Brazilian government has focused on encouraging innovation at the firm level, by improving its competence to produce higher added value goods, increasing technical skills and boosting entrepreneurship. The government has made adjustments to the institutional framework and in the legal apparatus, and created fiscal and financial incentives to support innovation.

In 1999, sectoral funds were established to fund strategic R&D, aimed at providing a more stable environment for innovative activities and at stimulating stronger connections between universities, research institutes and companies. These resources increased the financial capacity of the Brazilian Innovation Agency (FINEP), which provides financial support (grants and credit) to companies and institutions pursuing research activities or ready to build up cooperative innovative projects.[5]

In line with efforts to provide financial support to innovation initiatives, the National Development Bank (BNDES), a public institution which provides long-term credit to both productive and infrastructure investments, announced the creation of credit lines specifically designed to boost innovation. The financing packages offered by the BNDES supplement the resources provided by the FINEP and reinforce the availability of funds directed to innovative projects in Brazil. Between 2007 and 2009, BNDES support to innovation projects grew from R$923 million to R$1.5 billion. In the same period, the FINEP's financial resources expanded from R$2 billion to R$2.8 billion, sustained by sectoral funds. Brito Cruz and Mello (2006, p. 21) highlight the creation of venture capital funds by the BNDES, the FINEP and the Banco do Brasil in 2005 and 2006, but claim it is still too soon to evaluate the effects of these policies in encouraging start-up private investments.

With regard to institutional changes focused on innovation, it is important to mention two new supporting laws, launched in 2004 and 2005. The so-called "innovation law" (Law no. 10.973/2004) encourages public and private sectors to share staff, funding and facilities (such as laboratories). It allows private companies to give funds to public institutions to carry out research on their behalf, encouraging cooperation between research centers and the productive sector. Law no. 11.196/2005 (introduced one year later and known in Brazil as the "Lei do Bem") simplified

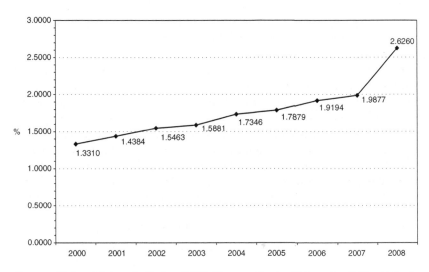

Source: National Science Indicators (NSI), Thomson Reuters/Science (available at http://
www.mct.gov.br). Elaborated by the authors.

*Figure 7.2   Share of Brazil in the world scientific papers indexed by the
ISI, 2000–2008*

procedures for firms to take advantage of existing tax breaks and sped up
and expanded fiscal incentives for investments in innovative activities. The
new rules reduced the bureaucracy of the former law, issued in 1993 (Law
no. 8.661/1993). According to the MCT, federal tax waivers associated to
this benefit were estimated to reach R$1.2 billion in 2010.[6] At the state
level, the spread of local institutions to provide funding to R&D activities
indicates that federal units are aware of this issue, even if the relatively low
resources allocated still suggest a lack of priority.

In spite of institutional and legal adjustments aimed at promoting innovation at the firm level, ST&I indicators suggest that a more successful
path was effectively observed for scientific indicators.[7] These include input
indicators such as qualified human resources, and output indicators such
as the number of scientific papers indexed by the Institute for Scientific
Information (ISI). The number of PhD researchers per 100 000 residents
more than doubled between 2000 and 2008, expanding from 17.10 to
40.10. In line with the increase in scientific infrastructure, the share of
Brazil in the number of world scientific papers indexed by the ISI similarly
increased, as shown in Figure 7.2.

Although ST&I policies have been successful in providing human
resources for research and increasing the national share in the output of

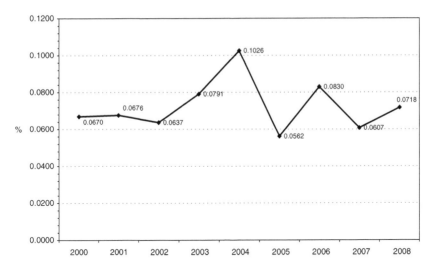

Source: National Science Indicators (NSI), Thomson Reuters/Science (available at http:// www.mct.gov.br). USPTO (available at: http://www.uspto.gov). Elaborated by the authors.

Figure 7.3 Share of Brazil in the world patents granted by USPTO, 2000–2008

world scientific papers, they have not been able to foster a meaningful innovation process. Not only are the technological inputs, such as private expenditures in R&D, relatively small, but also outputs, measured by the share of Brazil in world patents granted by the United States Patent and Trademark Office (USPTO), are low and, in addition, erratic, as shown in Figure 7.3.

The main challenge still remains: to make firms and the national innovation systems interact. In spite of widespread agreement on the positive association between knowledge, technological innovation and competitiveness, it remains to be shown how the "channels, mechanisms and conditions through which technological advances is translated into improved economic performance at the firm, regional and national level" (Oughton et al., 2002, p. 97). This is particularly true in environments marked by risk aversion and lack of an R&D tradition at the firm level, as seems to be the case in Brazil.

The successful cases of aircraft technologies, agriculture innovation and offshore oil extraction observed in Brazil reinforce this perception. In fact, the research networks surrounding Embraer, Embrapa and Petrobras have reached significant outputs.[8] All these cases have been marked by some sort of "embedded autonomy" (Evans, 1995), including long-term involvement of both government and industry, and an institutional network. Results still require a long time to appear, however.

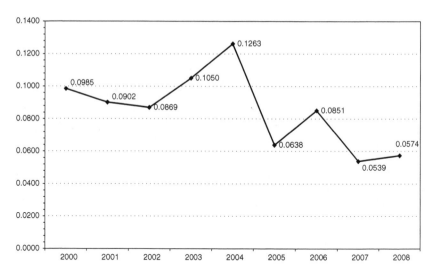

Source: National Science Indicators (NSI), Thomson Reuters/Science (available at http://
www.mct.gov.br) / USPTO (available at http://www.uspto.gov). Elaborated by the authors

Figure 7.4   Brazilian opportunity-taking indicator, 2000–2008

The erratic path of patents granted by the USPTO, combined with the accelerated growth scientific papers in Brazil indexed by the ISI, leads to a declining opportunity-taking indicator (OTI). This is defined by Albuquerque (1999) as the ratio between the two indicators, and is shown in Figure 7.4.

The trend in Figure 7.4 reinforces the perception that, in spite of relevant (though anecdotal) successful results, the adopted policies are still mainly directed to scientific research.

This overview of ST&I policies in Brazil will be useful in analyzing the regional distribution of resources directed to these activities in Brazil.

7.4   BRAZILIAN ST&I POLICIES AND THEIR REGIONAL IMPACTS

In this section, the regional impacts of the Brazilian ST&I policies are discussed. In subsection 7.4.1, an overview of the evolution of the ST&I regional inequalities in Brazil is presented. This overview supports subsection 7.4.2, where the regional distribution of federal resources directed to ST&I activities is discussed. It is assumed that the closer the distribution of the federal resources is to the distribution of the ST&I infrastructure in the country, the more neutral the policy. In other words, if the regional allocation of resources simply replicates the pre-existing ST&I basis, the ST&I policies might be considered passive. If the resources are directed to the federal units where a larger ST&I basis is installed, the policies tend to deepen regional inequalities (as the resources allocated to these regions will trigger the growth of the ST&I basis itself). This process may cause some sort of "cumulative causation", the concept of which was originally proposed by Myrdal (1960 [1957]) to explain inequality trajectories. If less developed federal units receive proportionally more resources than their ST&I basis, some sort of convergence process might take place. As a result, the ST&I infrastructure is both cause and consequence of the allocation of resources. In this chapter, the pre-existing infrastructure is used to check whether the distribution of resources follows a neutral, concentrating or deconcentrating path.

7.4.1 Evolution of the ST&I Regional Inequalities in Brazil

In this subsection, a brief overview of the ST&I regional inequalities in Brazil is presented. The analysis is based upon a series of data which reasonably reflect the scientific infrastructure in each federal unit on the one hand, and on the other, its technological and innovative development level.

Scientific infrastructure
The National Council for Scientific and Technological Development (CNPq) provides a direct measure of scientific infrastructure in each Brazilian federal unit based on the number of PhD researchers listed in the research groups census performed by the CNPq itself.[9] The choice of this indicator as a proxy of the scientific infrastructure implicitly assumes that the physical capital required to research activities is, on average, the same per capita level. If this assumption is valid, an indicator of human capital might be considered a reasonable proxy of the scientific infrastructure installed in each federal unit.[10] The indicator chosen in this chapter is available in the CNPq census for the years 2000, 2002, 2004, 2006 and 2008.

As mentioned in section 7.3, there was a considerable increase in scientific infrastructure (measured as the number of PhD researchers per 100 000 residents) in Brazil during the period 2000–2008. However, when the data are segmented by region, inequalities become apparent, as can be seen in Table 7.2.

The analysis of the data shown in Table 7.2 indicates that scientific inequalities are similar to the economic inequalities observed among the

Table 7.2   Number of PhD researchers per 100 000 residents, Brazilian macroregions, 2000–2008

	2000	2002	2004	2006	2008	Annual growth rate 2000–2008 (%)
North	5.42	8.65	12.32	15.78	18.88	16.89
Northeast	7.95	10.97	15.27	19.28	23.54	14.54
Center-West	16.33	20.20	29.53	33.63	40.28	11.94
Southeast	24.26	28.21	38.79	44.72	49.60	9.35
South	20.22	28.32	39.93	48.17	55.37	13.42
Brazil	17.10	21.33	29.68	35.08	40.10	11.24

Sources: IBGE / CNPq. Elaborated by the authors.

Brazilian federal units, as the share of each region in the total number of PhD researchers in Brazil is essentially the same as their share of the Brazilian GDP. As a result, both per capita income and the number of PhD researchers per resident in the Northeast, for example, is approximately half of the national average. The last column in Table 7.2 indicates a slow convergence process, as the growth rates of the regions with lower levels of PhD researchers are higher. A detailed analysis performed by Cavalcante (2011) using federal unit data and both Williamson and Theil inequality indexes confirms the convergence of the number of PhD researches per resident (both among and within regions). However, the convergence process was more accelerated in the early part of the decade.[11]

Technological efforts and innovative development
As shown in section 7.3, a reasonable proxy of the technological efforts is private internal and external R&D expenditures. However, in Brazil, data on private R&D expenditures are only available for the years 2000, 2003, 2005 and 2008, in which the Brazilian Innovation Survey (PINTEC) collected reliable information. In order to overcome this limitation, Araújo et al. (2009) proposed that the number of technical-scientific employees (PoTec) be used as proxy of the technological efforts of Brazilian firms.[12] Innovative development, in this chapter, refers to the number of firms which implemented innovations according to the criteria adopted in the PINTEC. As a result, data on innovative development are only available for the years 2000, 2003, 2005 and 2008, and for a limited number of federal units.[13]

The analysis of the relative shares of each federal unit in Brazilian technological efforts (measured by the PoTec) indicates a more asymmetrical distribution compared to the shares of GDP. The Southeastern region, which represents roughly 55 percent of Brazilian GDP, accounts for 75 percent of the national PoTec. The North and Northeast, which represent 5 percent and 13 percent of the Brazilian GDP, account for only 3 percent and 5 percent of the national PoTec, respectively. Table 7.3 shows the evolution of the PoTec for the Brazilian regions in the period between 2000 and 2007.

The evolution of the PoTec in the Brazilian macroregions suggests a process of deepening inequalities. Average rates of growth in the Northern and Northeastern regions are significantly smaller than those reported in the Southern and Southeastern regions.[14] This overall perception has been confirmed by Cavalcante (2010), who used both Williamson and Theil inequality indexes to validate the divergence process.

Data on the number of firms which implemented innovations according to the criteria adopted in the PINTEC are rare and temporally limited. In fact, the four available years cannot be considered a series that allows the path followed by the Brazilian macroregions to be analyzed. Table 7.4 shows the relative share of the Brazilian macroregions in the number of firms which implemented innovations between the years 1998 and 2008.

The data suggest a fairly stable path for the share of each Brazilian macroregion. The less developed regions (North, Northeast and Center-West) are represented proportionally less than their share in GDP, and there seems to be no consistent trend to revert this situation. These data are not enough to deny the divergence process indicated by the PoTec. As a result, the convergence process of the scientific infrastructure has not yet been capable of fostering a convergence process of the technological efforts in the country. The less developed regions rely not only on a smaller scientific infrastructure, but also on less effective transmission mechanisms between science and technology. Considering the increasing relevance of ST&I policies at the national level, this issue cannot be neglected in the formulation of regional development policies in Brazil.

7.4.2   Regional Distribution of the Federal Resources Directed to ST&I

Federal resources directed to ST&I are segmented into two parts: resources directed to researchers at universities and research centers ("scientific resources"), and resources directed to the productive sector ("technological and innovative resources"). This typology has been applied to the main financial and fiscal incentives provided by the Brazilian federal government and are shown in Table 7.5. In this table, the last column indicates the last available value involved in each instrument that can be segmented by federal unit.

As indicated above, financial incentives involve both grants and more favorable credit conditions. Grants are provided by the CNPq and the Coordination for the Improvement of Higher Education Personnel

Table 7.3 *Number of technical-scientific employees (PoTec), Brazilian macroregions, 2000–2007*

	2000	2001	2002	2003	2004	2005	2006	2007	Annual growth rate 2000–2007 (%)
North	1.657	1.820	2.154	1.436	1.657	1.886	2.382	2.461	5.81
Northeast	3.613	3.720	3.605	3.044	3.049	3.865	4.055	4.442	3.00
Center-West	852	1.084	1.223	1.107	1.219	1.787	1.680	1.991	12.89
Southeast	39.393	48.153	48.625	48.500	52.405	56.935	62.364	64.983	7.41
South	8.598	9.766	9.783	8.902	9.730	10.762	11.706	13.266	6.39
Brazil	54.113	64.543	65.390	62.989	68.061	75.234	82.189	87.143	7.04

Source: MTE / RAIS. Elaborated by the authors.

Table 7.4   *Firms that implemented innovations (share of Brazilian macroregions), 1998–2008 (%)*

	1998–2000	2000–03	2003–05	2005–08
North	2.59	3.11	3.11	3.24
Northeast	9.34	9.46	9.59	9.45
Center-West	4.39	4.98	4.78	6.03
Southeast	55.72	52.52	52.80	52.88
South	27.97	29.93	29.72	28.41

Source: IBGE. Elaborated by the authors.

(CAPES) and are mainly directed to researchers at universities and research centers. Resources provided by Brazilian sectoral funds to so-called cooperative projects are directed to universities, research centers, and firms. Grants directed only to firms are called "subvention funds" and are provided by sectoral funds through the FINEP. Credit provided by the FINEP is essentially directed to the productive sector. Fiscal incentives associated to the third chapter of the "Lei do Bem" also are directed to the productive sector.[15]

Table 7.6 provides an overview of the regional distribution of these resources among the Brazilian macroregions in the last available year for each of these instruments.

Table 7.6 suggests that the resources directed to scientific activities tend to reflect the pre-existing scientific infrastructure. In fact, the shares of each region both in the CNPq and the CAPES resources are essentially the same as those in the Brazilian scientific infrastructure. Data on cooperative projects (which to some extent mark a transition from science to technology) indicate more blurred results. In fact, while the Northeast and the Center-West are represented less than proportionally to their shares in Brazilian GDP, the share of the Northern region is above its economic representativeness. More developed regions show ambiguous signals as well: the shares of the Southeastern region are above, and the Southern region below, their share in Brazilian GDP. The three last columns, however, clearly indicate that the resources directed to technological and innovative activities tend to concentrate in more developed regions. In fact, while the share of the Southeastern region may reach values above 80 percent of the total, on several occasions the share of the less developed regions remains below 1 percent.

A way of analyzing the relationship between the pre-existing ST&I infrastructure (x_i) and the amount of federal resources directed to each

Table 7.5　Main financial and fiscal incentives for ST&I activities provided by the Brazilian federal government

Federal resources	Mainly addressed to:	Category	Total regionalized value, last available year (R$ millions current)
Financial incentives			
Grants			
CNPq	Universities and research centers	Science	1301 (2009)
CAPES	Universities and research centers	Science	820 (2008)
Sectoral funds cooperative projects	Universities, research centers and firms	Science / technology	249
Sectoral funds grants ("subvention funds")	Firms	Technology	519 (2007) 152 (2008)
Credit			
FINEP	Firms	Technology	837 (2008)
Fiscal incentives			
R&D fiscal incentives (Chapter 3 of the "Lei do Bem")	Firms	Technology	4096 (2008) (refers to the total value of the projects; tax expenditures estimated as 27.3% of this value) (Araújo, 2010).

Note:　BNDES credits especially directed to innovation were not included, as the data segmented by region were not available.

Source:　elaborated by the authors.

federal unit (y_i) is to plot a linear adjustment $\ln (y_i) = a \ln (x_i) + b$ which indicates whether the distribution of resources effectively reflects the ST&I relevance of each federal unit.[16] Values different from the unit for the slope a reflect an uneven distribution, benefiting the larger federal units if $a > 1$, and the smaller ones if $a < 1$. As suggested in the beginning of this section, the closer the slope a is to the unit, the more neutral the ST&I policy being analyzed.

An application of this procedure to the number of PhDs and the

Table 7.6   Regional distribution of ST&I resources among Brazilian macroregions, last available data (%)

	CNPq, 2009	Capes, 2008	Coop. Proj., 2008	Subvention funds, 2007	FINEP, 2008	"Lei do Bem", 2007
North	4.52	3.92	7.76	4.27	0.00	0.34
Northeast	15.55	16.82	11.21	8.74	0.12	2.79
Center-West	8.01	6.02	5.58	2.99	0.32	0.29
Southeast	54.83	55.08	61.63	66.43	48.96	83.09
South	17.09	18.16	13.82	17.58	50.60	13.48

Sources: CNPq / Capes / MTE / RAIS / FINEP / MCT.

resources allocated by the CNPq and CAPES in 2008 (Figure 7.5) indicates that resources directed to scientific activities tend to reflect pre-existing scientific infrastructure, as the coefficient obtained is 0.9816.

Analysis of the pre-existing scientific infrastructure and of the federal resources directed to science clearly indicates a neutral federal ST&I policy. As these resources become, at least in part, scientific infrastructure (for example, CNPq resources are used to support PhD formation), regional inequalities tend to perpetuate. This suggests that the convergence of scientific infrastructure might be slowing down.

An analysis of the relationship between technological efforts and resources directed to technological and innovative activities confirms their concentration in the more developed regions. In fact, seven states did not have access to any of the technological and innovative resources in the last year for which data are available; six federal units had access to only one of these instruments; another six states accessed two of them; and eight states (the three states that form the Southern region, three out of four states in the Southeastern region plus Bahia and Goiás) accessed all the instruments. When values associated to each instrument are considered, the high level of concentration becomes even more evident: the state of São Paulo, which represents around 33 percent of Brazilian GDP and 45 percent of the Brazilian PoTec, accessed 52 percent of the resources allocated for grants directed to firms, 45 percent of the credit provided by the FINEP and 40 percent of the fiscal incentives. These data reinforce the perception of concentration of the resources in the more developed regions even after controlling for the pre-existing basis.

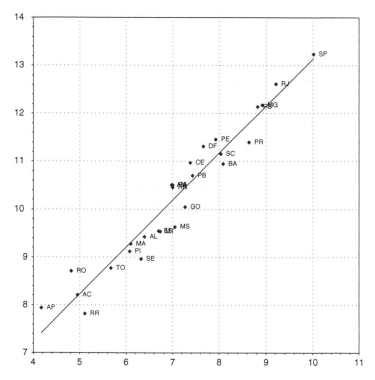

Source: elaborated by the authors.

Figure 7.5   Scientific infrastructure and CNPq + CAPES resources, 2008

7.5   CONCLUSIONS

In this chapter, Brazilian science, technology and innovation (ST&I) policies and the regional distribution of federal resources directed to these activities have been analyzed. The analysis was based on a litera-ture review of the association between ST&I and regional development (section 7.2) and on an overview of ST&I policies adopted in Brazil during the last decade (section 7.3). As shown in section 7.3, Brazilian ST&I poli-cies have increasingly recognized the systemic nature of the innovation process. Innovation policies have been increasingly considered by the federal government in the adoption of industrial policies. However, in spite of some successful cases, the analysis of the ST&I input and output indicators shows that the adopted policies are directed mainly to scientific research.

Data on the regional distribution of PhD researchers listed in the research groups census performed by the CNPq indicated that scientific inequalities are similar to economic inequalities observed among Brazilian federal units. Inequality levels are even higher when technological and innovative indicators are considered. In particular, the proxy for technological efforts – the number of technical-scientific employees – is more asymmetrically distributed among Brazilian federal units than the Brazilian GDP.

The analysis of the regional distribution of federal resources directed to ST&I in Brazil shows that: (1) resources directed to scientific activities (that is, mainly to researchers at universities and research centers) tend to reflect the pre-existing scientific infrastructure; and (2) resources directed to technological and innovative activities (that is, mainly to the productive sector) tend to concentrate in more developed regions, even after controlling for differences in pre-existing technological infrastructure. Technology and innovation policies, then, seem to be reinforcing regional inequalities among the Brazilian federal units, as market forces, scale economies and location decisions largely determine the allocation of resources.

Given the increasing relevance of ST&I policies in the current industrial policies of Brazil, it seems paradoxical that ST&I instruments have not been used as a way of reducing inequalities among Brazilian federal units. It is natural to assume that regional aspects could be taken into account in national industrial policies. In spite of the regional paradox mentioned in section 7.2 of this chapter, several experiences in other countries show that it is possible to promote ST&I and regional development simultaneously, working on both the demand and the supply side of the system. The creation of regionalized research centers (such as those created in the Southeastern states of the United States, or even those involving Brazilian agribusiness) might be a powerful instrument of regional development. It may increase resource destination to less developed regions without contradicting the meritocracy criteria that are to be applied in the allocation of these resources. This kind of instrument may be used to overcome the alleged contradiction between equity and efficiency in regional development policies.

NOTES

1. The funds include the Regional Development National Fund, the Funds for the Development of the Northeast and of the Amazonia, and the Constitutional Funds for the Northeast (FNE), the North (FNO), and the Center-West (FCO). Available at: http://www.integracao.gov.br/desenvolvimentoregional/pndr/ (accessed 18 October 2010).
2. The "red queen effect" derives from the Red Queen's race in Lewis Carroll's book

Through the Looking Glass. The Red Queen says: "it takes all the running you can do, to keep in the same place".

3. The model proposed by Kline and Rosenberg was used in the influential OECD report *Technology and the Economy: The Key Relationships* (OECD, 1992), expressing an important rupture with linear innovation models.

4. Comprehensive reviews of the Brazilian ST&I policies can be found in Amann and Baer (1999) for the period up to the late 1990s, and Cavalcante (2009) for the period up to the late 2000s.

5. FINEP is the executive secretariat of the Funding for Scientific and Technological Development (FNDCT). FNDCT was created in 1969 to support scientific research and, in 1999 was reinvigorated with new sources of the Sectoral Funds, which focus on fostering sector-specific ventures between companies and research institutions. Basically, these funds are nourished by contributions related to companies' invoicing and/or by earnings arising from the exploitation of natural resources belonging to the federal government (Uderman, 2010).

6. Available at: http://www.mct.gov.br/index.php/content/view/9252.html (accessed 20 October 2010).

7. Table 7.5, in the next section, presents a typology applied to the financial and fiscal incentives provided by the Brazilian federal government. Resources directed to researchers at universities and research centers are classified as "scientific resources", while resources mainly directed to the productive sector are classified as "technological and innovative resources".

8. Formerly a public company, Embraer has become one of the world's two leading producers of regional jet passenger aircraft; the Brazilian Agricultural Research Corporation (Embrapa) is a public company which provides solutions for the development of Brazilian agribusiness through technology generation and transfer; and Petrobras, one of the largest oil companies in the world, is controlled by the Brazilian federal government and is a world leader in offshore oil exploitation technology (see Amann, 2009).

9. Another measure of the scientific infrastructure is the number of research groups listed in each federal unit. As this measure leads to the same results as does the number of PhD researchers (Cavalcante, 2009), only the first indicator is used in this chapter.

10. This assumption does not take into consideration the distribution of researchers among scientific areas, although hard sciences probably require more physical infrastructure than social sciences.

11. Another caveat to the convergence process is the fact that only the aggregate data have been used in this analysis. If the number of PhDs, for example, were segmented by scientific area, the results could change. In fact, as the data on technological and innovative capabilities (shown below in this chapter) suggest, the number of PhDs allocated in industry might be diverging instead of converging. Further work may investigate whether the convergence process remains valid if, for example, the analysis is restricted to hard science PhDs.

12. The PoTec is simply defined as the sum of the number of researchers, engineers, R&D directors and managers and "scientific professionals" for each firm. In practice, some specific occupational groups of the Brazilian Classification of Occupations (CBO) are considered. Araújo et al. (2009) showed that the PoTec presents a correlation coefficient with internal and external R&D expenditures higher than 90 percent. Therefore, there is robust evidence that the PoTec is an appropriate proxy of technological efforts. Since the PoTec can be calculated based on the data from the Annual List of Social Information (RAIS), it is possible to follow its yearly evolution.

13. In the PINTEC 2008, disaggregated data are available just for Southern and Southeastern states, as well as for the states of Amazonas, Pará, Bahia, Ceará, Pernambuco and Goiás.

14. The higher growth rate of the Center-West region might be credited to its very low levels of PoTec (only 2.28 percent for a region which represents 8.87 percent of national GDP), and to its high GDP growth rates during the last years, due to the agribusiness pathway.

15. The third chapter of the "Lei do Bem" essentially replaces the Law no. 8.661, which provided fiscal incentives for R&D activities in Brazil.
16. See Fagundes et al. (2005) for details on the model used to analyze these data.

REFERENCES

Albuquerque, E.M. (1999), "National systems of innovation and non-OECD countries: notes about a tentative typology", *Revista de Economia Política*, **19** (4), 35–52.

Amann, E. (2009), "Technology, public policy, and the emergence of Brazilian multinationals", in L. Brainard and L. Martinez-Diaz (eds), *Brazil as an Economic Superpower? Understanding Brazil's Changing Role in the Global Economy*, Washington, DC: Brookings Institution Press.

Amann, E. and W. Baer (1999), "From technology absorption to technology production: industrial strategy and technological capacity in Brazil's development process", *Revista de Economia Aplicada*, **3** (1), 109–138.

Araújo, B.C. (2010), "Incentivos fiscais à pesquisa e desenvolvimento e custos de inovação no Brasil", *Radar: Tecnologia, Produção e Comércio Exterior*, **9**, 3–11.

Araújo, B.C., L.R. Cavalcante and P. Alves (2009), "Variáveis proxy para os gastos empresariais em inovação com base no pessoal ocupado técnico-científico disponível na Relação Anual de Informações Sociais (RAIS)", *Radar: Tecnologia, Produção e Comércio Exterior*, **5**, 16–21.

Baer, W. and W.R. Miles (1999), "The role of the state in United States regional development", *Revista Econômica do Nordeste*, **30** (2), 178–190.

Breschi, S. and F. Lissoni (2001), "Knowledge spillovers and local innovation systems: a critical survey", Liuc Papers, no. 84, Serie Economia e Impresa, 27, 2 marzo.

Brito Cruz, C.H. and L. Mello (2006), "*Boosting innovation performance in Brazil*", Organisation for Economic Co-operation and Development 6 December Economics Department Working Paper no. 532.

Bush, V. (1945), *Science: The Endless Frontier*, Washington, DC: United States Government Printing Office.

Cavalcante, L.R. (2009), "Políticas de ciência, tecnologia e inovação no Brasil: uma análise com base nos indicadores agregados", dez., Texto para discussão no. 1458, Rio de Janeiro: IPEA.

Cavalcante, L.R. (2011), "Desigualdades regionais em ciência, tecnologia e inovação no Brasil: uma análise de sua evolução recente", Texto para discussão, Rio de Janeiro: IPEA.

Chung, S. (2002), "Building a national innovation system through regional innovation systems", *Technovation*, **22** (8), 485–491.

Cook, P. and O. Memedovic (2003), "Strategies for regional innovation systems: learning transfer and applications", Vienna: United Nations Industrial Development Organization.

Doloreux, D. and S. Parto (2004), "*Regional innovation systems*: a critical review", INTECH (Institute for New Technologies). Discussion Paper Series. Maastricht, the Netherlands: United Nations University

Edquist, C. and L. Hommen (1999), "Systems of innovation: theory and policy for the demand side", *Technology in Society*, **21**, 63–19.

Evans, P. (1995), *Embedded Autonomy: States and Industrial Transformations*, Princeton, NJ: Princeton University Press.

Fagundes, M.E., L.R. Cavalcante and R.L. Ramacciotti (2005), "Distribuição regional dos fluxos de recursos federais para ciência e tecnologia", *Parcerias Estratégicas*, **21**, 59–78.

Hirschman, A.O. (1958), *The Strategy of Economic Development*. New Haven, CT: Yale University Press.

Kline, S.J. and N. Rosenberg (1986), "An overview of innovation", in R. Landau and N. Rosenberg (eds), *The Positive Sum Strategy: Harnessing Technology for Economic Growth*, Washington, DC: National Academy Press, pp. 275–306.

Kraemer-Mbula, E. and W. Wamac (2010), "Key issues for innovation and development", in OECD/International Development Research Centre (IDRC), *Innovation and the Development Agenda*, Ottawa, ON: OECD Publishing, pp. 29–38.

Luger, M. (1994), "Science and technology in regional economic development: the role of policy in Europe, Japan, and the United States", *Technology in Society*, **16** (1), 9–33.

Luger, M. and H. Goldstein (1991), *Technology in the Garden: Research Parks and Regional Economic Development*, Chapel Hill, NC: University of Northern Carolina Press.

Lundvall, B. (ed.) (1992), *National Systems of Innovation: Towards a Theory of Innovation and Interactive Learning*, London: Pinter.

Malecki, E.J. (1980), "Dimensions of R&D location in the United States", *Research Policy*, **9**, 2–22.

Malecki, E.J. (1987), "The R&D location decision of the firm and 'creative' regions – a survey", *Technovation*, **6**, 205–222.

MCT (2007), *Plano de ação de ciência, tecnologia e inovação (PACTI)*, Brasília: MCT.

MCT (2010), *Indicadores nacionais de ciência e tecnologia*, Brasília: MCT.

Myrdal, G. (1960), *Teoria econômica e regiões subdesenvolvidas*, Rio de Janeiro: UFMG Biblioteca Universitária, 1st edn 1957.

Nelson, R.R. (1993), *National Innovation Systems: A Comparative Analysis*, Oxford: Oxford University Press.

OECD (1992), *Technology and the Economy: The Key Relationships*, Paris: OECD.

OECD (2002), *Dynamising National Innovation Systems*, Paris: OECD.

Oughton, C., M. Landabaso and K. Morgan (2002), "The regional innovation paradox: innovation policy and industrial policy", *Journal of Technology Transfer*, **27**, 97–110.

Perroux, F. (1955), "O conceito de pólo de desenvolvimento", in J. Schwartzman (ed.), *Economia regional: textos escolhidos*, Belo Horizonte: CEDEPLAR.

Pilat, D. and A. Wyckoff (2010), "Innovation: sensible strategies for sustainable recoveries", *OECD Observer*, **279** (May), 27–29.

Putnam, R.D. (1993), "The prosperous community: social capital and public life", *American Prospect*, **13**, 35–42.

Schumpeter, J.A. (1950 [1942]), *Capitalism, Socialism, and Democracy*, 3rd edn, New York: Harper & Brothers.

Storper, M. (1994), "Desenvolvimento territorial na economia global do aprendizado: o desafio dos países em desenvolvimento", in Luiz Cezar de Queiroz Ribeiro and Orlando Alves dos Santos Júnior (eds), *Globalização, fragmentação e reforma urbana: o futuro das cidades brasileiras na crise*, Rio de Janeiro: Civilização Brasileira, pp. 23–63.

Uderman, S. (2010), "Financiamentos Reembolsáveis e o Estímulo à Inovação Empresarial no Brasil", paper prepared for the project Metodologia de avaliação dos resultados de conjuntos de projetos apoiados por fundos de Ciência, Tecnologia e Inovação.

Viotti, E.B. (2004), "Technological learning systems, competitiveness and development", Texto para Discussão no. 1057, Brasília: IPEA, Nov.

Woocock, M. (1998), "Social capital and economic development: toward a theoretical synthesis and policy framework", *Theory and Society*, **27**, 151–208.

8. FDI in Brazil from a regional perspective

Marcos C. Holanda and André Matos Magalhães

8.1 INTRODUCTION

Much has been said about the positive effects that foreign direct investment (FDI) can have on a recipient country's development effort.[1] Besides providing direct capital financing, FDI can be an important source for transfer of technology in that it creates and develops linkages with national firms. The perception that FDI can thus increase national productivity has led countries to offer incentives to attract foreign investments.

Between 1982 and 1993, the total FDI flow into developing countries has increased ninefold, whereas world trade of merchandise and services has only doubled in the same period. De Mello (1997) presents general numbers that help to confirm such behavior: over the period 1980 to 1994, "FDI inflows into developing countries have been concentrated in a few leading Southeast Asian and Latin American economies, and the rate of growth of FDI inflows as a share of exports into those economies has outpaced that of exports as a share of GDP". During the 1990s, the most important factors explaining the increase of FDI inflows into developing countries seem to be the foreign acquisition of domestic firms in the process of privatization, the globalization of production, and increased economic and financial integration (UNCTAD, 1996).

Brazil certainly benefited from this process. In this chapter, we focus on the distributions of FDI among Brazilian regions. To do so, we use the Census data on foreign-owned companies in Brazil from the Brazilian Central Bank. The Central Bank collects data every five years. We use available data for the first (1995) and last year (2005) and compare the distribution of FDI among regions and states within the regions (North and Northeast), as well as presenting some indicators of backward and forward linkages. Not surprisingly, the data show a strong concentration of FDI in the Southeast (more than 85 percent of the FDI is in this region). The data also show a significant increase (from four to nine times) in productivity, measured as gross revenue per job.

8.2 FDI MAIN DETERMINANTS AND REGIONAL POLICIES IN BRAZIL

FDI can be defined as a form of international interfirm cooperation that involves a significant equity stake in, or effective management control of, foreign enterprises (de Mello, 1997).[2] In a general sense, firms will engage in foreign investment either to serve a local market or to seek a more efficient base from which to export its goods. In the first case, the most important factors in explaining FDI are related to the size and the growth rate of the host country (Markusen, 1984; Markusen and Venables, 2000). In the second case, firms will exploit international factor price differentials (Helpman, 1984; Helpman and Krugman, 1985).

The literature on determinants of FDI can be divided into two broad categories: those which discuss the internal firm-specific factors that motivate a firm to become a multinational enterprise (MNE), and those which deal with the external factors that are likely determinants of the location and magnitude of FDI by MNEs.[3]

Given the difficulty in finding data that allow for testing on internal firm factors, empirical studies that attempt to estimate the importance of the different determinants of FDI tend to concentrate on external factors, that is, locational factors. The main factors usually considered are: human resource endowments; physical, financial and technological infrastructure; openness to international trade and access to international markets; development of the regulatory framework and economic policy coherence; and investment protection and promotion:

- Human resource endowments – cost and productivity of labor
  FDI can be considered an outcome of broad corporate strategies and investment decisions of profit-maximizing firms facing worldwide competition (MNCs), where significant differences in cost structures, due to factor productivity and remuneration differentials across countries, justify cross-border investment and production relocation. This is a view close to the international trade literature (Batra and Ramachandran, 1980; Grossman and Helpman, 1991).
- Physical, financial and technological infrastructure
  Infrastructural factors like the status of telecommunications and railways can play an important role in determining the foreign direct investor's decision to locate in a particular country. If the

infrastructural facilities are properly in place in a country, then that country tends to receive more foreign direct investment.

- Openness to international trade and access to international markets
  International agreements on trade and investment also influence the volume and patterns of FDI (Morrissey and Rai, 1995).
- Development of the regulatory framework and economic policy coherence
  The institutional features of the recipient economy can be important determinants of FDI, including the degree of political stability and government intervention in the economy (de Mello, 1997). The quality of institutions, particularly for less developed countries, tends to be an important determinant for FDI for several reasons. Poor legal protection of assets increases the chance of expropriation of a firm's assets, making investment less likely; poor quality of institutions necessary for well-functioning markets increases the cost of doing business, thereby reducing FDI activity; and poor institutions tend to lead to poor infrastructure, reducing expected profitability (Blonigen, 2005).
- Investment protection and promotion
  Country-specific FDI incentives are often mentioned among the policy-related institutional characteristics which promote FDI inflows. Policies such as fiscal incentives (tax rebates and exemptions), financial incentives (subsidized loans and grants) and non-financial incentives (for example, basic infrastructure provision) (Antoine, 1979; Chen and Tang, 1986) are among them. Fiscal incentives tend to prevail in developing countries in general, according to de Mello (1997). To a large extent, however, country-specific FDI incentives tend to reflect competition for foreign capital, and the effectiveness of beggar-thy-neighbor policies tends to be limited in scope and duration.

Although these determinants originally were intended to explain international flows of investments to a country as a whole, one also can use them to draw insights into the distribution of FDI within a country like Brazil. While development of the regulatory framework and economic policy coherence tend not to differ significantly throughout the country as a whole, the human resource endowments and the physical, financial and technological infrastructure determinants favor the Southeast, the most developed region in the country.

Brazil is a highly unequal country. The North and Northeast regions lag far behind the rich South and Southeast. The attraction of FDI to promote economic growth in poor regions is prevalent in many East Asian economies. The case of special economic zones in China is an example of this approach. In Brazil, only the North has an explicit policy for FDI promotion.

In the early 1970s, a free trade zone was created in the state of Amazon that offers fiscal incentives to foreign firms. The zone, known as the Zona Franca de Manaus, offers incentives to industries to produce goods that were formerly imported. Contrary to most free trade zones, it is an import-oriented as opposed to an export-oriented zone.

Among the incentives offered are: up to 88 percent reduction on import tax on inputs; tax exemption on the federal tax; 75 percent reduction on corporate federal income tax; and a tax exemption on the federal tax on production and social security.

8.3 THE DATA: THE CENTRAL BANK CENSUS OF FOREIGN CAPITAL

In order to study the distribution of FDI among the regions of Brazil, we made use of a specific database put together by the Brazilian Central Bank (the Bacen). Since 1995, the Brazilian Central Bank has been responsible for the Foreign Capital Census. The participants in the Census are companies that received foreign direct investments, companies that obtained foreign credit, and companies that present indirect foreign participation in its capital formation.[4]

The Bacen collects data on companies which receive foreign direct investment, where non-residents own at least 10 percent in stocks or quotas with the right to vote, or at least 20 percent of shares, direct or indirect,[5] in the total capital.[6] Since 1995, the Bacen has collected data from these companies in 1995, 2000 and 2005.

Non-residents were considered organizations with headquarters abroad, including multinational companies, private or state owned, as well those with more than one nationality or headquarters, even if one of the countries involved was Brazil.

In 1995, there were 6322 private companies under the definition provided by the Bacen. In 2005, this number was 17605 companies. The companies are asked to provide general information on address, economic activity, capital composition, market valuation, balance sheets, operational results, additional accounting information, and exports and imports. The information is made available at the national level by regions, states and economic sectors. The Bacen also makes available the origins of FDI by country.

In the next section, we present some key indicators constructed from the 1995 and 2005 Census and analyze their distribution among the Brazilian regions.

8.4   LOOKING AT SOME FDI INDICATORS FOR BRAZILIAN REGIONS

In this section, we analyze some economic indicators constructed from the Brazilian Census of Foreign Capital described in the last section. Here, we look at the FDI stock, gross revenue; the ratio of tax production over gross revenue; the ratio of income tax over gross revenue; the ratio of dividends, profits and royalties to residents over gross revenue; the ratio of imports over gross revenue; the ratio of exports over gross revenue; and the ratio of gross revenue over jobs created by foreign-owned companies in Brazil.

By looking at these data, we hope to observe the distribution and changes in patterns in FDI during this period; what have been the contributions of FDI in terms of backward and forward linkages in the regional economies; and whether there were any gains in productivity (gross product per job).

We begin by looking at FDI stock in Brazil in 1995 and 2005, as shown in Figures 8.1, 8.2 and 8.3.[7] During this period, the total FDI in Brazil increased from approximately R$65 million to R$162.8 million. It increased in all regions, but most of the FDI was concentrated in the Southeast (more than 88 percent in 1995 and 86 percent in 2005), that is, the FDI, as expected, went to the area with the largest market and better infrastructure. In terms of changes over this period, one should note the advance of FDI in the South. This could be related to the development of Mercosur.

Figures 8.4 through 8.9 show the distribution and values of the FDI stock within the North and Northeast regions. In the case of the North, the state of Amazonas experienced significant increase in FDI stock over the period, which coincides with the Zona Franca de Manaus. In the Northeast, the data show that the state of Bahia is the major recipient of FDI in the region. Its share is even higher in 2005 than in 1995. The increase of FDI stock in Pernambuco is also worth noting.

Figures 8.10 and 8.11 present the distribution of gross revenue for foreign-owned companies. From these figures, and the data on FDI stock, it is possible to observe significant changes in the Southeast and South regions. More specifically, in 1995, the Southeast received 88 percent of

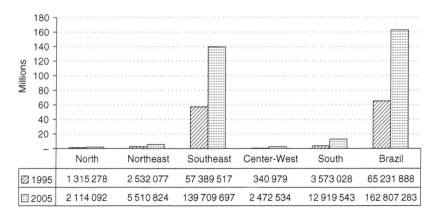

	North	Northeast	Southeast	Center-West	South	Brazil
▨ 1995	1 315 278	2 532 077	57 389 517	340 979	3 573 028	65 231 888
⊟ 2005	2 114 092	5 510 824	139 709 697	2 472 534	12 919 543	162 807 283

Source: Brazilian Central Bank FDI Census.

Figure 8.1   FDI stock in Brazil, 1995 and 2005 (R$1000; 2005 = 100)

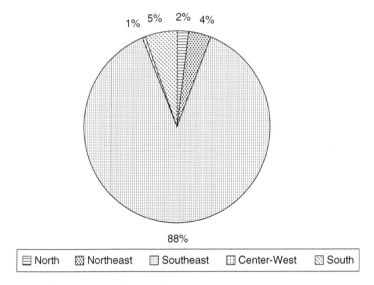

Source: Brazilian Central Bank FDI Census.

Figure 8.2   Distribution of FDI stock in Brazil by region – 1995 (%)

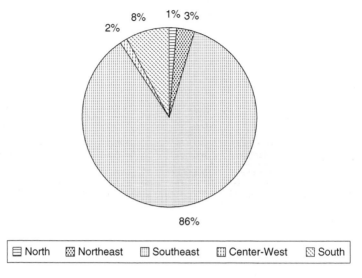

Source: Brazilian Central Bank FDI Census.

Figure 8.3   Distribution of FDI stock in Brazil by region – 2005 (%)

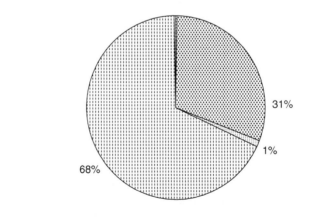

Source: Brazilian Central Bank FDI Census.

Figure 8.4   Distribution of FDI stock in Brazil's North region by state –
           1995 (%)

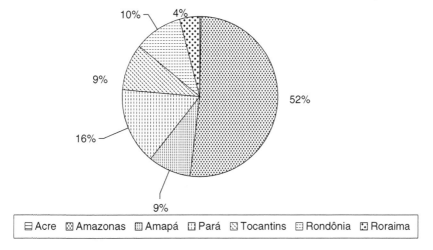

Acre ⊞ Amazonas ⊞ Amapá ⊞ Pará ⊠ Tocantins ⊞ Rondônia ⊡ Roraima

Source: Brazilian Central Bank FDI Census.

Figure 8.5   Distribution of FDI stock in Brazil's North region by state –
2005 (%)

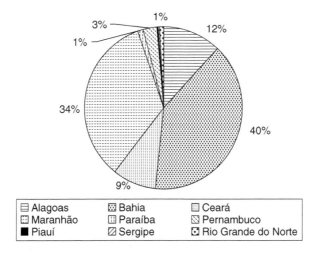

⊟ Alagoas   ⊠ Bahia   ⊞ Ceará
⊞ Maranhão   ⊞ Paraíba   ⊠ Pernambuco
■ Piauí   ⊘ Sergipe   ⊡ Rio Grande do Norte

Source: Brazilian Central Bank FDI Census.

Figure 8.6   Distribution of FDI stock in Brazil's North region by state –
1995 (%)

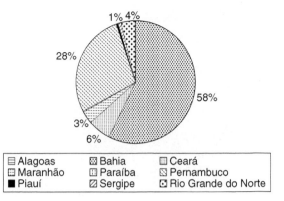

Source: Brazilian Central Bank FDI Census.

Figure 8.7   Distribution of FDI stock in Brazil's Northeast region by state – 2005 (%)

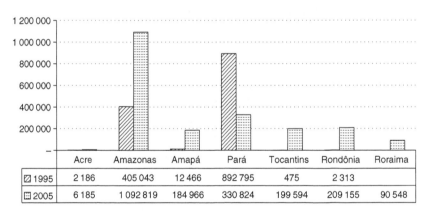

	Acre	Amazonas	Amapá	Pará	Tocantins	Rondônia	Roraima
1995	2 186	405 043	12 466	892 795	475	2 313	
2005	6 185	1 092 819	184 966	330 824	199 594	209 155	90 548

Source: Brazilian Central Bank FDI Census.

Figure 8.8   FDI stock in North states, 1995 and 2005 (R$1000; 2005 = 100)

the FDI stock and 87 percent of the gross revenue. In the same year, the South received only 5 percent of the FDI stock and 5 percent of the gross revenue. In 2005, the Southeast received 86 percent of the stock and only 68 percent of the gross revenue, while the South received 8 percent of the stock and 18 percent of the gross revenue. A similar movement occurred in the Northeast, although on a smaller scale (its share of the gross revenue

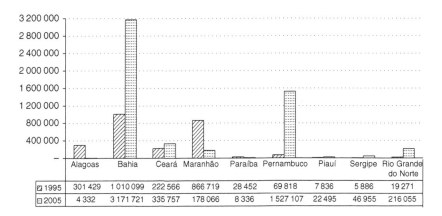

	Alagoas	Bahia	Ceará	Maranhão	Paraíba	Pernambuco	Piauí	Sergipe	Rio Grande do Norte
1995	301 429	1 010 099	222 566	866 719	28 452	69 818	7 836	5 886	19 271
2005	4 332	3 171 721	335 757	178 066	8 336	1 527 107	22 495	46 955	216 055

Source: Brazilian Central Bank FDI Census.

Figure 8.9   *FDI stock in Northeast states, 1995 and 2005 (R$1000; 2005 = 100)*

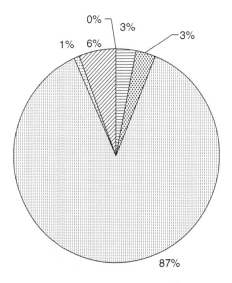

Source: Brazilian Central Bank FDI Census.

Figure 8.10   *Distribution of gross revenue of foreign-owned companies in Brazil by region – 1995*

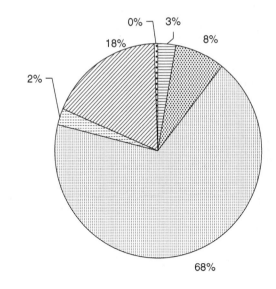

Source: Brazilian Central Bank FDI Census.

Figure 8.11   Distribution of gross revenue of foreign-owned companies in Brazil by region – 2005

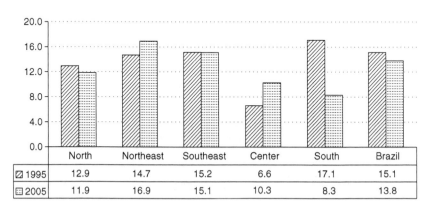

Source: Brazilian Central Bank FDI Census.

Figure 8.12   Total production tax – gross revenue ratio for foreign-owned companies in Brazil by region, 1995 and 2005 (%)

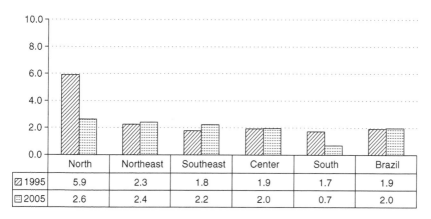

	North	Northeast	Southeast	Center	South	Brazil
1995	5.9	2.3	1.8	1.9	1.7	1.9
2005	2.6	2.4	2.2	2.0	0.7	2.0

Source: Brazilian Central Bank FDI Census.

Figure 8.13 Income tax – gross revenue ratio for foreign owned companies in Brazil by region, 1995 and 2005 (%)

increased from 3 to 7 percent, despite a decrease in its share of FDI stock from 4 to 3 percent). One could make the argument that, over this period, FDI that migrated to the South and Northeast was of greater aggregated value than FDI that went to the Southeast. An example of this high-value-added FDI is the Ford plant in Bahia.

Figures 8.12 and 8.13 present the ratios of production tax and income tax over gross revenue. Here we attempt to capture some indication of linkages with the internal market by using the measures of taxes that the FDI generates and that can be used to produce public goods for the local population. In both cases there was little or no advance in these indicators in the Northeast and Center-West. In the North and in the South, these ratios declined. This indicates that FDI did not benefit the regional economies through taxes.

On the other hand, when the ratio of dividends, profits and royalties over gross revenue is considered, one can observe some positive effect for the recipient regions (Figure 8.14). This was particularly true for both the Southeast and the Northeast, where we find a positive linkage between FDI and local economies.

We next look at the ratio of imports over gross revenue (Figure 8.15). This indicator gives us an indirect notion of backward linkages in the sense that a smaller percentage of imports could mean more participation of the domestic market supplying FDI companies. This seems to be the case for all regions during the analyzed period. From 1995 to 2005, FDI companies increased the share of supplies bought in the internal market. This change was especially significant in the Northeast.

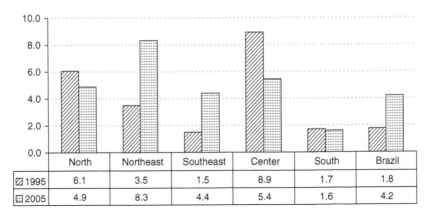

Source: Brazilian Central Bank FDI Census.

Figure 8.14   *Dividends, profits and royalties to residents – gross revenue ratio for foreign-owned companies in Brazil by region, 1995 and 2005 (%)*

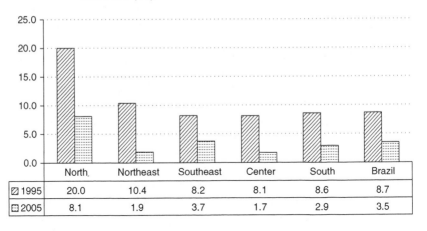

Source: Brazilian Central Bank FDI Census.

Figure 8.15   *Imports – gross revenue ratio for foreign-owned companies in Brazil by region, 1995 and 2005 (%)*

In Figure 8.16 we look at the ratio of exports over gross revenue as an indicator of the importance of the internal market to FDI companies. It is possible to observe that the internal market has increased its importance to these companies. The most significant change during the period from 1995 to 2005 was observed in the Northeast and South.

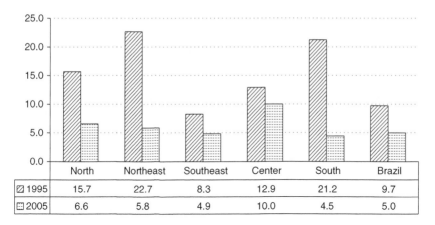

	North	Northeast	Southeast	Center	South	Brazil
1995	15.7	22.7	8.3	12.9	21.2	9.7
2005	6.6	5.8	4.9	10.0	4.5	5.0

Source: Brazilian Central Bank FDI Census.

Figure 8.16 *Export – gross revenue ratio for foreign-owned companies in Brazil by region, 1995 and 2005 (%)*

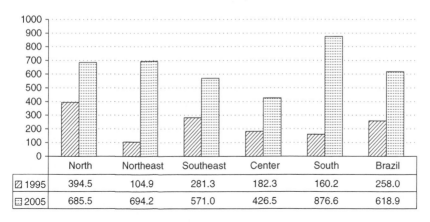

	North	Northeast	Southeast	Center	South	Brazil
1995	394.5	104.9	281.3	182.3	160.2	258.0
2005	685.5	694.2	571.0	426.5	876.6	618.9

Source: Brazilian Central Bank FDI Census.

Figure 8.17 *Gross revenue – jobs ratio for foreign-owned companies in Brazil by region, 1995 and 2005 (R$, base = 2005)*

Finally, in Figure 8.17, we present the ratio of gross revenue over jobs for foreign owned companies. With this ratio, we attempt to provide a measure of productivity for these companies. During this period, there were significant changes in this ratio for all regions. The highest gains in productivity were observed in the Northeast and South regions.

8.5   FINAL COMMENTS

In this chapter, we have examined foreign direct investment (FDI) to Brazilian regions using the census data from the Brazilian Central Bank. We used available data for the first (1995) and last year (2005) and compared the distribution of FDI among regions and states within the regions (North and Northeast), as well as presenting some indicators of backward and forward linkages.

Not surprisingly, as the country does not have a strong regional policy for FDI, the data show a strong concentration of FDI in the rich Southeast and South regions. Despite the significant differences in FDI concentration, there are no significant differences among the regions when some measures of backward linkages are taken into account. These measures show that the main FDI benefits to local economies come from the distribution of dividends and profits to residents, and from purchases of inputs. The data also show that the Brazilian internal market is the main destination of FDI production. Finally, FDI in Brazil has shown a significant increase in productivity from 1995 to 2005.

NOTES

1. See, for instance, Markusen (1995), Caves (1996) and de Mello (1997).
2. De Mello (1997) argues that because a formal clear-cut definition is difficult, FDI could be considered to encompass other, broader forms of non-equity cooperation involving the supply of tangible and intangible assets by a foreign enterprise to a domestic firm without foreign control. These broader collaborative associations would include most types of quasi-investment arrangements (such as licensing, leasing, franchising, start-up and international production-sharing agreements), joint ventures with limited foreign equity participation, and R&D cooperation. He argues that such a broad definition of FDI would be justified, given the growth of FDI in the service sector in recent years.
3. See for instance, Blonigen (2005) and Nonnenberg and Mendonça (2005).
4. Individuals; institutions from the federal, state and municipal governments; portfolio managers; mutual funds; real estate investment funds; and non-profiting organizations were not required to answer the Census.
5. With respect to the indirect participation of non-residents in institutions in the country, it was defined so that this participation would be measured by the property of stocks or quotas of social capital by institutions with headquarters in the Brazil, but which included among their partners non-resident individuals.
6. According to the methodological notes of the Bacen, this cut is consistent with the International Monetary Fund (IMF) guidelines on this matter.
7. Defined as capital stock held by non-residents.

REFERENCES

Antoine, R. (1979), *Tax Incentives for Private Investment in Developing Countries*, Boston, MA: Kluwer.

Batra, R.N. and R. Ramachandran (1980), "Multinational firms and the theory of international trade and investment", *American Economic Review*, **70**, 278–90.

Blonigen, Bruce A. (2005), "A review of the empirical literature on FDI determinants", *Atlantic Economic Journal*, **33** (4), 383–403.

Caves, R. (1996), *Multinational Enterprise and Economic Analysis*, Cambridge: Cambridge University Press.

Central Bank – Banco Central do Brasil. Metodologia do Censo de Capitais Estrangeiros no País (various years), http://www.bcb.gov.br/rex/Censo1995/Port/980527/metodolo.asp?idpai=CENSO1995P, accessed November 2010.

Chen, T.J. and D.P. Tang (1986), "The production characteristics of multinational firms and the effects of tax incentives: the case of Taiwan's electronics industry", *Journal of Development Economics*, **24**, 119–29.

de Mello Jr, Luiz R. (1997), "Foreign direct investment in developing countries and growth: a selective survey", *Journal of Development Studies*, **34** (1), 1–34.

Grossman, G.M. and E. Helpman (1991), *Innovation and Growth in the Global Economy*, Cambridge, MA: MIT Press.

Helpman, E. (1984), "A simple theory of international trade with multinational corporations", *Journal of Political Economy*, **92**, 451–72.

Helpman, E. and P.R. Krugman (1985), *Market Structure and International Trade*, Cambridge, MA: MIT Press.

Markusen, J.R. (1984), "Multinationals, multi-plant economies, and the gains from trade", *Journal of International Economics*, **16**, 205–26.

Markusen, J. (1995), "The boundaries of multinational enterprises and the theory of international trade", *Journal of Economic Perspectives*, **9**, 169–89.

Markusen, J.R. and A.J. Venables (2000), "The theory of endowment, intra-industry and multinational trade", *Journal of International Economics*, **52**, 209–34.

Morrissey, O. and Y. Rai (1995), "The GATT agreement on trade-related investment and their relationship with transnational corporations", *Journal of Development Studies*, **31** (5), 702–24.

Nonnenberg, M. and M. Mendonça (2005), "The determinants of foreign direct investment in developing countries", *Estudos Econômicos*, São Paulo, **35** (4), 631–55.

UNCTAD (1996), *World Investment Report*, Geneva.

9. Stabilization policies and regional development in Brazil

Alexandre Rands Barros

9.1 INTRODUCTION

Brazil has had a long history of inflation and, consequently, of stabilization policies. Since the period when the King came to live in Brazil and the country became a United Kingdom with Portugal, in 1808, inflation has been a frequent problem disturbing local economic life. Obviously, there was always fluctuation of inflation: in some periods it was higher, while it reached lower levels in others. Nevertheless, inflation was always an important feature of the Brazilian economic scene.[1]

Many stabilization policies were pursued along this long inflationary history. More orthodox strategies were part of many momentary recipes to control inflation, but also many heterodox plans were not only conceived but also implemented. A consequence of such varied experiments was that inflation and gross domestic product (GDP) growth have oscillated through Brazil's history. Inflation reached more than 1000 percent a year in some months and has been below 2 percent on an annual rate in other months. GDP has grown over 14 percent in some years and has contracted in others.

The results of such policies have varied a lot, as have their effectiveness concerning social and economic costs. This is a consequence of the well-known trade-off between inflation and economic growth.[2] Some stabilization plans had a very small negative impact on GDP and were successful in controlling inflation, at least for some time. Others had very high negative impacts on economic growth and very little ability to control inflation. Of course, there were also many stabilization policies that fitted well into the expected relationship between their impact on GDP and inflationary control efficacy.

Stabilization policies have not necessarily had the same impact on all regions and social groups in Brazil. Although it is possible to identify their impact on aggregate social welfare, under some assumptions, there are always relative winners and losers emerging from such policies. The existence of such asymmetry among individuals and economic groups is well known. Sometimes exporters gain, while on other occasions importers are those who benefit more. Some plans led to higher real wages, while others increased the share of profits and interest in GDP. Nevertheless, it is possible that regions also had gains and losses emerging from these policies. Such imbalances have not been the subject of many studies and this chapter aims to make a contribution to filling this gap in the literature.

9.2   STABILIZATION PLANS

Brazil has had several stabilization plans in its history.[3] In the colonial period, inflation was already a serious problem. Between 1815 and 1822, prices were rising. Figure 9.1 provides data on the growth rate of the money supply that gives support to this hypothesis. There is also evidence that there was some inflation in many periods in the late nineteenth century, as the exchange rate for the local currency, with respect to the British pound, devalued at high rates, as shown in Figure 9.2.

Many periods of high inflation ended with stabilization plans, which reduced the rate of inflation and usually altered other economic variables, such as the money supply, the exchange rate (see Figure 9.2) and

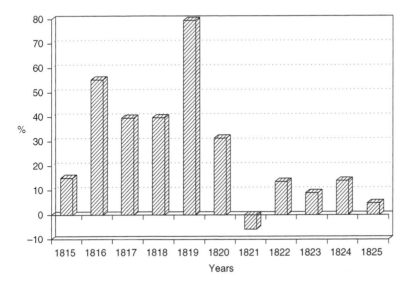

Figure 9.1   Annual rate of growth of money supply 1815–25 (%, high-powered money)

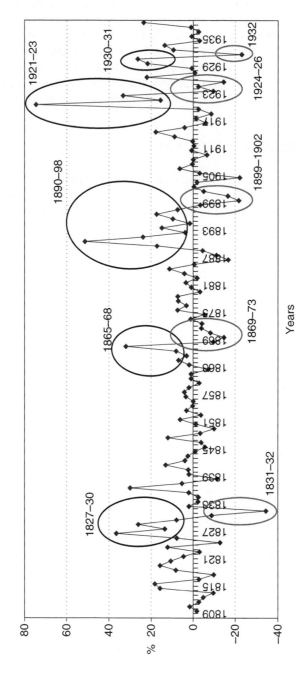

Figure 9.2   Yearly percentage change of exchange rate (local currency/British pound)

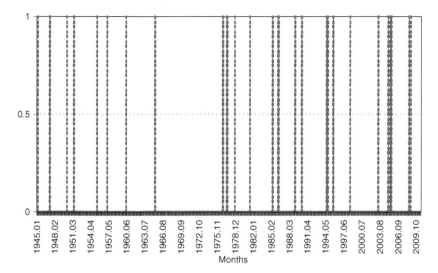

Figure 9.3   Identification of stabilization plans in Brazilian post-war history – 1945–2010

even real variables such as per capita GDP and interest rates. Figure 9.3 identifies stabilization plans from 1945 to 2010, using data for a general price index (IGP-DI). The strategy to identify these plans was to calculate a two-month average for the inflation rate (current and next), subtract the 12-month average inflation rate prior to the current month, and divide this difference by the standard deviation of the last 12 months' inflation rate. If this statistic was smaller than −1.645, the period was considered to be of a stabilization plan.[4]

This simple identification method generated 22 stabilization plans within the period 1945 to 2010. Many became popular because of their special features. For example, the Cruzado Plan (identified in Figure 9.3 as falling between March and May 1986), the Plano Verão (February 1989), the Collor Plan (April to May 1990) and the Plano Real (July to October 1994). There are also plans that were named and had special announcements, such as the Cruzadinho (July 1986), Cruzado II (November 1986) and Plano Bresser (June 1987), which did not manage to change inflation sufficiently to be identified as periods of stabilization by this simple method.

These stabilization plans relied on many different policy instruments. Actually, most of them relied on more than one. There were those that had a more orthodox bias, which normally relied on standard fiscal and monetary policies. Nonetheless, many heterodox plans were also implemented, which used price freezes, exchange rate and external trade controls and

partial asset freezes, depreciation or even confiscations. These stabilization plans and policies had as major similarities their goal to control inflation, although sometimes they were designed to ensure time consistency of
foreign balance, as happened in 1981.

It is not reasonable to assume that all the instruments relied upon had
the same impact on the performance of the different regions in Brazil.
Therefore, an evaluation of the potential impact of each is difficult to
assess. A possible solution, which restricts the scope of the chapter, is to
focus on the impact of successful policies. We shall therefore concentrate
our focus on an analysis of the impact of a decline in inflation on Brazil's
regional balance.

9.3   IMPACT OF INFLATION CONTROL ON REGIONAL DISPARITIES

The Brazilian economy has worked under a standard Phillips curve since
March 2003, as shown in Figure 9.4. This means that the higher the inflation rate, the lower is the unemployment rate.[5] As is common in many
economies, this curve sometimes moves. Thus, in the period between
March 2002 and August 2004, there was a higher rate of unemployment for each level of inflation than in the period from September 2004
to August 2010. Therefore, for the entire period there were two stable
Phillips curves.

A first glance at these data seems to suggest that there is a positive
relationship between inflation and economic growth, as a decrease in

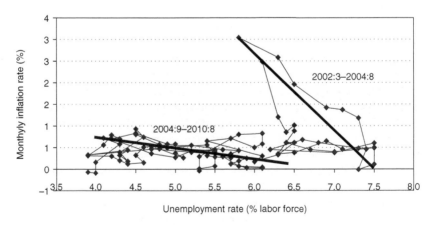

Figure 9.4   Brazilian Phillips Curve 2002:3 to 2010:8

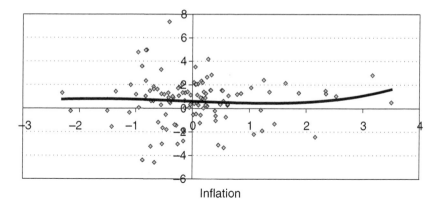

Inflation

Figure 9.5 *Relationship between quarterly GDP growth and inflation rate deviation from the last four quarters average*

unemployment tends to increase per capita GDP. These movements, however, are not identified in the direct relationship between these variables, as can be seen in Figure 9.5. Changes in productivity that arise from these movements in unemployment obscure the results.

In addition to changes in productivity, there is also the possibility that a positive short-run correlation could be reversed by future changes in GDP due to the initial movement of inflation. This fact has spawned a literature investigating the relationship between inflation and growth, which started in the 1960s and led to a new wave of research in the 1980s and 1990s. Some of the key contributions to this literature came from Fischer (1983) and Barro (1996).[6] There were both empirical and theoretical papers. The major results were that inflation causes growth and that the long-run effect is negative, at least when it is over some threshold level.[7] Therefore, these theoretical ideas and empirical conclusions imply that stabilization plans should have a long-term positive impact on GDP in Brazil, in spite of the short-term impact on unemployment.

There are three major explanations for a positive short-term impact of inflation on GDP appearing in the literature: (1) error in expectations will lead some firms to interpret the higher prices faced for their output as higher demand, and consequently they will increase their output;[8] (2) nominal wage rigidities could reduce real wages and consequently make it more profitable for firms to expand their individual output; (3) some key price rigidities could also improve the profitability of firms that can adjust their prices, and this would lead to their output increase.

In the long run, there is also more than one possible justification for the negative relationship between inflation and economic growth.

As higher inflation will require higher money growth in the long run, there are two relevant causes arising from this relationship.[9] The first is that this larger expansion of the money supply will increase the share of government in total income, and government resource allocation is less efficient. The second reason, also emerging from higher growth of money supply, is that the private sector will hold a larger share of its assets as money, so that the capital–labor ratio will be lower and, as a consequence, so will per capita output. Another crucial cause for lower growth when there is higher inflation is that it provokes a rise in uncertainty for private investors. This will lead to more changes in relative prices. Investments will be lower as a consequence and so will the growth rate of output.

To understand the impact of inflation control or stabilization plans on the regional production dispersion, it is necessary to see whether these short- and long-terms effects of lower inflation on GDP growth have diverse impacts on the many regions of a country and, consequently, whether they also affect regional balances. It is therefore necessary to understand the determinants of observed regional balances, in order to analyze the possibility that the identified sources of the effects of inflation on GDP growth would also affect the regional balance.

There are two major sources of regional imbalances found in the literature. The first one is difference in attributes of agents in many regions. For example, human capital availabilities could lead to differences in factor intensities among regions so that regional disparities would emerge.[10] The second source is the existence of increasing returns to scale associated with transport costs, which would generate a sort of circular cumulative causation process that concentrates more efficient production in some regions at the expense of others.[11] This would generate regional imbalances often found within countries.

If a stabilization plan could have a long-term or permanent impact on regional balance, it would need either to alter the balance among factors of production attributes, mainly human capital,[12] or to generate circular cumulative causation that would affect the relative scale economies among regions. To understand the potential to achieve the former impact, some further theoretical analysis would be necessary. For the second potential source of permanent impact, however, it is enough to have short-term impacts on the regional balances, as this should lead to changes in the relative scale effects. Therefore, discussion of potential short-term impacts is important before proceeding with further analysis of the potential permanent effect of stabilization plans on regional balance.

The short-term impact of inflation on GDP also generates three potential sources of short-term changes in regional balances as a consequence of stabilization plans. They are: (1) asymmetries in regional information levels; (2) asymmetries in nominal wage rigidities; and (3) differences in price rigidities among regions. The asymmetries in information levels could emerge because of differences in the relative sizes and sectorial proportion of firms in each region, in addition to the unequal social instruments providing information.

As information tends to be costly, larger firms tend to work with a higher informational level, as it is relatively cheaper for them to reach a given level of information per unit of output. There are also differences in informational availability by sector. Some sectors have more information than others. Some regions, for historical reasons, also have greater public investments in information generation. Firms in these regions will certainly also respond more promptly to news about price and quantity adjustments.

Asymmetries in nominal wage rigidities could also emerge from differences in sectorial compositions in each region, mainly arising from the share of the informal sector in each region. As workers in the informal sector are not protected by contracts, their labor relations tend to respond differently than the ones of those engaged in the formal sector. This tends to bring some asymmetries in their reactions to autonomous changes of inflation, which are often associated with stabilization plans.

If firms' size and managerial structures are different among regions, as well as their sources of raw materials and market structures, it is possible that price rigidities are different in these regions. Therefore, their final response in terms of output to autonomous inflation changes can also differ. These could justify differences in response to stabilization plans across regions in a country.

All these potential differences in short-term output responses to autonomous inflation movement make the short-term regional impact of stabilization plans an empirical matter. It is possible that there are short-term fluctuations in regional balances, but this has to be analyzed empirically, because the potential effect could in reality turn to be negligible. Furthermore, as a consequence of this and the "new geography" hypothesis on regional balances, the existence of long-term or permanent impact of stabilization plans on regional balances is also an empirical matter. The following two sections deal with these two empirical investigations.

9.4   LONG-TERM CHANGES IN REGIONAL DISPARITY IN BRAZIL

Stabilization plans always bring some political cost to governments. Most of them reduce employment and growth, and they sometimes rely on price control, which also can damage the image of a public administration. Therefore, they are only implemented in some particular periods when the costs of inflation and/or a collapse in foreign trade can bring an even higher political cost. Furthermore, the decision to design and introduce a stabilization plan is mainly political, so that it cannot be systematically predicted from any macroeconomic data. Therefore, they represent exogenous shocks to the economy that are fortuitous.

From the unit root literature, let us assume that the proportion of GDP (Y) in two regions could be represented by a time series such as:

$$\Delta Y_t = \alpha_0 + \alpha_1 Y_{t-1} + \sum_{i=1}^{k} \delta_i \Delta Y_{t-i} + \sum_{i=1}^{m} \phi_i D_i + e_t \qquad (9.1)$$

where Y_t is the proportion between the per capita GDP in regions N and S, respectively. The Greek letters are parameters and Δ is the first difference operator, so that $\Delta Y_t = Y_t - Y_{t-1}$. The error term is represented by e_t in this equation and it represents all the innovations that are not determined by Y_{t-i}, for any $i \in \aleph$, the set of natural numbers. D_i's are dummies for structural breaks that could appear in the series.

Under such specifications and the exogeneity of stabilization plans, they would enter the model defined in equation (9.1) through the error term e_t or through structural breaks represented through D_i. If stabilization plans could have a long-term impact on the proportion represented by Y_t, the error term e_t could also have it and the variable Y_t would have a long-term stochastic trend. When the impact of stabilization plans affects the proportion represented by Y_t through a structural break, its coefficient ϕ_i would be different from zero and such a structural break could be identifiable as resulting from a stabilization plan.

Under such specification, it is possible to test the hypothesis that there is a long-term impact of stabilization plans on regional balances through tests of the existence of a unit root in the series for Y_t or the existence of structural breaks that could be attributed to any of them. If there is not a unit root on Y_t or any structural break that is easily associated to any stabilization plan, it is possible to say that stabilization plans do not have any impact on the long-term regional equilibrium.

The series Y_t was built as the ratio of Northeastern to Brazilian per capita GDP. It was calculated with yearly data for the period 1939 to

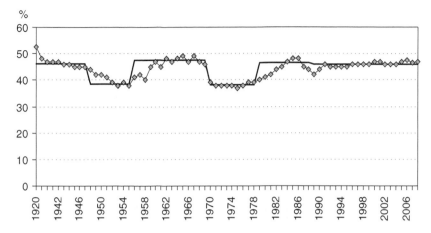

Source: IBGE, extracted from IPEADATA.

Figure 9.6 *Proportion between per capita GDP in Northeast and Brazil, 1920–2008*

2008.[13] The data for this time series appear in Figure 9.6. The series is plotted together with a hand-drawn trend in this figure, which will be useful in forthcoming arguments.

This time series was first submitted to a unit root test in which the null hypothesis was H_0: $\alpha_1 = 0$. This hypothesis was tested against the alternative H_A: $\alpha_1 < 0$. If the former case is true, the series will have a unit root and a stochastic trend. Therefore, shocks to this series, such as those introduced by stabilization plans, could have a permanent or long-term impact on the ratio of per capita GDP of the Northeast and Brazil. Under the latter hypothesis, this long-term impact would not exist.

The initial unit root tests were made under the simplifying assumption that $\phi_i = 0$ for all i. This assumption reduces the strength of the test because even when $\alpha_1 < 0$ the probability that $Y_{t+i} \neq Y_{t+j}$, for i < j, is higher if there is a structural break between the periods $t + i$ and $t + j$. Therefore, the rejection of the null hypothesis becomes less probable.[14] Nevertheless, it is a good starting point for the tests. Two alternative tests were used, which were the Augmented Dickey and Fuller (ADF) and Phillips and Perron tests. The results are presented in Table 9.1.

These tests indicate that the null hypothesis that there is a unit root or a stochastic trend is rejected at a 5 percent significance level through the ADF. Nevertheless, it is not rejected at any standard p-value through the Phillips and Perron tests. Although this latter test is less powerful than

Table 9.1   Augmented Dickey and Fuller (ADF) and Phillips and Perron tests for models with five lags and no deterministic trend and no structural breaks

	Estimated statistics	Critical values		
		1%	5%	10%
T statistics for ADF test	−3.30	−3.51	−2.89	−2.58
Phillips and Perron statistics	−2.51	−3.53	−2.90	−2.59

Source: Own estimates.

Table 9.2   Results for Lee and Strazicich unit root tests when there are structural breaks

Number of structural breaks	Estimated statistics	Critical values		
		1%	5%	10%
1	−3.5376	−4.24	−3.566	−3.211
2	−3.9488	−3.61	−3.047	−2.763
3	−4.1372			

Note: Critical values were estimated for a sample of T = 100. They were extracted from Lee and Strazicich (2003, 2004).

Source: Own estimates.

the former, the model specification is more important for the ADF test. Therefore its results would be more reliable if the five lags used are correct. Nevertheless, there is no way to be sure that this is the case, even if selection has relied on Akaike criteria.

As a consequence of the uncertainties generated by these tests, a second group of tests was made, which allowed for the existence of structural breaks in the series, or $\phi_i \neq 0$ in equation (9.1). The tests suggested by Lee and Strazicich (2003, 2004) were the ones used. The null and alternative hypotheses continue to be exactly the same as before. The results appear in Table 9.2.

They indicate that under the hypothesis that there are two structural breaks, the null hypothesis that there is a unit root or long-term stochastic trend in the series is rejected even at a 1 percent significance level. This means that such tests reject the hypothesis that stabilization plans or any other autonomous shocks change the long-term ratio of Northeastern per capita GDP to that of the whole of Brazil. This certainly indicates

Table 9.3   *Years with a structural break in the proportion of Northeastern per capita GDP to the Brazilian one and the minimum lag of years with stabilization plans before them (period 1945 to 2008)*

Years with a structural break	SP1: Minimum lag of years with a stabilization plan	SP2: Minimum lag of years with at least two stabilization plans
1956	1	5
1959	2	8
1962	2	11
1970	5	5
1987	1	1

Source: Own calculation.

that stabilization plans do not have any long-term impact on regional balances.

Although this conclusion is general and we only need two structural breaks to reach such a result, there are still two structural breaks that could be justified by stabilization plans. Furthermore, the fact that only two structural breaks are necessary to conclude that there is no long-term persistence of shocks in the Y_t series does not mean that it only has two structural breaks. Others could be identified, as the simple observation of the series indicates. The handmade shifts introduced in Figure 9.6 bring five structural breaks. This is a much smaller amount than the number of stabilization plans identified in Figure 9.3 between 1945 and 2009, which was 22. Therefore, most of the potential generation of structural breaks accruing from stabilization plans would not be observable, if they were by any chance responsible for such breaks.

To take a deeper look at the possibility that structural breaks could be caused by stabilization plans, a more rigorous identification of them was used. A structural break was identified as a shift in the variable Y_t ($Y_t - Y_{t-1}$) that was big enough to fall outside the 80 percent interval around the mean of the distribution of the shift, under the assumption that this distribution is normal. Such a rule of identification pointed to five structural breaks, as can be found through a simple observation of the series presented in Figure 9.6. These breaks were in the years 1956, 1959, 1962, 1970 and 1987. Identification considering shifts in two and three periods were tried and the results were the same, so that these years can be considered as those in which there were structural breaks.

To build Table 9.3 the monthly stabilization plans identified in Figure

9.3 were gathered under two statistics. The first one, which was called SP1, identified the years which had at least one stabilization plan. The second one, called SP2, identified the years which had two or more stabilization plans. Between 1945 and 2008 there were 24 years identified through SP1 and 15 years through SP2. These data indicate that there is often a second tightening in policies in the same year when there is a former one. With these two statistics, Table 9.3 brings the minimum lag in which there were stabilization plans before a structural break in Y_t, the ratio of Northeastern per capita GDP to that of the whole country.

Four out of five structural breaks were preceded by at least one stabilization plan in one or two years. This might indicate that there is a tendency to have structural breaks in Y_t, one or two years after stabilization plans. Nevertheless, when the amount of stabilization plans is raised to at least two in the same year, this apparent systematic behavior disappears. Furthermore, when we also consider that there were 24 years with stabilization plans, and only four of them could have generated structural breaks within two years, any possible relationship between these two events seems to be accidental. Additional statistical exercises described below give further support for the hypothesis that there is no relationship between stabilization plans and structural breaks.

9.5   STABILIZATION PLANS AND SHORT-TERM CHANGES IN REGIONAL DISPARITY IN BRAZIL

To verify the possibility that there are short-term impacts of stabilization plans in regional disparities, some simple statistical tests were pursued. The identification of years with stabilization plans pursued in the previous section generated dummy variables, called SP1 and SP2, in which there was 1 in years with stabilization plans and 0 otherwise. If there was at least one stabilization plan in the year, the value of SP1 in this year is 1, and 0 otherwise. If there were at least two stabilizations plans in a specific year, SP2 would have 1 this year, and 0 otherwise.

These dummies were included in autoregressive time series models for Y_t. As there was no reason to have a priori definition of the number of lags for Y_t in these models, several lag structures were tried. The basic results appear in Table 9.4, for both SP1 and SP2. The results indicate that only with three lags of Y_t, SP1 and SP2 have coefficients significantly different from zero at standard p-values (10 percent). This seems to indicate that there are short-term impacts of stabilization plans on the regional equilibrium in Brazil, although the evidence is not strong.[15]

Table 9.4 Estimated equations for Y_t with SP1 and SP2 as the stabilization plan indicators

Model	Variable	Constant	Y_{t-1}	Y_{t-2}	Y_{t-3}	Y_{t-4}	$SP1_t$	$SP2_t$	R^2	Durbin–Watson
SP1.1	Coeff.	0.44					0.004		0.00	0.233
	t-Stat.	10.01					0.439			
	p-value	0.000					0.661			
SP1.2	Coeff.	0.047	0.89				0.005		0.78	1.842
	t-Stat.	2.07	17.08				1.366			
	p-value	0.038	0.000				0.172			
SP1.3	Coeff.	0.05	0.97	−0.09			0.005		0.78	2.032
	t-Stat.	2.20	8.66	−0.77			1.306			
	p-value	0.028	0.000	0.441			0.191			
SP1.4	Coeff.	0.07	0.94	0.13	−0.22		0.006		0.79	2.095
	t-Stat.	2.33	8.17	0.72	−1.37		1.706			
	p-value	0.020	0.000	0.472	0.17		0.088			
SP1.5	Coeff.	0.08	0.89	0.14	0.036	−0.26	0.005		0.81	1.974
	t-Stat.	2.99	7.87	0.84	0.16	−1.75	1.418			
	p-value	0.003	0.000	0.404	0.877	0.080	0.156			
SP2.1	Coeff.	0.44						0.011	0.02	0.251
	t-Stat.	87.40						1.165		
	p-value	0.000						0.244		

Table 9.4 (continued)

Model	Variable	Constant	Y_{t-1}	Y_{t-2}	Y_{t-3}	Y_{t-4}	$SP1_t$	$SP2_t$	R^2	Durbin–Watson
SP2.2	Coeff.	0.05	0.88					0.005	0.78	1.784
	t-Stat.	2.26	16.87					1.383		
	p-value	0.024	0.000					0.167		
SP2.3	Coeff.	0.06	0.98	−0.12				0.005	0.78	2.036
	t-Stat.	2.40	8.49	−0.95				1.422		
	p-value	0.017	0.000	0.340				0.155		
SP2.4	Coeff.	0.07	0.96	0.09	−0.22			0.007	0.79	2.100
	t-Stat.	2.53	7.10	0.48	−1.34			1.871		
	p-value	0.012	0.000	0.629	0.180			0.061		
SP2.5	Coeff.	0.09	0.91	0.11	0.04	−0.26		0.006	0.81	1.988
	t-Stat.	3.16	7.71	0.62	0.16	−1.77		1.520		
	p-value	0.002	0.000	0.535	0.875	0.077		0.129		

Note: Estimation was made by OLS with correction for heteroskedasticity by the method of White (1980). Yearly data for period 1945 to 2008.

The estimated impacts of stabilization plans are positive, so that these results indicate that when they happen (which means that when inflation falls), the per capita GDP in the Northeast rises relative to that of the other regions. Thus, if these stabilization plans reduce per capita GDP, as they normally do, this fall is higher in the non-Northeastern regions than in the Northeast. This impact, however, only holds in the short term, as was seen in the previous section.

The major potential explanations for such results, according to arguments forwarded in section 3, are that: (1) wages and salaries are less rigid in the Northeast than in other regions, especially the Southeast; (2) firms in the Northeast are smaller than in other regions, especially in the Southeast; and (3) price adjustments have higher costs in other regions than in the Northeast because of market structures, which are more organized in the rest of the country. Although such regional comparisons are not made formally, they are normally taken to be true when the Northeast is compared with the Southeast and the South. Therefore, the results found are as expected from theory and regional features in Brazil.

Two other exercises, very similar to the first one, were also made. One included a one-year lag of SP1 or SP2. The second included these variables lagged two years in each equation. If there is any persistence of the impacts, the null hypothesis of no impact of stabilization plans should also be rejected. If the persistence is higher, they would be rejected for both one and two lags. If such persistence is lower, the null hypothesis could be rejected for one lag only. These exercises could also identify the existence of a sluggish impact of stabilization plans on the regional equilibrium, which cannot be ruled out a priori.

The results of these two exercises are presented in Tables 9.5 and 9.6, for SP1 and SP2. They indicate that either there is no persistence, or it is sufficiently low that there is no statistically significant impact of lagged stabilization plans on the regional balance in Brazil. These results strengthen the conclusion of the previous section that there is no persistence of stabilization plan impacts on regional balances. They also indicate that if there is any sluggish response, it is weak enough to lead to no rejection of the null hypothesis of no impact.

9.6 CONCLUSIONS

Brazil has had several stabilization plans during its post-Second World War history. Even before that, in the nineteenth century, there were periods in which inflation fell abruptly, which were probably a consequence of

Table 9.5 Estimated equations for Y_t with one lag of SP1 or SP2 as the stabilization plan indicator

Model	Variable	Constant	Y_{t-1}	Y_{t-2}	Y_{t-3}	Y_{t-4}	$SP1_{t-1}$	$SP2_{t-1}$	R^2	Durbin–Watson
SP1.1	Coeff.	0.44					0.00		0.00	0.24
	t-Stat.	73.51					0.29			
	p-value	0.000					0.771			
SP1.2	Coeff.	0.05	0.89				0.00		0.78	1.81
	t-Stat.	2.16	16.61				0.04			
	p-value	0.031	0.000				0.965			
SP1.3	Coeff.	0.06	0.98	-0.11			-0.00		0.78	2.04
	t-Stat.	2.34	8.50	-0.95			-0.11			
	p-value	0.019	0.000	0.344			0.916			
SP1.4	Coeff.	0.07	0.97	0.07	-0.19		-0.00		0.79	2.08
	t-Stat.	2.43	8.21	0.40	-1.26		-0.37			
	p-value	0.015	0.000	0.692	0.209		0.711			
SP1.5	Coeff.	0.09	0.91	0.09	0.08	-0.28	0.00		0.80	2.00
	t-Stat.	3.08	7.79	0.54	0.38	-1.92	0.25			
	p-value	0.002	0.000	0.589	0.705	0.054	0.800			

SP2.1	Coeff.	0.44					0.01	0.01	0.25
	t-Stat.	85.37					0.83		
	p-value	0.000					0.408		
SP2.2	Coeff.	0.05	0.89				−0.00	0.78	1.80
	t-Stat.	2.14	16.57				−0.15		
	p-value	0.032	0.000				0.879		
SP2.3	Coeff.	0.06	0.99	−0.11			−0.00	0.78	2.04
	t-Stat.	2.29	8.41	−0.93			−0.23		
	p-value	0.022	0.000	0.354			0.820		
SP2.4	Coeff.	0.07	0.96	0.07	−0.19		−0.00	0.79	2.09
	t-Stat.	2.36	7.99	0.38	−1.18		−0.13		
	p-value	0.018	0.000	0.705	0.239		0.894		
SP2.5	Coeff.	0.09	0.90	0.10	0.08	−0.28	0.00	0.80	1.99
	t-Stat.	3.12	7.63	0.59	0.37	−1.94	0.47		
	p-value	0.002	0.000	0.558	0.715	0.053	0.638		

Note: Estimation was made by OLS with correction for heteroskedasticity by the method of White (1980). Yearly data for period between 1945 to 2008.

155

Table 9.6 Estimated equations for Y_t with the second lag of SP1 or SP2 as the stabilization plan indicator

Model	Variable	Constant	Y_{t-1}	Y_{t-2}	Y_{t-3}	Y_{t-4}	$SP1_{t-2}$	$SP2_{t-2}$	R^2	Durbin–Watson
SP1.1	Coeff.	0.43					0.01		0.01	0.24
	t-Stat.	73.41					1.01			
	p-value	0.000					0.313			
SP1.2	Coeff.	0.05	0.88				0.01		0.78	1.77
	t-Stat.	2.16	16.53				1.35			
	p-value	0.031	0.000				0.177			
SP1.3	Coeff.	0.06	0.98	-0.11			0.01		0.79	2.01
	t-Stat.	2.32	8.50	-0.96			1.37			
	p-value	0.020	0.000	0.338			0.172			
SP1.4	Coeff.	0.07	0.96	0.05	-0.17		0.01		0.79	2.06
	t-Stat.	2.35	8.17	0.29	-1.11		1.21			
	p-value	0.019	0.000	0.775	0.267		0.225			
SP1.5	Coeff.	0.08	0.92	0.07	0.07	-0.25	0.00		0.81	1.97
	t-Stat.	3.06	8.03	0.46	0.31	-1.73	0.87			
	p-value	0.002	0.000	0.647	0.753	0.083	0.382			

SP2.1	Coeff.	0.44					0.01	0.01	0.25
	t-Stat.	84.34					0.66		
	p-value	0.000					0.511		
SP2.2	Coeff.	0.05	0.89				0.00	0.78	1.81
	t-Stat.	2.15	16.76				−0.25		
	p-value	0.031	0.000				0.803		
SP2.3	Coeff.	0.06	0.98	−0.11			0.00	0.78	2.04
	t-Stat.	2.30	8.34	−0.88			−0.18		
	p-value	0.022	0.000	0.378			0.857		
SP2.4	Coeff.	0.07	0.96	0.08	−0.19		0.00	0.79	2.09
	t-Stat.	2.38	7.98	0.41	−1.19		−0.28		
	p-value	0.017	0.000	0.685	0.235		0.776		
SP2.5	Coeff.	0.09	0.91	0.09	0.07	−0.27	0.00	0.80	1.99
	t-Stat.	3.11	7.84	0.56	0.31	−1.85	−0.22		
	p-value	0.002	0.000	0.578	0.757	0.064	0.825		

Note: Estimation was made by OLS with correction for heteroskedasticity by the method of White (1980). Yearly data for period between 1945 to 2008.

anti-inflationary policy strategies. Thus, such stabilization plans have a very long history in Brazil. There were also anti-inflationary stabilization plans that did not generate any relevant impact on inflation itself, so that there were more plans than the data on inflation movements reveal.

Stabilization plans normally also have an impact on per capita GDP and other economic variables, such as unemployment. Nonetheless, there is no reason to think that these anti-inflationary policies have the same impact on all regions within a country with such a high degree of spatial economic diversity as Brazil. The reasons that are normally given by theory that anti-inflationary policies have short-term impacts on unemployment and GDP are not evenly distributed among regions in Brazil. The existence of contracts, information on macroeconomic developments and the ability of firms to adjust prices quickly, which is often associated to their size, are not attributes equally distributed among regions.

The poorest regions usually have a lower share of formal labor relations, which reduces the wage rigidities to which they are subject; and firms are smaller, which gives them more flexibility to respond to price adjustments to news on macroeconomic developments. On the other hand, these smaller firms have less information on relevant new macroeconomic facts, and there is no reason to suppose that they are less subject to regulated prices. Therefore, stabilization plans can move the regional balances in Brazil in both directions, at least in the short run.

As concerns the long run, there are different views coming from theory. The first one argues that such policies do not have any effect on the determinants of long-term regional equilibrium, which is mainly determined by relative availability of some key factors of production, especially human capital. In this sense, they should not have any long-term impact on the regional balance. Nevertheless, there are some economists of the new economic geography who have argued that economies of scale are the most relevant determinants of equilibrium among regions. In this case, accumulation of short-term fluctuations could have a long-term impact, as they can change the relative existence of scale among regions. So long-term impacts of stabilization plans on regional balances are also not a priori defined by theory.

Empirical investigations conducted in this chapter have shown that there is some short-term effect of stabilization plans on the regional balance in Brazil. Regressions which used dummies for years in which there were sharp falls in inflation to explain the ratio of Northeastern to Brazilian per capita GDP were estimated. They indicated that such phenomena had an impact on that ratio in the year in which they occur, although in subsequent years it disappears. This impact is such that stabilization plans increase the ratio of Northeastern per capita GDP to the Brazilian one. Therefore, the lower ratio of economic relationships governed by contracts and smaller firms prevails over the impact of informational asymmetries.

The unit root tests gave support to the hypothesis that there is no long-term impact of stabilization policies on the regional balance. Therefore, the hypothesis of relative availability of factors of production and its tendency to persist is more important to determine the regional balance in Brazil than the scale effects stressed by the new economic geography. Such a relative role of these two determinants has already been stressed by Barros (2011) and it was again confirmed by the empirical analysis presented here.

Overall, the major conclusion of this chapter is that stabilization plans and short-term macroeconomic policies in a more general framework seem to have a negligible impact on regional balances in Brazil. Therefore, concerns with this problem should focus on development policies, rather than on stabilization policies, as instruments that could affect the economic inequalities among regions.

NOTES

1. See, for example, Pelaez and Suzigan (1981) and Goldsmith (1986).
2. See Fischer (1983) and Barro (1996) for seminar contribution stating this hypothesis.
3. Baer (2008) provides an analysis and description of many of these more recent plans.
4. This method implies that if the 12 months' previous inflation rate was normally distributed, a stabilization plan would exist if the mean for the two next monthly inflation rates lies outside a confidence interval of 95 percent of this distribution.
5. Mazali and Divino (2010), through more formal estimation procedures, also have shown that there is an identifiable Phillips curve in the Brazilian economy.
6. For more recent contributions, see Andres and Hernando (1999), Bruno and Easterly (1998) and Kremer et al. (2009).
7. See Vale (2005) for a test of this hypothesis with Brazilian data that gives support to it.
8. This idea comes from Lucas (1972, 1973) models.
9. They were initially forwarded by Fischer (1983).
10. See Barros (2010, 2011) for more rigorous discussions of this source.
11. This source is more rigorously analyzed in Fujita et al. (1999) and Fujita and Thisse (2002).
12. Barros (2011) has shown that Brazilian regional disparities can be plainly explained by differences in human capital availability.
13. Data were from IBGE, extracted from IPEADATA.
14. For a more detailed presentation of the econometrics behind this loss of strength of unit root tests when there are structural breaks, see Perron (2006).
15. Rejection of the null hypothesis of no impact of stabilization plans was not verified at 5 percent or 1 percent, as normally happen with hypotheses with strong empirical support.

REFERENCES

Andres, J. and I. Hernando (1999), "Does inflation harm economic growth? Evidence for the OECD", in M. Feldstein (ed.), *The Costs and Benefits of Price Stability*, Chicago, IL: University of Chicago Press, pp. 315–348.

Baer, W. (2008), *The Brazilian Economy*, 6th edn, Boulder, CO: Lynne Rienner Publishers.

Barro, R. (1996), "Inflation and Growth", *Federal Reserve Bank of St. Louis Review*, May/June, 153–169.

Barros, A. (2010), "Um Teorema da Não Convergência das Rendas per capita Regionais", mimeo, Department of Economics, Federal University of Pernambuco, Recife-PE, Brazil.

Barros, A. (2011), *Desigualdades Regionais no Brasil*, Rio de Janeiro: Campus-Elsevier.

Bruno, M. and W. Easterly (1998), "Inflation crisis and long-run growth", *Journal of Monetary Economics*, **41**, 3–26.

Fischer, S. (1983), "Inflation and growth", NBER Working Paper 1235, Cambridge, MA.

Fujita, M. and J. Thisse (2002), *Economics of Agglomeration, Cities, Industrial Location and Regional Growth*, Cambridge: Cambridge University Press.

Fujita, M., P. Krugman and A. Venables (1999), *The Spatial Economy*, Cambridge, MA: MIT Press.

Goldsmith, R.W. (1986), *Brasil 1850–1984: Desenvolvimento Financeiro sob um Século de Inflação*, São Paulo: Editora Harper & Raw do Brasil.

Kremer, S., A. Bick and D. Nautz (2009), "Inflation and growth: new evidence from a dynamic panel threshold analysis", School of Business & Economics Discussion Paper, 2009/9, Freie Universitat.

Lee, J. and M. Strazicich (2003), "Minimum LM unit root test with two structural breaks", *Review of Economics and Statistics*, **85** (4), 1082–1089.

Lee, J. and M. Strazicich (2004), "Minimum LM unit root test with one structural break", Appalachian State University Working Paper.

Lucas, R. (1972), "Expectations and the neutrality of money", *Journal of Economic Theory*, **4** (2), 103–124.

Lucas Jr., R. (1973), "Some international evidence on output-inflation tradeoffs", *American Economic Review*, **63** (3), 326–334.

Mazali, A. and J. Divino (2010), "Real wage rigidity and the new Phillips curve: the Brazilian case", *Revista Brasileira de Economia*, **64** (3), 291–306.

Pelaez, C.M. and W. Suzigan (1981), *História monetária do Brasil*, Brasília: Universidade de Brasília.

Perron, P. (2006), "Dealing with structural breaks", in T. Mills and K. Patterson (eds), *Palgrave Handbook of Econometrics: Econometric Theory*, Vol. 1, London: Macmillan, pp. 278–352.

Vale, S. (2005), "Inflation, growth and real and nominal uncertainty: some bivariate Garch-in-Mean evidence for Brazil", *Revista Brasileira de Economia*, **59** (1), 127–145.

White, H. (1980), "A heteroskedasticity-consistent covariance matrix estimator and a direct test for heteroskedasticity", *Econometrica*, **48** (4), 817–838.

10. The use of native forests versus economic growth in Brazil: is it possible to reach a balance?

Carlos José Caetano Bacha

10.1 INTRODUCTION

This chapter analyzes the unsustainable use of Brazilian native forests and how this process is associated with Brazilian economic growth. For this purpose, the chapter focuses on the period between 1930 and 2011.

The use of native forests in Brazil is regulated by forest policy. This is implemented through a series of Acts intended to control the deforestation process, to regulate the sustainable use of the remaining native forests, and to encourage reforestation. Brazil's forest policy has been systematic since 1934, when the first forest code came into effect. It was strengthened in the 1960s and the 1990s, when new amendments to the forest policy were issued and specific legislation concerning the use of water resources, and environmental crime in connection with forest legislation, came into effect. This legislation has created a complex legal framework that, in principle, would control deforestation in Brazil if all the aforementioned legislation were obeyed. However, deforestation continues to occur at different paces among the Brazilian states, and without respect for existing forest legislation.

The forest policy for the control of deforestation is classified as an incomes policy, which is constituted in a series of regulations that restrict the production and trade of products. Other examples of incomes policy are: labor legislation, defining rules for the use of the workforce and wages; zoning policies for the use of land, defining what share of a physical territory can be used and how it can be used; and price-setting policies (such as price freezing plans). An incomes policy is established by legislation that defines what, when and how something can be done.

The goal of forest policy in Brazil is not to eliminate deforestation totally, but rather to control it. Nevertheless, the policy has not been satisfactorily complied with, and deforestation has reached significant levels in several Brazilian states. For this reason, this chapter seeks to demonstrate that the effort to control deforestation has been only partially effective, and attempts to explain the causes of its failure.

The study suggests two hypotheses to explain the partial ineffectiveness of forest policy in Brazil:[1]

1. The destruction of Brazilian forest resources, and the unsustainable use of remaining native forests, is connected with Brazilian developmental policies. These, in turn, have been based on the prevailing macroeconomic models in vogue at different points in time among Brazilian policymakers.
2. Even though measures to control and regulate deforestation have been ineffective, those responsible for defining forest policy have continued to issue increasingly detailed and restrictive legislation without creating significant monetary stimulus that makes the preservation and conservation of native forest a profitable and competitive activity in relation to other types of economic exploration of the land.

10.2   THE IMPORTANCE OF FORESTS TO A NATION

Forests can be used to produce ecological benefits, such as ecotourism and the production of forest commodities. According to Camino (1999, p. 101), "non-market ecological benefits produced by forests include carbon storage and fixation from the atmosphere, preserving water resources and watersheds, protecting species with pharmaceutical values, and regulating the climate". These services are provided free of charge; but if a charge could be applied, the revenue derived from native forests would increase substantially. According to Camino (1999, pp. 101–102):

> Owners of private forests in Mexico are losing a minimum of $4 billion every year of the nonmarket components of the forest's total economic value . . . Estimates of the total economic value of Costa Rican forests . . . show that owners of forested areas (including the state) fail to receive approximately 82 percent of the value of all forests (including protected areas), and 72 percent of the value per hectare from productive forests

Ecotourism brings travelers to tropical forests, preserved flora and fauna sites, beaches, and other locations with little changed natural vegetation. This type of tourism has been shown to be economically viable in a number of cases. In 1992, it accounted for 7 percent of international tourism. Furthermore, it helps to preserve natural forests (Dourojeanni, 1999, p. 90). In Brazil, there are now farms dedicated to ecotourism.

Tradable forest-based products are divided into two groups: (1) wood and paper-based products; and (2) non-wood-based products (Simula, 1999, p. 197). The first group includes: (1) low-processed goods, such as firewood, charcoal, roundwood and wood chips; (2) products resulting from the first industrial handling of roundwood, such as lumber, wooden panels, cellulose and paper; and (3) more elaborate and added-value products such as lumber for construction, furniture, paper products and cardboard.

Non-wood-based forest products "include a wide range of items from medicinal and aromatic plants to nuts, fruit, resins, tannin, wax and hand-craft products" (Simula, 1999, p. 200).

The importance of forests, as outlined above, has led many countries to make efforts to avoid losing them or to restore them. According to the Food and Agriculture Organization (FAO) (2010), Canada and Japan did not alter their forest coverage between 1990 and 2010. Forests covered 34 percent of Canadian territory and 66.1 percent of Japanese territory in 2010. The USA increased their forest coverage during the same period, increasing from 30.8 to 31.6 percent of their territory. European countries similarly increased their forest coverage (both native and planted) by 15.5 million hectares between 1990 and 2010. In 2010, forests covered 43.8 percent of European territory, compared to 42.9 percent in 1990. China increased its forests by 49.7 million hectares, and India by 4.5 million hectares, during the same time period.

Brazil, in contrast, was the largest destroyer of native forests worldwide between 1990 and 2010. It lost 55.3 million hectares. Indonesia came second on the list, with a loss of 24.1 million hectares (according to FAO, 2010).

It could be imagined that Brazil has an above-average forest coverage in comparison with other countries, which could account for this loss of native forests. Indeed, in 2010, 61 percent of Brazilian territory was covered with forests (FAO, 2010). However, a high percentage of forest coverage can also be found in other countries that did not lose their forest coverage. In 2010, 65.5 percent of Finland was covered with forests, 62.6 percent of Sweden, and 66.1 percent of Japan. Even countries less developed than Brazil maintain a high percentage of forest coverage, such as French Guyana (96.3 percent) and Surinam (90.4 percent).

It could also be claimed that forests have no economic importance for Brazil. This is also incorrect. Wood-made products accounted for 8.7 percent of Brazilian exports in 1999, and were directly and indirectly responsible for 1.8 million jobs (Bacha, 2001).

From the above information, one can see that forests have not been used in Brazil in such a way as to maximize their possible economic and environmental benefits. In order to understand this process, it is important to make a historical analysis of how deforestation in Brazil has taken place.

10.3   THE EVOLUTION OF DEFORESTATION IN BRAZIL

Deforestation is not a new phenomenon in Brazil. In fact, the country has destroyed its native forests throughout its economic development. Although most attention is currently paid to the Legal Amazon region, deforestation rates have actually been higher in other regions, where the ecological benefits of native forests and other natural vegetations have largely been lost.

Since the Portuguese discovered Brazil in 1500, natural forests and other forms of natural vegetation have been removed to make way for farming, industry, mining, economic infrastructure (roads, dams, and so on) and urban expansion. According to the SOS Mata Atlântica Foundation (1998), the Southern and Southeastern Brazilian states had approximately 48.9 and 33.9 million hectares of forest coverage in 1912, respectively. By the late 1950s and early 1960s, these numbers had fallen to 11.7 and 11.1 million hectares, respectively. During this time, the most developed regions of Brazil lost 60 million hectares (an area almost equal to the size of France).

Since the mid-1970s, deforestation has intensified in the Legal Amazon region. Between 1975 and 2010, the region lost 62.7 million hectares (INPE, 2000, 2011), almost equal again to the territory of France.

This loss of forest resources could be considered normal for a country that is expanding its farming, industry and urban sectors. However, the intensity of the process, the way it has been carried out, the forecasts of further deforestation, and no guarantee that the remaining forests will be sustainably used in the future, are in absolute contrast to the importance that forests have for the economy.

The rate of deforestation differs from one Brazilian state to another. Tables 10.1, 10.2 and 10.3 show the shares of the Brazilian states' surfaces that were covered with forests or other native vegetation in selected years.

The data in these tables permit the following conclusions. Firstly, the Southern and Southeastern states lost more forest coverage (Table 10.1). In some cases, forest coverage is below the minimum levels recommended by international agencies. The United Nations Environment Program (UNEP) suggests that at least 10 percent of a region's territory be preserved with native vegetation. This does not include what should be maintained for sustainable forest exploitation. In the Southern and

Table 10.1 Shares of the Southeastern and Southern Brazilian states covered with native forests in selected years (%)

State	1500	1912	Late 1950s and early 1960s	2005	2010
Minas Gerais	51.76	47.50	9.89[e]	4.55	4.47
Espírito Santo	86.81	64.98	29.69[d]	10.33	10.31
Rio de Janeiro	98.27	82.06	25.33[g]	18.51	18.48
São Paulo	82.39	58.42[a]	13.72[f]	9.30	9.29
Paraná	84.20	82.86	27.91[g]	9.77	9.71
Santa Catarina	81.48	78.65	29.99[c]	22.84	22.55
Rio Grande do Sul	39.76	35.13[b]	9.58[c]	3.58	3.56

Notes:
a. data for 1907;
b. data for 1940;
c. data for 1959;
d. data for 1958;
e. data for 1961;
f. data for 1962;
g. data for 1960.

Source: SOS Mata Atlântica Foundation (1998, 2002, 2009, 2010).

Table 10.2 Shares of Amazonian states covered with native forests in selected years (%)

State	1500	1975	1990	2000	2010
Acre	98.9	98.1	92.2	88.76	85.52
Amazonas	97.94	97.89	96.52	95.99	95.48
Roraima	76.85	76.82	75.16	74.06	72.93
Rondônia	95.93	95.42	81.88	71.57	62.27
Pará	92.77	89.52	81.20	77.04	72.27
Amapá	85.45	85.34	84.53	84.18	83.94
Tocantins	99.46	98.16	90.98	88.98	89.43
Maranhão	90.64	66.17	54.75	51.25	47.87
Mato Grosso	97.73	96.58	87.31	79.58	72.46
Legal Amazon region	94.89	92.44	86.43	83.00	79.65

Source: INPE (2000, 2011).

Table 10.3   Shares of Northeastern and Center-Western states' territories covered with natural vegetation (forests, cerrado, caatinga, prairie and swamps)

State	1500	1970s[a]	1980s
Piauí	93.13	90.68	56.57[b]
Ceará	93.46	73.24	15.66[b]
Rio Grande do Norte	97.01	69.44	43.46[b]
Paraíba	98.98	53.55	30[b]
Pernambuco	96.30	58.27	49.41[b]
Sergipe	96.86	–	37.6[b]
Alagoas	98.69	–	22.8[b]
Bahia	95.29	64.53	48.08[b]
Goiás	–	–	27.1[c]
Mato Grosso do Sul	97.23	–	44.89[d]

Notes:
a.   for Piauí and Paraíba, this information is for 1971–73. For the other states, it is for 1977–81;
b.   for 1988/89;
c.   for 1983;
d.   for 1982.

Source: Bacha (1995), using data from different publications.

Southeastern regions, only the states of Rio de Janeiro, Espírito Santo and Santa Catarina meet this minimum.

Secondly, the Northeastern states saw great changes in their natural coverage in the 1970s and 1980s (Table 10.3). This process has not been widely reported in the literature.

Thirdly, the states that make up the Legal Amazon region still have widespread forest coverage. However, there has been intense deforestation in some of these states, and they have faced a rapid drop in their forest coverage. The states of Maranhão, Mato Grosso, Pará and Rondônia (where farming is expanding rapidly) are responsible for 89.1 percent of the deforestation in this region from 1991 through 2010, despite the fact that these states make up only 48.4 percent of the region's territory. This deforestation process is what attracts attention from the international community. What happened in the rainforest (especially the Mata Atlântica) is now being repeated in the Legal Amazon (Viana, 2002, p. 4).

Fourthly, the aggregate deforestation at the state level does not reveal the inequality of this phenomenon within each state. For instance, in the

Legal Amazon, "many districts and towns have already seen deforestation levels of over 50% and some have reached levels similar to those of the rainforest" (Viana, 2002, p. 1).

Deforestation has taken place in a disorderly manner. The richness of the native forest has mostly been burnt, without the wood being put to good use. Ecosystems have been destroyed and can never be fully recovered. The abundance of land in Brazil, associated with the expanding transport system, has allowed increased farming production. New frontier areas have been converted to crop production, while already deforested land continues to be underutilized.

10.4 EVOLUTION AND BACKGROUND OF FOREST POLICY AIMING TO CONTROL DEFORESTATION

As emphasized in the introduction to this chapter, the policy to control deforestation is an incomes policy that has been implemented through forest legislation. The latter has been in existence since 1934, and has been gradually improved over time. However, it remains to be enforced in its entirety. According to Alencar et al. (2004, p. 13), "Brazilian environmental legislation is currently one of the most sophisticated in the world and provides a potentially very efficient legal basis for the occupation of new frontiers in an orderly manner and a reduction in deforestation, especially when it is illegal and inadequate". However, as shown in section 10.3, deforestation is not slowing down and new frontiers have not been occupied in an orderly fashion. The question must be asked: why is forest legislation not entirely enforced in Brazil?

During the colonial and imperial periods in Brazil, the central government was concerned with restricting deforestation to avoid wasting logs that could be of interest to the Portuguese Crown, the sovereignty of the nation, or to avoid scarcity of roundwood in the future. These factors account for a number of Acts aimed at restricting the use of native forests, and the central government imposed a monopoly on the trade of some types of logs (see Castro, 1975; Zaniolo, 1988; Azeredo, 1988). Nevertheless, the expansion of farming led to a great deal of deforestation in areas close to the Brazilian coast.

In the building of houses in Brazil, preference has been given to stone, bricks and sand as the main building inputs. Timber is not the material used most for building houses. The lack of knowledge concerning Brazilian trees had led to the use of imported wood. According to Zenid (1997, p. 16):

despite the fact that there were wide areas of forest available and production of pine lumber had begun, the first two decades of the twentieth century were marked by the significant amounts of imported and processed lumber from the Northern hemisphere to meet demand in the cities of Rio de Janeiro and São Paulo.

10.4.1   Time Period from 1930 to 1964

The first broad set of Acts to protect Brazil's natural resources was issued in the 1930s. The Great Depression, coupled with skepticism of the main economic ideas of the time (before John Maynard Keynes's *General Theory*) enabled the authoritarian government of Getulio Vargas to prepare a number of codes to protect natural resources. These included: the First Forest Code (Decree # 23 793 of 23 January 1934); the Waters Code (Decree # 24 643 of 10 July 1934); the Fishing Code (Decree-Law # 794 of 19 October 1938); and the Mining Code (Decree-Law # 1985 of 29 January 1940).

The idea behind these codes was to put limits on the use of natural resources. These would be in accordance with what was discussed in the theory of externalities (Pigou, 1932), with theoretical formulations concerning the limit of the natural resource use (such as the model prepared by Hotteling in 1931), and recognizing that the price mechanism does not lead to the optimum allocation of abundant natural resources.

The 1934 Forest Code established the following measures aimed at controlling deforestation:

- Limits on the use of land within each farm, which would be divided into three areas: one free for exploitation; another kept as forest reserve (at least 25 percent of each rural property area formerly covered with native forests); and the third comprising of forests bordering rivers and waterways (riparian forests) which could not be exploited.
- An obligation for rural landowners to request a prior license from the federal government forest bureau in order to exploit areas with native forests bordering navigable rivers and lakes or railroads.
- An obligation for large-scale industrial consumers of forest products (such as steelmakers and railroad companies) to maintain their own forests for the sustainable supply of firewood or charcoal. This meant that these companies had to replace the native trees they had cleared from natural forest.
- The creation of conservation units to protect certain ecosystems in areas undergoing rapid deforestation, including public wood forests (future national forests), parks and protective forests. The latter served to conserve waterways, avoid land erosion by natural agents,

fix dunes, help defend frontiers, ensure public health conditions, protect natural beauty spots and harbor rare species of native fauna.

Note that only bans and obligations involving land use were created. No monetary stimuli to encourage landowners to maintain native forests were established.

The National Pine Institute (INP) was the agency in charge of ensuring compliance with the 1934 Forest Code (also known as the 1st Forest Code). This task was later forwarded to the Department of Renewable Natural Resources, a branch of the Ministry of Agriculture.

The 1934 Forest Code was insufficiently enforced. The country was growing, and preference was given to industrial and urban activities, which required a certain amount of deforestation. To finance these activities, the state adopted exchange rate and taxation policies that transferred a share of potential farmer's income to industry (see Baer, 2001). Ensuring the expansion of farming (and the occupation of land previously covered with forests) was an important element within this development policy,[2] and explains why the federal government did not allocate resources to enforce the regulations contained in the 1934 Forest Code.

It is important to point out that during the 1940s, 1950s and 1960s the main macroeconomic model advocated by macroeconomic policymakers was the Keynesian theory (today a part of the neoclassical synthesis). It divides the economy into five markets (product, money, bonds, labor and foreign currency exchange market), paying no attention to the role of natural resources within the economy.

The product market balance equation is:

$$Y = C + I + G + X - M$$

In this equation, Y is the gross domestic product (GDP), C is private sector consumption, I is private sector investment, G is government expenditure, X refers to exports and M to imports.

Taking into account only the product market, the following development policies were coherent with this model:

- New investments for the purpose of converting forest-covered land into farmland (increase in I).
- Increased government expenditure necessary to build new roads and power plants, leading to further deforestation (increase in G).
- Companies exploiting forests in an unsustainable way, to obtain more products for the purpose of increasing exports (X) or reducing imports (M).

Consequently, farmland increased at the expense of forest. According to Brazilian agricultural census data, 3 million farming establishments were created between 1940 and 1970, and the total area given over to farming rose by 100 million hectares. The style of growth in farming production contributed significantly to deforestation in Brazil. Between 1940 and 1970, the expansion in farming was due to growth in farmland. Goldin and Rezende (1993, pp. 15–16) – based on Melo (1987) – claim that the growing area of farmland was responsible for 72 percent of the growth in agricultural production in the 1950s and 65 percent in the 1960s. From 1938 to 1964, 356 000 kilometers of roadways were built (an increase of 185 percent)[3] due to government investments in this type of infrastructure. Exports were encouraged by activities that could deplete forest resources, such as mining, farming and forest exploitation. Concerning the latter, the exploitation of pine in the South generated foreign currency for the country through exports.

10.4.2   Time Period from 1965 to 1988

From 1965 to 1988, a new phase of Acts to monitor and control deforestation was introduced, but again no monetary stimuli were given to preserve native forests. On 15th September 1965, law number 4771 (also known as the 2nd Forest Code) was issued, aiming to create more detailed and strict rules than the 1934 Forest Code. The main changes can be seen in Table 10.4. The most important are: (1) an increase in the areas given over to permanent preservation; (2) different sizing of legal reserves according to the location of the property among the Brazilian regions; (3) a requirement of government license to exploit all remaining native forests; (4) requirement of management plans prior to exploiting forests in the Northeastern, Northern and Center-Western regions; (5) a requirement for all consumers (in addition to large-scale industrial consumers) of forest products to replace exploited forests.

Forest policy was implemented by the Brazilian Forest Development Institute (IBDF), which was created on 28 February 1967, and succeeded the Renewable Natural Resources Department of the Ministry of Agriculture.

Although more strict, the 2nd Forest Code rules were largely overlooked as they were not in accordance with other measures adopted by the federal government to stimulate economic growth, such as:

● Monetary stimuli (through rural credits and a guaranteed prices policy) to expand farming in the 1970s and early 1980s. This accounts for the growth in farming in the Center-West region, which automatically increased deforestation in this region.

Table 10.4   Comparison between the 1934 and 1965 Forest Codes

Topic	1934 Forest Code	1965 Forest Code
Types of area inside each farm	Three areas: one is for free exploitation, other is maintaining with native forests on at least 25% of the total farmland (called as forest reserve), and the third one is the riparian forests (not allowed to be exploited).	Three areas: permanently preserved forests (which include riparian forests and others), the legal reserve (formally called forest reserve) and areas for free agricultural exploitation.
Size of legal reserve	At least 25% of each farm formerly covered with native forests. This percentage was unique for the entire country.	At least 20% of property in the Southeast and South and part of the Center-West, and at least 50% of property located in the Northern part of the Center-West region and the North region. Initially, this restrictive zoning was established for farms previously covered with native forests, but latter this zoning was extent for all farms independently of their former native vegetal coverage.
Requirement for management plan	None	Required for exploiting native forests in the Northeast, North and Center-West.
License requirement to exploit the remaining native forests	For forests located near rivers and railroads	Required for exploiting all native forests.
Replacement of native forests	Required only for large consumers of forest products	All consumers of forest products should replace the forests that have been exploited. Large consumers should have their own sustainably managed plantations of trees or native forests.
Areas for preservation	Riparian forests	Riparian forests, areas on hilltops and steeped side of mountains.

Source: prepared by the author based on Decree 23.793/34 and Law 4.771/65.

- Governments at the federal, state and local levels building more roads. Total length of roads increased from 548 000 kilometers in 1964 to 1 502 000 kilometers in 1988. The new roads provided access to previously isolated and forest-covered areas.
- The federal government provided monetary incentives to agricultural and industrial projects in the Amazon and the Northeast region. These projects received incentives from SUDAM and SUDENE and implied further deforestation.[4]
- Several conflicts arose between forest legislation and other federal legislation. For instance, the Land Statute Act (Estatuto da Terra) assures ownership to those who have improved the land. One definition of improvement was clearing the land, that is, chopping down native forests.

In the early 1970s, criticisms of Keynesian economics concentrated on the lack of microeconomic bases in the macroeconomic framework and the lack of rational expectations in the same framework. The new classic and new Keynesian models arose to overcome these deficiencies, but they did not consider natural resources to be significantly relevant. The same applied to the neoclassical synthesis model.[5] Natural resources were included in supply shock models (for example, an exogenous oil price shock), which accounted for the stagflation that developed countries faced during the 1970s (Blanchard, 2006, Chapter 7).

During the 1970s and early 1980s, there were at least two attempts to incorporate natural resources into macroeconomic models. The first introduced natural resources into the neoclassical growth model. Stiglitz (1974) claimed that this model has no equilibrium, but Cigno (1981) proved that it does. The second was Sachs's (1990) proposal which used Michael Kalecki's growth equation to show how the rational use of natural resources can permit the product to increase in value. However, neither of these two models was considered fundamental for policymakers when defining macroeconomic and sector policies.

10.4.3 Period After 1988

In October, 1988, the new Brazilian Constitution was drafted and approved, guaranteeing the right of Brazilian states to implement stricter laws protecting forest resources. This enabled the Brazilian states to create their own forest legislation which, like the federal legislation, have emphasized controls over deforestation. However, a new instrument was created to encourage towns to preserve riparian forests or conservation units. This instrument is the state-charged Added Value Tax (known as

ICMS Ecologico in Portuguese) which allocates a share of the tax money collected by state governments to cities where farmers are allocating areas to protect commonly used resources, such as conservation units and riparian forests surrounding water reservoirs and their tributary rivers. ICMS Ecologico is a form of compensation for cities due to the ecological benefits that their forests provide to their neighbors.

The ICMS Ecologico was first implemented in the state of Paraná in 1992, followed by the states of São Paulo (1994), Minas Gerais (1996), Rondônia (1997), Rio Grande do Sul (1999) and Mato Grosso do Sul (2002), while other states are still considering it (Bacha and Shikida, 1999).[6] The results of this measure have not been extraordinary, but they are helping to preserve native forests both inside and outside conservation units.

Despite its creativity at the state level, the federal government has maintained its policy of controlling deforestation, broadening previously established measures and seeking to make them more restrictive. Law enforcement, however, continues to be a problem.

Eight important measures were taken after 1988:

1. Definition of a global policy for the environment, recognizing that all natural resources interact with each other. This led to the creation of the Ministry of the Environment and Natural Resources (MMA, in Portuguese).
2. Reorganization of federal environmental agencies. In February 1989, the Brazilian Institute for the Environment and Renewable Natural Resources (IBAMA) was created to unite the responsibility of the federal agencies that monitored specific resources, such as the Brazilian Institute for Forest Development (IBDF), the Rubber Inspectorate (SUDHEVEA), Fishing Inspectorate (SUDEPE), and the Special Environmental Secretariat (SEMA). In November 1992, the Ministry of the Environment and Natural Resources (MMA) was created, and the IBAMA became a branch of the MMA. In August 2007, the Chico Mendes Biodiversity Conservation Institute was created, also connected to the MMA, and it has managed and monitored the conservation units since.
3. Requirement of environmental impact reports (EIRs) on projects affecting the environment, such as the building of roads and power plants, mining and large farming projects. EIRs are a way to impose measures on economic projects in order to minimize environmental damages.
4. New forest legislation was issued which made it compulsory to replace native forestland that had been depleted. This legislation consisted

of the case of riparian forests surrounding water reservoirs (Law # 7754 of 14 April 1989), and the Legal Reserve (Law # 8171 of 17 January 1991 and Decree # 2166). These Acts, together with the Environmental Crime Law (Law # 9605 of 12 February 1998), define more clearly the individualization of environmental crime responsibility. The last law was sanctioned eight years after its introduction in Congress and became regulated only in 2000.

5.   Abolition of SUDAM and SUDENE tax incentives for farming involved in the deforestation of the Legal Amazon.

6.   Increase in the size of legal reserves. From 25 July 1996 to 24 August 2001, 67 *Medidas Provisorias* (preliminary laws issued by the Federal Government) were issued, increasing the size of legal reserves. The last *Medida Provisoria*, number 2166-67, has been in force since 24 August 2001, and states that all farms in Brazil must have a legal reserve, irrespective of the region's native vegetation and the size of the farm. The size of the legal reserve was increased to 80 percent of the total area of each farm originally covered with forest and situated inside the Legal Amazon region (possibly reduced to 50 percent if the farm is located inside regions subject to ecological-economic zoning); 35 percent in areas covered by *cerrado* vegetation inside the Legal Amazon; and 20 percent for other rural properties in the rest of Brazil (covered with *cerrado*, prairie, forests or *caatinga*). If a rural property has no legal reserve, the owner has 30 years to replace it, planting at least one-tenth of the required missing forestland every three years.

7.   Establishment of criminal procedures and fees for negative environmental actions by farmers and other perpetrators by improving the Environmental Crime Law (Law # 9605 of 12 February 1998). Decree # 6514 – issued on 22 July 2008 – clearly defines the fees for any person who chops down trees inside preservation areas or without a government license. Fees are also established if the farmer does not re-establish legal reserves and other preservation areas (cited in items 4 and 6 above). Enforcement of Decree # 6514 was postponed to 13 December 2010, and again to 13 June 2011. In mid-2011, the Brazilian Congress was discussing amendments to the 2nd Forest Code that would ease the replacement of preservation areas and legal reserves and reward farmers who replaced them. Among the ideas being discussed are: that small family farms (from 20 to 400 hectares) would be exempted from replacing legal reserves if they had chopped down all their native forests before 2008; some perennial crops, such as coffee and apple trees, would be allowed to keep their crops on the steeper side of the mountain; and a proposal that farmers deduct the amount spent in replacing riparian forests from their banking rural

loans. These and other amendments may form part of the 3rd Forest Code as soon as the Brazilian Federal Congress achieves a final agreement about them and the Brazilian President agrees. It is a novel to be continued throughout 2012.

8. Creation of a specific federal file for each farm concerning its environmental areas. Decree # 7029 – issued 10 December 2009 – created the Federal Program to Support Environmental Regulation of Rural Properties, called the Environmental Program (Programa Mais Ambiente). The farmer has the obligation to register Preservation Areas and Legal Reserve and to replace areas cited in items 4 and 6 above.

Forest legislation up to 2010 requires replacement of land that should not have been deforested. Fees would be charged if the farmer did not fulfill the requirements of forest legislation. No nationwide monetary rewards – such as seedling grants, free technical assistance or monetary payments to preserve native forests – have been created to help farmers fulfill forest legislation. There is also no incentive to integrate farming and industry in order to make the replacement of legal reserves viable, and to ensure their use in the future.

Measures to monitor and control deforestation do not always achieve expected results in Brazil. One example of the ineffectiveness of forest legislation in the country is the enforcement of legal reserves. In the Legal Amazon, all properties should have had a legal reserve since 1934, as they have forest coverage. However, this never happened. In fact, there has been a decrease in the number of properties with legal reserves. According to Incra's Registration Statistics, 93.03 percent of rural properties in the state of Rondônia had a legal reserve in 1978. In 1998, this had declined to 5.02 percent.

In 1998, only 7.04 percent of rural properties in Brazil had legal reserves. Therefore, around 93 percent were legally responsible to replace it. In 1998, 39.8 million hectares were declared legal reserves. If properties in the North should have 50 percent of their areas given over to legal reserves, and in other regions 20 percent, there should be in total 111 million hectares of legal reserves (according to the INCRA dataset) – 71.2 million hectares of arable farming land have to be transformed into legal reserves. On the whole, this is not impossible to achieve because 73.4 million hectares of arable farming land located inside the Brazilian farms was declared exploitable but was left unused in 1996. Therefore, all that has to be done is to plant forests in these areas in order to recuperate the legal reserves.

But this situation can vary from one region to another and implies an alteration in the technology used in farming to implement legal reserves. Bacha (2004b) considers the 48 cities that make up the Piracicaba River Basin (a strip stretching from São Paulo state to Minas Gerais state) and finds that replacement of the legal reserves could be achieved if grassland areas were reduced by 32.8 percent. This could be achieved if the number of cows per hectare of pasture increased by 48.8 percent, which was not impossible at the beginning of the 2000s, considering the existing technological pattern of livestock grazing in Brazil.

Emphasis on these control measures, focused on disciplining deforestation in terms of each farm, did not halt deforestation in Brazil. What has attracted the attention of the domestic and international community is the destruction of 32.17 million hectares of native forests in the Legal Amazon between 1991 and 2010 (equivalent to half the size of France). Of no less importance are the 11.5 million hectares of forests lost in the South and Southeast between the late 1950s and 2010.

The question remains: why does a country with detailed and strict forest legislation like Brazil not achieve its goals? The answer is that these goals are not implemented in tandem with other development goals and policies adopted by policymakers.

In the 1990s, Brazil adopted measures in line with the Washington Consensus (neoliberal policies). These policies sought: (1) fiscal discipline, redirecting public expenditure priorities to health, education and infrastructure; (2) tax reforms; (3) a flexible exchange rate; (4) a guarantee of property rights; (5) deregulation of sectors driven by the state; (6) reduction of the state's participation in production by privatizing state-owned companies; and (7) capital flow liberalization among countries (see Baumann, 2000, p. 13). These reforms were to take place gradually.

The Washington Consensus made no reference to the preservation or conservation of natural resources. Indeed, some of its measures meant further destruction of natural resources in developing countries. The guarantee of property rights, capital flow liberalization and flexible exchange rates in Brazil would mean increased exports of minerals and agricultural commodities. Brazil has a comparative advantage in these products, and the result has been further deforestation. According to Prates (2008), expanding production of these products would imply further deforestation, particularly in the Amazon region.

At the same time, the need to control the public deficit and the need to increase Brazilian exports led to the weakening of public agencies that inspect the destruction of natural resources, particularly forests. Thus, priority was given to activities that would increase exports, such as the expansion of farming in the Center-West and North, even though this would lead to more deforestation.

Natural resources have still not been given an important role in mainstream macroeconomic models, despite being an important part of other economic models. Despite this, a wide range of literature on sustainable development and sustainability has arisen (see Rocha, 1999, pp. 16–24). This literature offers no consensus on how to achieve sustainable development, but has made an impact by raising awareness among economic policymakers of the sustainability of economic development. It has led to the reformulation of forest legislation, increasing the size of the legal reserve and transforming it from a forest reserve into a reserve for sustainable use. This literature on sustainable development has also had an influence on the creation of the National Water Resources Policy (Law # 9433 issued 1 August 1997). This normative Act states that "water is a public domain commodity" (Article 1, paragraph I) and the National Water Resources Policy should "guarantee that current and future generations will have access to water of adequate standard and quantity for their respective uses" (Article 2, paragraph I).

Efforts have been made to change how macroeconomic variables are measured in order to calculate sustainable income. The latter is estimated by deducting the depreciation of natural resources and the environment from the conventional measures of income. Daly (1992), Harrison (1992) and El Serafy (1992) propose different methodologies for calculating sustainable income. Some studies have been done for Brazil considering specific sectors (such as Motta and Young, 1991; Bastos Filho, 1995) and have found that sustainable income is lower than that obtained by the traditional System of National Accounts. Nevertheless, the values calculated by the System of National Accounts are the most frequently used when evaluating economies.

10.5   FINAL CONSIDERATIONS

The destruction of native forest resources in Brazil, and the unsustainable use of remaining native forests, has always been associated with development policies, which in turn have been influenced by popular, mainstream macroeconomic models. Even with the ineffectiveness of measures to control and regulate deforestation, those responsible for defining the forest policy have continued to issue increasingly detailed and restrictive legislation without creating the monetary stimulus that would make the preservation and conservation of forest resources profitable and competitive for farmers in relation to other types of economic exploitation of the land.

It is true that the preference for development policies can be attributed to interest groups which dominate the agencies formulating economic policy. But how can the situation be changed? Five propositions can be considered.

The first would be to change the economic models on which macro-economic policies are backed, giving priority to those that consider the rational use of natural resources, such as forests. So far, no widely accepted macroeconomic model has been developed that includes natural resources among its main macroeconomic variables (such as product, prices, interest rates and exchange rates). Nevertheless, current models can be reworked to include natural resources as a variable that restricts the aggregate supply curve.

Most of the macroeconomic aggregate supply curve models consider the labor market equilibrium, taking a production function where the natural resources are not explained or appear to be added to the capital, for which there is no restricted use (see Branson and Litvack, 1981; Dornbusch et al., 2009). One alternative in order to consider natural resources clearly in these models is to include them in the production function alongside labor and capital as production factors. Furthermore, one can consider that the cost of natural resources will increase the more they are used, because control policies limit their exploitation. Therefore, an aggregate supply curve that grows steeper at every point until it becomes totally vertical will be observed.

The second possibility is to focus on the control of deforestation in each Brazilian region. In this sense, ecological–economic zoning (EEZ) would be an alternative because it can define regions due to their economic aptitude and the ecological benefits that stem from the vegetation. By using this zoning, economic policies could differ from one region to another depending on how they are defined by EEZ.

EEZ on a nationwide scale in Brazil could define at least three areas: area for free exploitation; forest area for sustainable exploration; and a share for preservation. To this end, one can consider the current experiments and proposals of EEZ in order to learn more about its benefits and weak points. There are some EEZ proposals in Brazil, such as the Planafloro in the state of Rondônia and a system of national forests in the Legal Amazon region (Veríssimo et al., 2000). The Planafloro has not had satisfactory results, in part because federal policies have not adopted it. The National Forest proposal for the Legal Amazon (Flonas) has identified 1.15 million km^2 in the Legal Amazon (23 percent of the region) that are not protected areas and remain untouched, but have a high potential for wood. These areas, if transformed into national forests, will enable roundwood production in a sustainable system capable of meeting the demand for roundwood in the forest industry of the Legal Amazon, and enable a rise of 60 percent in this industry's production capacity.

To adopt EEZ in Brazil, farming policy can differ from one region to another. For example, if a certain region in the Amazon is given over to conservation or preservation of native forest resources, rural credits, minimum pricing of agricultural products, and infrastructure for transport and storage should not be offered for farming activities. However, these services and products should be offered in areas where farming is already under way. To compensate states and districts for preserving forests and environmental benefits, a special environmental allowance could be given when it comes to distributing federal taxes among the states. Similar to the ICMS Ecologico system, states and cities would receive a larger share of national income tax revenue and taxes charged on industrial goods due to their preservation and conservation of native forests. To achieve this, the National Institute of Colonization and Agrarian Reform (INCRA) files about farms could be used to compute how much each city has given to its legal reserve and permanent preservation in Brazil.

The third possibility is to make the enforcement of forest legislation more effective. This could be done without allocating a great additional amount of money to environmental agencies. All that is required is to integrate further the information systems of federal agencies.

It has been claimed that greater enforcement can only be achieved with further financial and human resources for the agencies involved in establishing and enforcing forest policy. According to Alencar et al. (2004. p. 13):

> What has hindered effective action against deforestation is the weakness of the institutions responsible for monitoring the frontier, victims of over ten years of policies to curb federal government expenditure. INCRA and the Brazilian Institute for the Environment and Renewable Natural Resources (IBAMA) are unable to carry out their job adequately. Massive long-term investments will be required, investments in manpower, equipment, and funding in the field to guarantee the effective presence of the government on the expanding pioneer fronts. Without strengthening these institutions, there is no chance of ordering the expansion of the frontier and reducing deforestation.

However, an examination of the degree of computerization of the activities of the environmental agencies and their interrelations shows that they are rudimentary and could be improved with few additional resources in order to facilitate electronic checking and avoid falsification of documents issued by the IBAMA.

Another flaw in the inspection system is that the farmers' files of public agencies – such as the IBAMA (and similar state agencies), the INCRA and Brazil's Internal Revenue Service – are not interconnected. When registering with the INCRA, landowners have to declare whether or not they have a legal reserve. If a landowner declares that he does not have a legal reserve, then the IBAMA would know that the landowner has admitted that he is not complying with forest legislation. Furthermore, when dealing with the Internal Revenue Service, the landowner has to declare his Rural Land Tax (ITR) and income tax. The Rural Land Tax on the legal reserve is not charged and depends on how the land is being used. If the landowner declares on his Land Tax form that he has a legal reserve (so that he can pay less tax) and does not declare it to the INCRA, this would be recognized as tax fraud. As a result, he would be automatically fined. Therefore, electronic inspections can be conducted and would be a powerful instrument to bring farmers into line when it comes to complying with forest legislation. To make this system workable, all that is required is an interconnection and exchange of information among federal public agencies.

Finally, on-site inspections have been hindered by inadequate and ludicrous procedures on the part of the IBAMA. This agency, when confiscating illegally harvested roundwood, has nominated the person responsible for this illegal act as the trustee, and this person ends up "doing away with" the roundwood. According to Veja (2004. p. 33):

> around 48 000 cubic meters of logs, confiscated by IBAMA last year during the Forever Green operation, disappeared from the yards of five lumber companies charged with illegal deforestation in the state of Pará. The thousands of logs were stored in the yards of the same companies that were being fined

The IBAMA claims that it does not have enough resources to store the logs by itself. So why not auction it and deposit the money? In the example above, the vanished logs had an estimated value of R$10 million, equivalent to two-thirds of the money the IBAMA spent on airline tickets in 2003.

The fourth possibility is to provide monetary compensations for rural landowners to protect forests. The introduction of monetary rewards to preserve and/or conserve forests is already a reality in countries such as the United States of America (USA), Finland, Austria and United Kingdom (UK), but is still being scarcely tested in Brazil.

The fifth possibility is to change the concept and valuation of farmers and consumers concerning the importance of natural resources, such as forests. This is already the case for farmers who seek environmental certification and consumers who favor ecologically friendly products. Some European countries are already more focused to consume sustainably forest products. This awareness has to be heightened in Brazil's domestic market. Demand for certification is high. The FSC-Brazil (Forest Stewardship

Council), in May 2004, had 1 578 213 hectares of certified forests in Brazil, of which 38.6 percent (608 678 hectares) were native forests. The certification process facilitates the enforcement of forest legislation because the certification process evaluates the compliance with this legislation.

NOTES

1. The first hypothesis has already been examined by Bacha (2004a), but the second one has not. Therefore, the present chapter expands the analysis of the former paper, focusing only on the use of native forests and broadening the discussion of policies that enable balance between economic growth and the sustainable use of native forests.
2. The colonization of the north of Paraná state in the 1950s and 1960s, sponsored by the government at the time, is an example of how native forests in this state were substituted by coffee plantations to generate exports.
3. According to the *Brazilian Statistical Yearbook* (several issues), on 31 December 1938 there were 192 612 km of roadways in Brazil, and on 31 December 1964 this had grown to 548 510 km.
4. SUDENE and SUDAM (Development Agencies for the Northeast and North regions of Brazil, respectively) handled fiscal incentives programs during the 1970s and 1980s to promote economic growth in the Northeast and North of Brazil in order to reduce inequality among the Brazilian regions. Among these were farming and livestock projects, leading to more deforestation.
5. The neoclassical synthesis incorporated some of the criticisms of the new classicists to the constructions of the Keynesian theory.
6. The years mentioned in this paragraph are the ones when the ICMS Ecologico was implemented in each mentioned Brazilian state. The laws that created this tax stimulus were issued in earlier years.

REFERENCES

Alencar, A., D. Nepstad, D. McGrath, P. Moutinho, P. Pacheco, M.D.C.V. Diaz and B. Soares Filho (2004), *Desmatamento na Amazônia: indo além da "emergência crônica"*, Belém: Instituto de Pesquisa Ambiental da Amazônia.
Azeredo, N.R.S. (1988), "O Brasil e o mercado mundial de produtos de madeira", *Anais do 1st Encontro Brasileiro de Economia Florestal*, Curitiba, 23–27 May, pp. 391–418.
Bacha, C.J.C. (1995), "A Evolução do Desmatamento no Brasil", *Revista de Economia e Sociologia Rural*, Brasília, **34** (2), 111–135.
Bacha, C.J.C. (2001), "O Sistema Agroindustrial da Madeira no Brasil", *Revista Econômica do Nordeste*, Fortaleza, **32** (4), 975–993.
Bacha, C.J.C. (2004a), "O Uso de Recursos Florestais e as Políticas Econômicas Brasileiras – Uma Visão Histórica e Parcial de um Processo de Desenvolvimento", *Estudos Econômicos*, **34** (2), 393–426.
Bacha, C.J.C. (2004b), "Análise da eficácia da política de reserva legal no Brasil", XLII Congresso Brasileiro de Economia e Sociologia Rural, Cuiabá, Mato Grosso, 25–28 July.

Bacha, C.J.C. and P.F.A. Shikida (1999), "Experiências brasileiras na implementação do ICMS Ecológico", in F. Casimiro Filho and P.F.A. Shikida (eds), *Agronegócio e Desenvolvimento Regional*, Toledo: Edunioeste, pp. 179–207.

Baer, W. (2001), *The Brazilian Economy: Growth and Development*, 5th edn, Westport, CT: Praeger Publishers.

Bastos Filho, G.S. (1995), "Contabilizando a erosão do solo: um ajuste ambiental para o produto bruto agropecuário brasileiro", MSc Dissertation, "Luiz de Queiroz" College of Agriculture, University of São Paulo, Brazil.

Baumann, Renato (2000), "O Brasil nos Anos 1990: uma Economia em Transição", in R. Baumann (ed.), *Brasil – Uma Década em Transição*, Rio de Janeiro: Editora Campus, pp. 11–53.

Blanchard, O. (2006), *Macroeconomics*, 4th edn, Upper Saddle River, NJ: Pearson Education.

Branson, W.H. and J.M. Litvack (1981), *Macroeconomics*, New York: Harper & Row.

Camino, Ronnie de (1999), "Sustainable management of natural forests: actors and policies", in Kari Keipi (ed.), *Forest Resource Policy in Latin America*, Washington, DC: Inter-American Development Bank, pp. 93–109.

Castro, C.M. (1975), "Ecologia – a redescoberta da pólvora", *Revista de Administração de Empresas*, **15** (5), 6–19.

Cigno, Alessandro (1981), "Growth with exhaustible resources and endogenous population", *Review of Economics Studies*, **48** (2), 281–287.

Daly, H.E. (1992), "Toward a measure of sustainable social net national product", in Y.J. Ahmad, S. El Serafy and E. Lutz (eds), *Environment Accounting for Sustainable Development*, 3rd edn, Washington, DC: World Bank, pp. 8–9.

Dornbusch, R., S. Fischer and R. Starts (2009), *Macroeconomics*, 10th edn, New York: McGraw Hill.

Dourojeanni, Marc J. (1999), "The Future of Latin America's natural forests", in Kari Keipi (ed.), *Forest Resource Policy in Latin America*, Washington, DC: Inter-American Development Bank, pp. 79–92.

El Serafy, S. (1992), "The proper calculation of income from depletable natural resource", in Y.J. Ahmad, S. El Serafy and E. Lutz (eds), *Environment Accounting for Sustainable Development*, 3rd edn, Washington, DC: World Bank, pp. 10–18.

FAO (2010), *The Global Forest Resources Assessment 2010 – Main Report*, Rome: Food and Agriculture Organization, October (available at http://www.fao.org/docrep/013/i1757e/i1757e.pdf).

Goldin, I. and G.C. Rezende (1993), *A agricultura brasileira na década de 80 – crescimento numa economia em crise*, IPEA, série IPEA 138, Rio de Janeiro.

Harrison, A. (1992), "Introducing natural capital into the SNA", in Y.J. Ahmad, S. El Serafy and E. Lutz (eds), *Environment Accounting for Sustainable Development*, 3rd edn, Washington, DC: World Bank, pp. 19–25.

Hotelling, H. (1931), "The economics of exhaustible resources", *Journal of Political Economy*, **39**, 137–175.

INPE (2000), *Monitoramento da Floresta Amazônica brasileira por satélite 1999–2000*, São José dos Campos: Instituto Nacional de Pesquisas Espaciais, May (available at http://www.inpe.br).

Instituto Nacional de Pesquisas Espaciais (INPE) (2011), Homepage, http://www.inpe.br (accessed February 2011).

Melo, F.H. (1987), "Export-orientated agricultural growth: the case of Brazil", World Employment Programme Research Working Paper, September, Genebra.

Motta, R.S. and C.E.F. Young (1991), "Recursos naturais e contabilidade social: a renda sustentável da extração mineral no Brasil", in *Proceedings of the 19th Encontro Nacional de Economia*, Curitiba, 3–6 December, Vol. 2, pp. 235–252.

Pigou, A.C. (1932), *The Economics of Welfare*, London: Macmillan.

Prates, R.C. (2008), "O desmatamento desigual na Amazônia brasileira: sua evolução, suas causas e conseqüências sobre o bem-estar", PhD thesis, "Luiz de Queiroz" College of Agriculture, University of São Paulo, Brazil.

Rocha, D.P. (1999), "Evolução e sustentabilidade do setor industrial madeireiro no Estado de Rondonia", MSc Dissertation, "Luz de Queiroz" College of Agriculture, University of São Paulo, Brazil, November.

Sachs, Ignacy (1990), "Recursos. emprego e financiamento do desenvolvimento: produzir sem destruir – o caso do Brasil", *Revista de Economia Política*, **10** (1), 111–132.

Simula, Markku (1999), "Trade and environmental issues in forest production", in Kari Keipi (ed.), *Forest Resource Policy in Latin America*, Washington, DC: Inter-American Development Bank, pp. 195–230.

SOS Mata Atlântica Foundation (1998), *Atlas da evolução dos remanescentes florestais e ecossistemas associados no domínio da mata atlântica no período 1990–1995*, Fundação SOS Mata Atlântica, Instituto Nacional de Pesquisas Espaciais e Instituto Socioambiental, São Paulo.

SOS Mata Atlântica Foundation (2002), *Atlas dos Remanescentes Florestais da Mata Atlântica – Período 1995/2000*, São Paulo: Fundação SOS Mata Atlântica e Instituto Nacional de Pesquisas Espaciais.

SOS Mata Atlântica Foundation (2009), *Atlas dos Remanescentes Florestais da Mata Atlântica – Período 2005–2008 – RELATÓRIO PARCIAL*, São Paulo (available at http://mapas.sosma.org.br/site_media/download/atlas%20mata%20atlantica-relatorio2005-2008.pdf).

SOS Mata Atlântica Foundation (2010), *Atlas dos Remanescentes Florestais da Mata Atlântica – Período 2008–2010 – Dados parciais dos estados avaliados até maio de 2010*, São Paulo (available at http://mapas.sosma.org.br/site_media/download/atlas-relatorio2008-2010parcial.pdf).

Stiglitz, J.E. (1974), "Growth with exhaustible natural resources: the competitive economy", *Review of Economic Studies* (Symposium), 139–152.

Veja (2004), "Ouro para o bandido 1", *Revista Veja*, **37** (26), 33; 30 June.

Veríssimo, A., C. Souza Júnior and P.H. Amaral (2000), *Identificação de Áreas com Potencial para a Criação de Florestas Nacionais na Amazônia Legal*, Ministério do Meio Ambiente, Brasília, September, Research report UTF/BRA/047.

Viana, V.M. (2002), "As florestas brasileiras e os desafios do desenvolvimento sustentável: manejo, certificação e políticas públicas apropriadas", thesis, "Luiz de Queiroz" College of Agriculture, University of São Paulo, Brazil, April.

Zaniolo, A. (1988), "Análise setorial das exportações brasileiras da indústria da madeira", *Proceedings of the 1st Encontro Brasileiro de Economia Florestal*, Curitiba, 23–27 May, pp. 171–194.

Zenid, G.J. (1997), "Identificação e Grupamento das Madeiras Serradas Empregadas na Construção Civil Habitacional na Cidade de São Paulo", "Luiz de Queiroz" College of Agriculture, MSc Dissertation, University of São Paulo, Brazil.

11. Regional development and agricultural expansion in Brazil's Legal Amazon: the case of the Mato Grosso frontier

Charles C. Mueller

11.1 INTRODUCTION

This chapter examines the recent expansion of the agricultural frontier region of Mato Grosso, an important state of the so-called 'Legal Amazon' region of Brazil, from the standpoint of the theory and analysis of regional development. It begins with a conceptual discussion of the extent to which this entity – the Legal Amazon – can be considered an organic region. It examines the main factors that have facilitated or hindered the expansion of the agricultural frontier in this region, highlighting two basic determinants: regional development policies and market conditions. The effects of the latter are observed in two contrasting periods: the 1999–2005 phase of increasing world and/or domestic prices of agricultural commodities, and the 2005–06 period of sharply decreasing prices. Section 11.2 contains a conceptual discussion; section 11.3 analyzes the effects of stimuli and obstacles on the evolution of agricultural activity fronts in the Mato Grosso frontier region; and section 11.4 has concluding comments.

11.2 AGRICULTURAL EXPANSION AND UNDERDEVELOPED REGIONS IN BRAZIL: A CONCEPTUAL INCURSION

11.2.1 The Regional Design in Brazil

Agricultural activities are essentially space-users. In evaluating the effects of development policies on the agriculture of a region with a substantial potential for agricultural expansion, it is important to establish what is meant by "region", and what has been the nature of the progression of agriculture in its space.

Defining "system" as an aggregate of interconnected elements forming a complex, organic whole, a region can be viewed as a living system.[1] Its elements are the various sectors and subsectors that operate in a territory endowed with natural resources and with a given constructed structural basis (transport infrastructure, urban networks and institutional foundations). Given these, the elements of the regional system interact and operate as a complex living organization. The regional system is open and interrelates with other systems. Over time, an organic region tends to change, to expand and to evolve.

A regional strategy can be seen as a set of measures or policies designed to interfere in the process of regional change, and which aim at certain development goals. In a region of substantial agricultural potential, certain courses of action will promote regionally focused agricultural growth. They could involve measures to improve the region's foundations, such as investments in transport infrastructure, incentives to attract factors of production (labor and capital) and the implementation of institutional reform (land reform and establishing uncontested property rights). The strategy may involve policies to facilitate the operation of agriculture in the region (regionally focused credit, price support and promotion of technical change). But it is important to distinguish regional policies from those policies which have a broader (national) focus.

How does this relate to Brazilian regional delimitation and to its strategies for regional development? Have regional development policies been established in this context? Is the expansion of agriculture in regions with large endowments of unused land the result of policies geared towards the formation of organic regional systems? Other queries soon present themselves when considering these issues: how was official regional delimitation established? Can the country's official regions be considered even remotely organic regions?

As indicated by Cunha el al. (2005), until early in the twentieth century, the role of natural resources in the economic expansion of most countries led to an emphasis on natural resource endowments in their regional definition. Socio-economic features were not ignored but natural endowments tended to prevail. This was the "natural determinism" approach; it inspired the Institutio Brasileiro de Geografia e Estatística (IBGE)'s definition of Brazil's physiographic macro regions in 1942.[2] However, as the result of spatial patterns of expansion of the Brazilian economy since then, this regional configuration was deemed inadequate, and in the 1970s, the IBGE established the current regional design: North,

Northeast, Southeast, South and Center-West. But this new arrangement was – to some extent – inspired by another type of determinism: "economic determinism". The configuration of the two huge and, from the perspective of the 1970s, almost "empty" macro regions – the North and the Center-West – was influenced by natural considerations; and that of the Northeast was influenced by a natural phenomenon, that of recurring droughts. Nevertheless, more complex socio-economic factors were said to have prevailed (IBGE, 2010).

The huge macro regions defined in the 1970s were far from organic spatial systems. Moreover, the territory of each region was to remain unchanged, an exception being made for the internal division of the macro regions, based on the criterion of the productive structure. Each macro region was subdivided in mezzo regions and micro regions and, in principle, this subdivision was allowed to change, taking into account the dynamic interactions occurring inside the macro regions (IBGE, 2010).

When the current territorial configuration was established, there had been a considerable revision in the way geographers considered a "region". The "natural determinism" approach had been replaced by the Marxist-inspired outlook of the constructed or used territory. According to this outlook, an "empty" territory is of no consequence. What are relevant are the portions of a territory that, as a result of the evolution of conditions of production, experience the expansion of productive forces (see Santos and Silveira, 2003). This engenders the construction of space, and in the era of globalization and vigorous technological change the process is seen as having little to do with natural conditions.

Considering the case of Brazil, it is hard to disagree with the statement of Diniz that, whatever the IBGE's motivations in the 1970s, "the current regionalization with the five macro regions, which continues the base of regional policies, is not functional and should be replaced" (Diniz, 2009, p. 244). However, can the necessary political coalition be assembled for this to be accomplished?

11.2.2   Agriculture in Underdeveloped Regions

Cunha et al. (2005) argue that it is important to focus on aspects of the construction of a territory when establishing territorial units, but that it is a mistake to ignore natural features. Spatial analysis should replace the question "What is a region?" by a far more pertinent question: "What are the reasons for segmenting a space?" This question is particularly relevant in an analysis of the recent spread of agricultural fronts in the regional complex of Amazônia – a significant area of frontier expansion in Brazil.

The so-called "regional policies" for the Northeast and the Amazon consider the agriculture of each of these regions to be an important component, either explicitly or implicitly, and that the performance of this sector could be improved by the implementation of certain strategies. However, if we examine the processes that unfolded in these regions, the forms of organization of agricultural production present, the flows of output to the main markets and the policies implemented, it becomes evident that an organic system approach was never implemented.

The Northeast is mentioned because it was the cradle of regional development policies in Brazil. In the 1950s the report of the Grupo de Trabalho para o Desenvolvimento do Nordeste (GTDN), coordinated by Celso Furtado, offered a development strategy for the region, conceived specifically to counter the exploitation of the Northeast by the industrializing Southeast (Diniz, 2009). The strategy emphasized endogenous industrial development, but agriculture also played an important role. Measures were proposed to transform agriculture radically in the region's more humid band, to improve the agricultures of the *caatinga* and of the *semi-arido*, based on family farms, and to promote the expansion of the agricultural frontier in order to absorb demographic surpluses of the region's more settled areas. However, the Northeast was composed of the traditional *zona da mata*, the *caatinga* and the *sertão* according to the GTDN strategy, and the proposed locus of frontier expansion was the state of Maranhão, then still sparsely settled. The Cerrado (savannahs) of the official Northeast, currently important areas of agricultural expansion, were not on the radar.

With the inception of the military regime in 1964, the strategy for the Northeast was altered. The GTDN strategy focused on a smaller portion of the current official Northeast, treated as a territory which should be made organically operational by the implementation of the proposed regional development strategy. This approach was discarded, but it produced the idea that there should be development strategies for other macro regions, particularly those with sizeable 'empty' portions of the Amazon. In 1966, the Superintendência para o Desenvolvimento da Amazônia (SUDAM) was created, together with the Banco da Amazônia (analogous to the Banco do Nordeste, the financial arm of the Northeast development strategy). These organizations were intended to focus on the official North region, but later a larger entity emerged: the "Legal Amazônia" (Diniz, 2009), and the area of attention was in part diverted from the territory of the North to that of the "Legal Amazônia".[3]

There are, therefore, two different regional entities of development programs for Amazônia: while SUDAM and the Ministry of Regional Development have been stressing the official North region,[4] the Legal

Amazon region includes, in addition to the North, the huge Center-West state of Mato Grosso and parts of the state of Maranhão in the Northeast. This spatial entity has been the object of official consideration. In the 2009 Copenhagen Summit, for instance, the Brazilian government pledged to reduce its greenhouse gas emissions by between 36.1 percent and 38.9 percent by 2020; this is to be achieved by policies expected to generate an 80 percent decrease in the rate of deforestation, predominantly in Amazônia.[5] The announced goal was based on estimates by Brazil's National Institute of Space Research (INPE, 2009), which in turn were based on trends of deforestation in the Amazon between 1999 and 2008. The Amazônia of this pledge, and of the INPE surveys, is the "Legal Amazon".

The Legal Amazon regional entity has been the recipient of many programs and incentives established to spur the settlement of remote portions of Brazil, prompted mostly by the expansion of agricultural fronts (Mueller, 1980, 1984). Several of these incentives have remained in place, albeit with modifications.[6] The Legal Amazon comprises an area of 5.1 million km², which includes not only 4.1 million km² of the Brazilian Amazon biome, but also considerable portions of the Cerrado (savannah) biome in the states of Mato Grosso, Maranhão, and Tocantins. Being the locus of incidence of special incentives, powerful political forces emerged which would oppose meaningful changes to this territorial arrangement.

It is important to emphasize that neither the North nor the Legal Amazon is close to constituting an organic region. Both are artificial cuts in the vast northern portion of Brazil. If one considers the programs specially geared to the North region, they stress the two major urban poles of Belém and Manaus, and a few subregional centers such as Porto Velho (Rondônia), Rio Branco (Acre), and Santarém and Marabá in the state of Pará (IBGE, 2008). But the interconnection between these urban centers, and of each of them with the North's extended hinterland, is tenuous. Distances are vast and the difficulties of organically integrating them are enormous. The Legal Amazon entity includes the huge state of Mato Grosso, a dynamic unit whose main economic links are with São Paulo and the Center-South, not the North (IBGE, 2008).

11.3   AGRICULTURE, REGIONAL POLICIES AND MARKETS IN THE MATO GROSSO FRONTIER REGION

This section evaluates the role of frontier expansion in the conversion of Mato Grosso into a major supplier of agricultural commodities and cattle ranching for national and external – not regional – markets. But first I outline the regional policies that helped to erect the current structural foundation of the state, and emphasize the role of market conditions in recent years.

Following Sawyer (1983), I consider the agricultural frontier as a potential space, and not as a line determined by transportation costs, as in the von Thünen model (Ferreira, 1988). It is regarded as a portion of previously unoccupied or marginally occupied space which acquires the potential for agricultural exploitation. This is shaped not only by investments in transportation infrastructure, but also by the penetration and development of markets of commodities, land, services, labor and inputs, and financing; by the availability of unused or unoccupied land; and by the formation of a minimally adequate institutional foundation. These factors establish conditions for the expansion in the potential space of the frontier of activity fronts, that is, of concrete forms of undertakings that spread in the frontier. This can happen in different ways: an activity front may start precariously but evolve into established forms of enterprise, but it may also gradually fizzle out. It may expand in a sustained fashion or it may center on short-run gains, overlooking future consequences.

Agricultural expansion in the Legal Amazon frontier region has resulted from the intertwined interaction of activity fronts such as legal and illegal logging; the formation of cattle ranches, large agricultural ventures, small-scale agricultural official and private settlements; and the action of land speculators, among others (Mueller, 1984). Some of the activities undertaken in these remote areas have been illegal (Viola, 2009, p. 180); and some evolved simultaneously in space, favoring conflict and violence.

There are, however, considerable subregional differences. Two of the largest Legal Amazon states – Mato Grosso and Pará – have contrasting histories of frontier expansion. In Mato Grosso, the occupation of land was preceded by the establishment of property rights, which remain largely uncontested. In the 1970s, after the failure of "model colonization projects" – established by the military government to settle portions of the "empty" north – it was decided to make land available in parts of Mato Grosso's Amazon and northern Cerrado areas for cooperatives and private colonization ventures, which sold medium-sized to large plots to experienced farmers from the center and south of Brazil. Measures carried out to establish firm property rights of land helped to prevent disputes and violence, and expansion of agriculture and of cattle ranching took place in an orderly manner (Mueller, 1980, 1984). The state of Pará, in contrast, is notorious for problems regarding property rights and the lack of unbiased legal enforcement. Conflicts and violence have been frequent and intense (Alston et al., 2000) and have held back the expansion of its agriculture.

I focus here on events that took place in the frontier of Mato Grosso

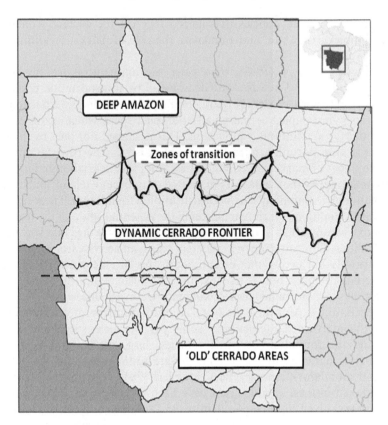

*Figure 11.1   Brazil's state of Mato Grosso: the dynamic Cerrado frontier,
the zones of transition and the Deep Amazon*

(Figure 11.1). With 903.6 thousand km², this state occupies 10.3 percent
of the total geographical area of Brazil – an area almost the size of that
of France and of Germany combined. Mato Grosso contains sections of
three major Brazilian biomes: the Amazon in the north; the Cerrado in the
center and southeast; and the Pantanal biome in the southwest. The agricultural frontier has expanded vigorously over the past two decades and
now occupies lands in both the Cerrado and Amazon biomes.

In 1985, the agricultural frontier was located in the state's southeastern
portion. It was well endowed with transport infrastructure, but the region
still exhibited low yields (Cunha et al., 1994). In 1985 the three major commercial crops – cotton, soybeans and corn – occupied areas of less than 2
percent of the national total area in these crops. The share of the area in
rice was higher (almost 6 percent). By 2008, Mato Grosso had become a

major producer of cotton (52.3 percent of the country's total), soybeans (29.1 percent) and corn (13.2 percent).[7] Commercial crops had expanded to the center and center-north of the state. Crop production had reached portions of Mato Grosso's Amazon biome.

Figure 11.1 shows the location of the agricultural frontier in Mato Grosso. The settled Cerrado areas to the south of the state remain major producers of commercial crops and beef cattle, but the "dynamic Cerrado frontier" in the center and northwest of the state underwent spectacular growth (Mueller and Martha Jr, 2008). Around the line separating the two biomes in Figure 11.1[8] are the "transition" areas, while further to the north is the Deep Amazon subregion; part of its originally lush forests have been cleared and opened for beef cattle ventures (more on the subregions below).

It is essential to stress the role of technical change in these developments. In 1985, agriculture in Mato Grosso was laggard. The savanna soils are acidic and feature low natural fertility, requiring considerable technology and the consistent use of modern inputs to generate acceptable yields. After 1985, EMBRAPA – the Brazilian agricultural technical change organization – generated and made available technologies that enabled a considerable spread of high-yield agriculture in the Cerrado, including the recent dynamic Cerrado frontier and transition areas.

Cattle ranching has also expanded in Mato Grosso. The state's herd increased from 6.5 million head in 1985 (5.1 percent of Brazil's total) to over 26 million head in 2008 (12.9 percent of the country's total).[9] There are two categories of cattle ranching in Mato Grosso: in the more settled areas of the south, the activity is undertaken under fairly modern management; in the transition and Deep Amazon frontier subregions, cattle ranching is usually extensive.

11.3.1 Regional Development Policies

Policies and programs of the past were important for the construction of potential space in the Mato Grosso frontier region. They created a transport infrastructure, to enable the expansion of agriculture to the remote areas of the territory, and established uncontested property rights to land. Moreover, they provided various incentives to convert lands in the Cerrado, and even parts of the Amazon, rapidly into agricultural and cattle ranching ventures. However, these policies and programs were not part of a strategy aimed at establishing an organic Amazon region, and were mainly guided by geopolitical concerns. Most were introduced by the military government in the 1970s to occupy the "empty" spaces of the Amazon and Cerrado. In the Amazon, major examples include the road construction carried out under the Programa de Integração Nacional; the

Proterra land redistribution initiative; the fiscal incentives program, which promoted large-scale cattle ranching; the official colonization schemes; and the Poloamazônia. In the Cerrado, the Polocentro program, favored minimum prices and subsidies of diesel fuel aimed at inducing agricultural expansion.[10] General agricultural policies and subsidies of the 1970s and 1980s, in addition to the "tropicalization" of soybeans by EMBRAPA, also had significant effects but again were not regionally focused.

In recent years, while there still are regionally oriented credits of the Fundos Constitucionais for the North and Center-West, credit of the broad agricultural policy and of the Brazilian Development Bank (BNDES) programs has been more significant.[11] Among the projects of the federal program for the Acceleration of Growth (PAC) is the improvement of roads connecting frontier areas. One example is the project to renovate the road from Cuiabá, in the south of Mato Grosso, to the port of Santarem on the Amazon River. Once concluded (the project is still in progress) this road will have a considerable impact on agricultural expansion in the Mato Grosso frontier region.

When exploring the effects of more recent regional policies in the Mato Grosso frontier region, it becomes clear that these policies were not the main driving force behind the expansion of agriculture and cattle ranching that took place over the decade of the 2000s. Instead, one must look at the effects of overall market conditions for agricultural commodities. These conditions have affected the movement of commercial crops and cattle ranching fronts. To establish this, I outline recent agricultural price movements and trends in cattle prices and examine their effects in terms of the expansion or retraction of agricultural fronts in the Mato Grosso frontier region.

11.3.2 Market Conditions and the Use of Land in the Mato Grosso Frontier Region

In order to evaluate the effects of the recent movements of agricultural and cattle prices, the Mato Grosso frontier was subdivided into three subregions: the Cerrado dynamic frontier; the transition areas between the Cerrado and the Amazon; and the Deep Amazon (Figure 11.1).[12] Regional subdivision did not strictly follow the limits between the Cerrado and the Amazon biomes, since most of the available disaggregate data were for *municípios* (counties) and some of the *municípios* of the north of Mato Grosso are large and contain considerable segments of the two biomes. Furthermore, the transition subregion is not strictly the area of biological transition between the two biomes; this would be difficult to fit into the existing municipal subdivision. In fact, the transition subregion includes important portions of the Amazon biome that were occupied and cleared

Table 11.1   *Mato Grosso subregions: geographical area, population (2004), annual rate of population growth (1999–2004) and the 2004 demographic density*

Subregion	Geographical area (1000 ha)	Population 2004	Annual rate of growth 1999–2004 (% a.a.)	Demographic density (pop./km²) 2004
Cerrado frontier	16 897.6	297 163	4.8	1.8
Transition zones	20 793.2	337 244	2.6	1.6
Deep Amazon	19 103.2	246 704	1.6	1.3

Source: Basic data from IBGE database (www.sidra.ibge.gov.br).

in the 1970s and 1980s as a result of private settlement programs implemented by the military government.

The total geographical areas of the three subregions are: 16.9 million hectares in the Cerrado frontier region; 19.1 million hectares in the Deep Amazon; and 20.8 million hectares in the transition region (Table 11.1). The 2004 population and demographic densities were quite low in all subregions. The 1999–2004 annual rate of population growth was considerable only in the Cerrado frontier region (4.8 percent p.a.), but this is mostly due to a small initial base; in absolute terms there was an increase of less than 63 000 persons there in the period. As can be seen in Table 11.1, in the other two regions the rates of population growth were modest for frontier areas. The limited demographic response in areas of rapid expansion of agricultural fronts is due mainly to the adoption of a highly mechanized agricultural technology, which is particularly well suited to the topography of important parts of the Cerrado and transition subregions, resulting in low labor requirements. In addition, the labor intensity of cattle ranching in the frontier region tends to be low.

11.3.3   The Time Frame

Two contrasting periods were considered: the 1999–2005 period of favorable and increasing world and/or domestic prices of agricultural commodities grown in the Mato Grosso frontier region; and the 2005–06 period, in which these prices experienced sharp declines; in this period a drought and other tribulations compounded the problems brought about by price reductions. Cattle prices in both periods experienced a declining trend.

Figure 11.2 depicts the 1996–2008 movement of soybean prices in Chicago

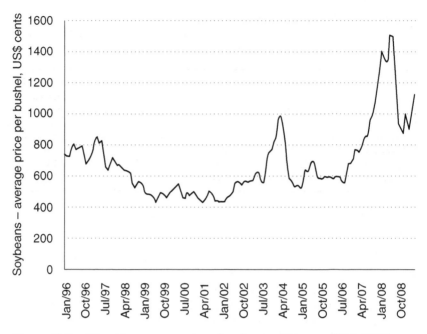

Figure 11.2   Monthly average price of soybeans, Chicago, 1996–2006

– a major commodity in Mato Grosso's recent agricultural expansion (Mueller, 2005).[13] We can observe an initial decline from a peak in 1996, but the price of the commodity has stabilized by 1999; in 2001, it increased again, reaching another peak in 2003–04. The fact that the world price remained largely stable between 1999 and 2002 did not discourage Brazilian producers, since a significant devaluation of the Brazilian currency in 1999 was responsible for a sharp increase in domestic soybean prices (Agroanalysis, 2006).

Figure 11.3 shows the 1998–2006 movement of domestic soybean prices in real terms, in two commodity marketing hubs: Maringá, in the southern state of Paraná; and Rondonópolis, in the southeast of Mato Grosso.[14] Devaluation in 1999 generated noticeable domestic price increases, even in years of fairly stable world prices, and domestic prices remained high until 2004, after which they declined sharply.

The Maringá price line is above that of Rondonópolis because Maringá is situated fairly close to Brazil's main markets and ports. In Brazilian terms, Rondonópolis is fairly well endowed with transport infrastructure, but considerable distances from markets and ports mean that transportation costs are higher than those of Maringá. The Rondonópolis farmer, therefore, receives less for his soybeans than a farmer in Maringá.

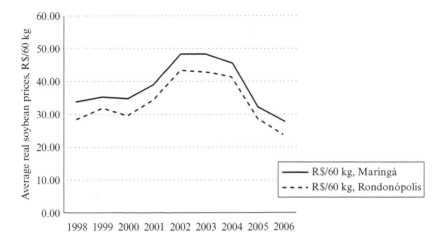

Figure 11.3 Brazil: annual average real soybean prices relevant to procedures in Maringá PR, and in Rondonópolis (MT), 1998–2006

Comparable price data for the frontier subregions were not available but, given the distances and the often precarious state of transport infrastructure linking these areas to markets, the price lines of sites in the Mato Grosso frontier would surely be below that of Rondonópolis. The price lines of sites in the Cerrado dynamic frontier would be above those in the transition region and in the Deep Amazon.

Price movements were similar for other agricultural commodities – especially cotton and corn. It is worth stressing that the 1999–05 commodity boom in Brazil was outstanding not only for its high prices but also for its duration. Agriculture in the country has seldom experienced five years of continuous prosperity. In contrast, the country's gross domestic product (GDP) real growth averaged only 1.8 percent between 1999 and 2004 (Mueller and Mueller, 2004).

Given that the expansion of cattle ranching has been significant in parts of the Mato Grosso frontier, it is important also to examine movements of beef cattle prices in the 1999–2005 period. As shown by Martha Jr and Vilela (2007), the real prices of fattened steers in two important cattle marketing areas of the Center-West – the Minas Triangle and the south of Goiás – exhibited a declining trend, lasting from 2001 to 2004.[15] These two areas are important due to their relative proximity to the Mato Grosso frontier; they are markets for steers produced in Mato Grosso, with effects on all three frontier subregions. The declining trend was reversed only by mid-2005; by then, soybean prices were in a phase of sharp reduction.

Table 11.2   *Mato Grosso frontier subregions: area in annual crops (1999,*
2005 and 2006); annual rates of growth of the area in annual
crops (1996–2005 and 2005–06); proportion of the total
geographical of the 2005 area in annual crops; and proportion
of the area in annual crops planted in soybeans (1999 and 2005)

Subregion	Area in annual crops (1000 hectares)			Annual rate of growth of the area in annual crops (% a.a.)		% of the area in crops of the total geographical area	% of the area in crops of the area in soybeans	
	1999	2005	2006	1999–2005	2005–06	2005	1999	2005
Cerrado frontier	2509.4	4747.2	4521.4	10.6	−4.9	28.1	67.5	74.6
Transition zones	249.0	1284.6	938.5	27.3	−31.4	6.2	29.7	59.2
Deep Amazon	106.6	102.7	87.0	−0.5	−16.6	0.5	0.2	15.9

Source: Basic data from IBGE database (www.sidra.ibge.gov.br).

11.3.4   Agricultural Expansion in the Mato Grosso Frontier Region During the 1999–2005 Commodity Boom

To examine the effects of the favorable market conditions of this period, I employed IBGE's yearly estimates of the municipal areas in annual crops (available both for the total of crops and for individual items). In the case of cattle ranching, it would have been ideal to work with information on the municipal area in planted pastures at each year. Since this information was not available, municipal estimates of the number of heads of cattle were the proxies employed to establish the expansion of beef cattle activity fronts in the three sub regions.

In Table 11.2, we see a remarkable 10.6 percent annual increase in the Cerrado dynamic frontier between 1999 and 2005, from little more than 2.5 million hectares to over 4.5 million hectares in crop production. Moreover, as a result of consistent gains in yields for most crops in the Cerrado (Mueller and Martha Jr, 2008), the increase in production proceeded progressively faster in this period. In the transition Cerrado–Amazon region, the rate of growth in crop area was also substantial (27.3 percent per annum), but was smaller than that in the Cerrado frontier region; its crop area increased from 249 000 hectares in 1999 to nearly 1.3 million hectares in 2005. As for the Deep Amazon, the area in annual crops remained insignificant; in 2005, it was only 102 700 hectares, a mere 0.5 percent of the region's geographical area.

The role of soybeans in the expansion of annual crops in the Cerrado frontier should be stressed; we see in Table 11.2 that the proportion of land planted with soybeans to the total crop area, which was already large in 1999 (67.5 percent), continued to increase, reaching 74.6 percent in 2005 (Table 11.2). In the transition region, this proportion escalated noticeably, from 29.3 percent in 1999 to 59.2 percent in 2005. However, in the Deep Amazon, the proportion of the total area in annual crops planted in soybeans was only 15.9 percent in 2005.

This contradicts the common belief that the Amazon region is being overrun by soybean plantations. As a whole, the expansion of annual crops in the Deep Amazon was quite modest. In the 1999–2005 period, this expansion was not an important driver of deforestation (at least directly); but this was surely not the case in the other two frontier sub-regions. In 2005, the proportion of the area in annual crops of the total geographical area of the Cerrado frontier region was a high 28.1 percent, and in the transition zones a more modest, but still considerable, 6.2 percent.

The proportion of the area in annual crops of the Deep Amazon was only 0.5 percent, but this does not mean that the Deep Amazon is immune from pressures of commodity booms; with good prices and improvements in transport infrastructure,[16] deforestation may escalate. Part of the 1999–2005 expansion of soybeans in the transition region occupied areas that were originally densely forested but which, as indicated, had been partly cleared in earlier times, mostly for the formation of pastures.

Table 11.3 examines the change in the beef cattle herds during the period. The pattern of progression was the reverse of that of annual crops. The 2000–2005 rate of growth of the herds in the Cerrado frontier was the lowest of the three subregions, 4.0 percent annually; it was 5.2 percent in the transition region, and an impressive 10.7 percent in the Deep Amazon region. In absolute terms, the increase was also larger in the latter sub-region: the cattle herd of the Deep Amazon increased almost 2.3 million head in the period, from 3.2 million to 5.5 million head. In the transition region, the increase was of a little less than 1 million head, from 3.4 million to 4.4 million head; while in the dynamic Cerrado frontier region, the increase totaled only 482 900 head, from 2.2 to 2.7 million head. In fact, some of the municipalities of the Cerrado frontier showed declines in the size of their cattle herds in the period.

Table 11.3   *Frontier subregions of Mato Grosso: head of beef cattle (2000 and 2005); the 2000–2005 annual growth of the cattle herd; the 2005 cattle density*

Subregion	Estimate of the cattle heard (1000 head)		Growth of the cattle herd (% a.a.) 2000–05	Beef cattle density (head/100 hectares) 2005
	2000	2005		
Cerrado frontier	2172.2	2655.1	4.0	12.9
Transition zones	3362.7	4355.9	5.2	16.2
Deep Amazon	3205.9	5485.9	10.7	16.8

Source: Basic data from IBGE database (www.sidra.ibge.gov.br).

Given the undeveloped management that prevails in the cattle ranches of frontier areas, the high rates of growth of the cattle herds of the Deep Amazon and transition regions, and even of some of the municipalities of the dynamic Cerrado, are much larger than those that would have resulted exclusively from the natural growth of their herds. These sub-regions have obviously received large inflows of cattle from the southern portions of Mato Grosso and from other parts of the Cerrado and Brazil.

In the long 1999–2005 period of high and increasing crop prices, the motivation for holding cattle in the main crop expansion areas was quite different from that in the Deep Amazon. As the domestic crop prices started rising, the opportunity cost of holding cattle on low-carrying-capacity pastures in areas favorable for crop expansion increased, and it became more profitable to sell the cattle and convert pastures to crop production. This was reinforced by the 2000–2005 decrease in real cattle prices. A significant number of cattle were purchased by ranchers of the Deep Amazon. They were not stirred by the growing commodity prices because transportation costs and other factors did not allow them to compete in the production of agricultural crops. However, land was cheap in the Deep Amazon and the low price of cattle presented an opportunity to expand their herds. Cattle and land are viewed as assets, the values of which are expected to increase in the long run. Additionally, as shown by Arima et al. (2005), there were already four modern slaughter plants operating in the Deep Amazon in 2004, processing this region's cattle for national markets and aspiring to export.

11.3.5   Impacts of the 2005–06 Phase of Price Declines

In 2005, there were sharp reductions in the prices of agricultural commodities – especially of soybeans.[17] Prices started to fall in 2004 but this intensified during 2005 and 2006. The effects of these declines were magnified by factors such as the appreciation of the Brazilian currency, which negatively affected producers of export crops; unfavorable climatic conditions; a fungus infestation in parts of Mato Grosso; and the excessive indebtedness of many farmers, which led to a decrease in the area planted with commercial crops, especially in the Cerrado frontier region and the transition region.[18]

As a result, there were negative rates of growth in the area of annual crops in 2005–06 in all three regions (−4.9 percent in the Cerrado frontier region, a massive −31.4 percent in the Transition region, and −16.6 percent in the Deep Amazon). In absolute terms, the 2005–06 area changes were −225 800 hectares in the Cerrado frontier; −346 100 hectares in the transition region; and −15 700 hectares in the Deep Amazon (Table 11.2). The area decreases were especially large in the transition region, because as commodity prices began to fall, transportation costs became amplified. This also occurred in the Cerrado frontier region, but to a lesser extent, since its distances to the main markets were smaller and the conditions of its transport infrastructure somewhat better.

As for the effects of the reduction of agricultural prices on cattle ranching, since they were short lived – commodity prices began recovering in 2007 – it was impossible to detect significant changes in this segment. Frontier cattle ranching tends to react to price changes at a slower pace than crop production activities; low agricultural relative prices would have to remain in place for a long period to generate significant impacts. This happened in the booming price phase but not in the short 2005–06 period. At any rate, the prices of products of cattle ranching began increasing in 2006 (Martha Jr and Vilela, 2007); if this continues, the motivation for the expansion of cattle ranching activities in the Mato Grosso frontier region, particularly in the Deep Amazon, will most likely be reinforced.

11.4   CONCLUDING REMARKS

My analysis of the spread of activity fronts in the agricultural frontier of the Legal Amazon highlights the lack of functionality in Brazil's regional definitions. For instance, what exactly is "Amazônia"? Does it consist of the official North macro region? Or the policy entity called the Legal

Amazon, which includes parts of Maranhão and the huge Center-West state of Mato Grosso in addition to the North?

This study has focused on the Mato Grosso frontier region, which contains a part of the Amazon biome and important areas of the Cerrado savanna. In the 1970s and early 1980s the Legal Amazon was the locus of structuring measures with considerable long-term effects; however, most of these were implemented to promote the occupation of "empty" spaces in portions of the center and north of Brazil – and not to contribute to the formation of an organic Amazônia. These measures undoubtedly had important effects on the expansion of agricultural fronts in the Legal Amazon, despite the fact that structuring policies had faded; they were recently replaced by the inducements and constraints of unique market conditions. I focused three adjacent subregions of Mato Grosso's agricultural frontier – the dynamic Cerrado frontier, the transition areas and the Deep Amazon – and examined the behavior over time of agricultural commodity and cattle ranching fronts. The time frame encompassed the 1999–2005 period (favorable agricultural commodity prices, but declining prices for cattle products); and the 2005–06 period (sharp decreases in agricultural prices).

As a result of the 1999–2005 boom in commodity prices, there was a sizeable expansion of commercial crops in the dynamic Cerrado frontier region, a less impressive absolute increase in the intermediary transition areas, and very modest growth in the Deep Amazon. The direct land use effect was important in areas of the frontier fairly accessible to markets, but almost zero in the remote Deep Amazon. There was, however, evidence of an important indirect land use effect. In spite of – or perhaps due to – the 1999–2005 declining trend in beef cattle prices, there was an impressive increase in the cattle herd of the Deep Amazon; I contend that this was largely influenced by the process of conversions of land in pastures to crop production in the Cerrado frontier and in parts of the transition areas. To a large extent, cattle ranching activities were transferred from these frontier subregions to the Deep Amazon. Moreover, the ongoing high and rising prices of both agricultural commodities and cattle products are probably, through the indirect land use effect, reinforcing the motivation to clear land for cattle ranching activities in the Amazon biome.

The role of market conditions in the cultivation of agricultural commodities in the Mato Grosso frontier region was highlighted by the effects of the 2005–06 phase of declining prices. There was a sizeable reduction of crop area in the Cerrado frontier, but this occurred more intensely in the more remote transition areas.

Lastly, the sensitivity of economic agents in the frontier region to price incentives indicates that if there is a desire to preserve or conserve portions of the Amazon and Cerrado biomes, there should be a substantial overhaul of the transport infrastructure projects in the Legal Amazon. Booming commodity markets provide important incentives, but the difficulty of access acts as a deterrent to the expansion of agricultural activity fronts in the region. Opening and improving roads which connect and cross fragile areas – as is being done – makes such expansion virtually impossible to control in favorable periods. Effective containment and repression become very difficult and expensive under such circumstances.

NOTES

1. Based on von Bertalanffy (1958) see also Branco (1989).
2. IBGE (2010). In 1942 the country's macro regions were: North, Northeast, East, South and Center-West.
3. In 1989 the North region was augmented by the incorporation of the newly created state of Tocantins, previously the northern portion of the Center-West state of Goiás.
4. A similar position is that of the strategy for the development of the Amazon outlined in Albuquerque (2010) – a suggestion for the President elected in 2010. In it the Amazon is the North region; the natural continuity of the North's southern borders with portions of the Center-West was ignored.
5. Concerns about the trends of deforestation there reside on two negative environmental impacts it engenders: the release of greenhouse gases, and the reduction of biodiversity.
6. The system of fiscal incentives, instituted in the 1960s, has been one of the main instruments in the regional development strategy for the Legal Amazon.
7. Proportions calculated based on data from the IBGE, *Anuário Estatístico* (IBGE, 1985), and from www.sidra.ibge.gov.br (for 2008).
8. The line separating the Cerrado from the Amazon biome in Figure 11.1 is roughly the "official" boundary between them, established by the IBGE.
9. Data on livestock from www.sidra.ibge.gov.br.
10. For details, see Mueller (1980, 1984, 1990), Mueller and Martha Jr (2008) and Rezende (2003).
11. In the commercial fronts of the Mato Grosso frontier region, soybean cultivation began with modern inputs and practices, and it benefited substantially from subsidized credit, such as that offered by the BNDES for investment (agricultural equipment). But again, this was not part of a regional development policy.
12. The delimitation of the subregions was based on a scrutiny of municipal data, gathered by the IBGE and by other statistical organizations, and of other disaggregated information. The official, widely accepted, classification of the Cerrado municipalities is from the IBGE.
13. International soybean prices from www.abiove.com.br/english/cotações – Chicago monthly average prices (first delivery) of the Soybean Complex (soybean, meal and oil) surveyed by Abiove with data from CBOT.
14. Soybean prices in Brazil for various marketing points gathered by Abiove (www.abiove.com.br).
15. The declining trend in cattle prices resulted basically from the operation of the cattle cycle (Martha Jr and Vilela, 2007).
16. In the case of soybeans, the development of varieties that generate acceptable yields in the Deep Amazon would also be required. This is not yet the case.
17. After 2006, commodity prices recovered – see Figure 11.2 – but this occurred outside this study's time frame.
18. See, for instance, Agroanalysis (2006).

REFERENCES

Agroanalysis (2006), "Soja: ascensão e queda", *Agroanalysis*, Rio de Janeiro, Fundação Getúlio Vargas, **26** (7), 19–20.

Albuquerque, Roberto Cavalcanti de (2010), "Amazônia: oportunidades de desenvolvimento", in Forum Nacional – Cúpula Empresarial (ed.), *Plano Nacional de Desenvolvimento: a Hora e a Vez do Brasil – Colocando o Brasil no Século XXI*, Rio de Janeiro: INAE, pp. 288–308.

Alston, L., G. Libecap and B. Mueller (2000), "Property rights to land and land reform: legal inconsistencies and the sources of violent conflict in the Brazilian Amazon", *Journal of Environmental Economics and Management*, **39**, 162–188.

Arima, E., P. Barreto and M. Arito (2005), *Pecuária na Amazônia: tendências para a conservaçao ambiental*, Belém: Instituto do Homem e meio Ambiente da Amazônia (Imazon).

Bertalanffy, L. von (1958), "General system's theory", *General Systems*, **1** (1), 1–10.

Branco, S.M. (1987), *Ecossistêmica – uma abordagem integrada dos problemas do meio ambiente*, São Paulo: Editora Elgard Blücher Ltda.

Cunha, Aércio S., Charles Mueller, Eliseu R.A. Alves and José Eurípedes da Silva (1994), *Uma Avaliação da Sustentabilidade da Agricultura nos Cerrados*, Brasília: IPEA and PNUD.

Cunha, Alexandre Mendes, Rodrigo Ferreira Simões and João Antonio de Paula (2005), "Regionalização e história: uma contribuição introdutória ao debate teórico-metodológico", Belo Horizonte, CEDEPLAR/FACE/UFMG, Texto para Discussão no. 260, May.

Diniz, Clélio Campolina (2009), "Celso Furtado e o desenvolvimento regional", Belo Horizonte, UFMG, *Nova Economia*, **19** (2), 227–249.

Ferreira, Carlos Maurício de Carvalho (1988), "As teorias da localização e a organização espacial da economia", in P. Haddad, C.M. Ferreira and T.A. Andrade (eds), *Economia Regional: Teoria e Métodos de Análise*, Fortaleza: Banco do Nordeste do Brasil, pp. 67–197.

Institutio Brasileiro de Geografia e Estatística (IBGE) (1986), *Anuário Estatístico do Brasil, 1985*, Rio de Janeiro: IBGE.

IBGE (2008), *Regiões de Influência de Cidade 2007*, Rio de Janeiro: IBGE.

IBGE (2010), "Divisão Regional", www.ibge.gov.br/home/geociências/geografia (accessed 09 October 2010).

Instituto Nacional de Pesquisas Espaciais (INPE) (2009), *Estimativas das Emissões de CO_2 por Desmatamento na Amazônia Brasileira – Relatório Técnico Sintético* (www.inpe.br/noticias/arquivos/pdf/Emissões_CO2_2009.pdf).

Martha Jr, Geraldo Bueno and Lourival Vilela (2007), "Uso de fertilizantes em pastagens", in G.B. Martha Jr, Lourival Vilela and Djalma de Souza (eds), *Cerrado: uso eficiente de corretivos e fertilizantes em pastagens*, Planaltina, DF: EMBRAPA Cerrados, pp. 17–42.

Mueller, Charles C. (1980), "Recent frontier expansion in Brazil: the case of Rondônia", in Françoise Barbira-Scazzocchio (ed.), *Land, People and Planning in Contemporary Amazonia*, Cambridge: Centre of Latin American Studies, pp. 141–153.

Mueller, Charles C. (1984), "El estado y la expansion de la frontera agrícola en la Amazonia", in Comision Economica para America Latina (CEPAL) y Programa de las Naciones Unidas para el Medio Ambiente (PNUMA),

Expansion de la Frontera Agropecuaria y Medio Ambiente en America Latina, Madrid: Naciones Unidas y CIFCA, pp. 37–78.

Mueller, Charles C. (1990), "Políticas governamentais e a expansão recente da agropecuária no Centro-Oeste", *Planejamento e Políticas Públicas*, **3** (June), 45–75.

Mueller, Charles C. (2005), "Impacts of the soybean boom on the Cerrado of Brazil's Center West region", in Annual Meeting of the Society for Conservation Biology, Brasília, DF: Universidade de Brasília, September.

Mueller, Charles C. and Geraldo Bueno Martha Jr (2008), "A agropecuária e o desenvolvimento socioeconômico recente do Cerrado", in Fábio G. Faleiro and Austeclínio L. de Farias Neto (eds), *Savanas: desafios e estratégias para o equilíbrio entre sociedade, agronegócio e recursos naturais*, Brasília: Embrapa, pp. 35–99.

Mueller, Charles C. and Bernardo Mueller (2006), "The evolution of agriculture and land reform in Brazil, 1950–2006", in H.S. Esfahani, G. Facchini and G.J.D. Hewings (eds), *Economic Development in Latin America*, Basingstoke and New York: Palgrave Macmillan, pp. 133–162.

Rezende, Gervásio (2003), "Ocupação agrícola, estrutura agrária e mercado de trabalho rural no Cerrado: o papel dos preços da terra, dos recursos naturais e das políticas públicas", in S. Helfland and G. Rezende (eds), *Região e Espaço no Desenvolvimento Agrícola Brasileiro*, Brasília: IPEA, pp. 173–212.

Santos, Milton and Maria Laura Silveira (2003), *O Brasil: Território e Sociedade no Início do Século XXI*, Rio de Janeiro and São Paulo: Record.

Sawyer, Donald (1983), "Ocupación y desocupación de la frontera agrícola en el Brasil; un ensayo de interpretación estructural y espacial", in CEPAL/PNUMA (eds), *Expansión de la Frontera Agrícola y Medio Ambiente en América Latina*, Madrid: Naciones Unidas/CIFCA, pp. 79–104.

Viola, Eduardo (2009), "The great emitters of carbon and the perspective for an agreement on mitigation of global warming", in Paulo Leite da Silva Dias, Wagner Ribeiro, João Lima Sant'Anna Neto and Jurandir Zullo Jr (eds), *Public Policy, Mitigation and Adaptation in South America*, São Paulo: Instituto de Estudos Avançados da Universidade de São Paulo, pp. 9–25.

12. Embrapa: its origins and changes

Geraldo B. Martha Jr, Elisio Contini and Eliseu Alves[1]

12.1 INTRODUCTION

Brazilian agriculture is a success story. The country that until the 1960s systematically received food donations from abroad, and up to the 1980s was still a large food importer, had its agriculture profoundly changed. The traditional agriculture that prevailed in Brazil until the 1970s was progressively transformed in the following decades into a modern and highly competitive agriculture based on science. Along with this structural transformation in the primary sector, the industry and service sectors directly linked to agriculture also became two of the world's biggest and most competitive. Furthermore, as food production increased at higher rates than food demand over time, food prices decreased.[2] These gains in consumer surplus took place due partially to lower income for Brazilian farmers.[3]

Brazil is now recognized as the sole agricultural power in the tropics.[4] According to recent estimates, on a country basis, Brazil's share in world agricultural markets (8 percent) is only second to that of the United States (17 percent) (Liapis, 2010) and some analysts already suggest that Brazil's share will be similar to that of the US in the next 10 to 15 years. The Organisation for Economic Co-operation and Development (OECD) and the Food and Agriculture Organization (FAO), from the United Nations, in their 2010 joint agricultural outlook projected that Brazilian agricultural production will increase 38 percent from 2010 to 2019 (OECD/FAO, 2010). This huge increase in agricultural production is nearly twice the global average and several times higher than the figures prospected for giants in world agriculture such as the United States, Canada and the European Union.

12.2 THE DEVELOPMENT OF BRAZILIAN AGRICULTURE[5]

12.2.1 A General Overview

Until the mid-1980s, the industrial sector was granted a series of advantages that discriminated against agriculture. These distorting policies against rural areas were translated into an accelerated rural–urban migration process starting in the 1950s. After the 1990s, the urbanization process lost impetus, in part because the rural–urbanization cycle was almost complete in the South, Southeast and Midwest regions (Alves et al., 1999), but also because of the low economic growth rates in the country during the 1980s and the 1990s that weakened the attractiveness of the cities.

The percentage of urban population in Brazil rose from 31.2 percent in 1940 to 84 percent in 2010. Alves and Rocha (2010) showed that from 1991 to 2000 the percentage of migrants from rural to urban areas was 24.7 percent of the rural population; between 2000 and 2007, the migration process dropped to 12.5 percent of the rural population.

The development of a modern agriculture in Brazil was initially prompted by the industrialization policy, especially after the late 1960s, which through urbanization[6] created higher per capita income, accelerated population growth and a strong demand for the agricultural sector.[7] In addition, opportunities for agribusiness product exports were then identified to generate funds to finance imports of technology and capital for the emerging industry.

At the same time, it became clear that the opportunities for agricultural expansion in traditional areas were becoming limited. Increasing productivity in already opened areas, and incorporating the "unproductive" Cerrado – the savannah-type biome in Brazil – was perceived as a means to guarantee the increase in agricultural production and to ensure food to the growing urban population at affordable prices. Thus, it was necessary to improve agricultural land and labor productivity significantly.

The government's response to the challenge of creating a new era in agriculture resulted in the creation in 1973 of the Brazilian Agricultural Research Corporation, Embrapa, a "research arm" of the Ministry of Agriculture, Livestock and Food Supply. This institution was given the mission of coordinating the Brazilian Agricultural Research System, composed of state agricultural research organizations, universities (agricultural colleges) and Embrapa itself.

From the mid-1990s onwards, macroeconomic stability, better relative prices for agricultural commodities in the world markets, and the maturation of tropical agricultural technologies generated in the preceding two decades settled the basis for a new era in Brazilian agribusiness. The sector moved forward fast from a traditional to a science-based agriculture.

12.2.2   Policies

Three policies played a central role in the agricultural modernization process: (1) subsidized credit, mainly for capital financing and for purchasing modern inputs; (2) rural extension; and (3) support to agricultural research, under Embrapa's leadership.

Agricultural credit
Beginning in the mid-1960s, agricultural credit was mainly provided by the federal government through the Banco do Brasil and the Banco do Nordeste. The private sector had little participation in the loans to farmers until the late 1980s. Interest rates were more heavily (financially) subsidized from 1970 to 1985 (Coelho, 2001). Agricultural credit peaked in 1979, at US$75.8 billion.[8] Then, as a part of the imposed macroeconomic adjustment in the 1980s and early 1990s, it quickly declined to around US$11.5 billion in 1995–96; and then slowly increased to US$43 billion in 2009.[9]

Policies toward agricultural modernization did not achieve the objective of reaching most of the producers in the 1950–85 period. Limited financial resource availability, farmers' low schooling, and lack of legally regularized land ownership hampered a widespread adoption of technologies. As a consequence, rural credit was in certain terms not inclusive and benefited privileged farmers, mainly those coming from the South-Southeast regions (Contini et al., 2010).

Rural extension
In the 1950–70 period, policymakers placed a lot of emphasis on rural extension, and neglected efforts in research. Their hypothesis was that a vast array of technologies was already available for adoption. In the early 1970s, empirical evidence proved that this hypothesis was false. A virtuous cycle of tropical agricultural research was then considerably expanded and strengthened, and science-based technologies fuelled the extension service.

In this context, governmental agricultural credit was associated with public and private technical assistance. The idea was to strengthen human capital to utilize better the investments being made available for the acquisition of capital goods and modern inputs. The association of technical assistance with rural credit was compulsory until the 1990s, being paid by the farmer through a fee. In the 2000s this association was only mandatory for a few credit lines. Farmers who are well integrated into markets have been predominantly using private technical assistance.

Agricultural research

In the late 1960s, Brazilian policymakers realized that the strategy to increase food supply through the expansion of cultivated area and the adoption of practices of limited technological content should be revised. This perception prevailed in spite of the fact that more than half of the national territory remained untouched and could be occupied. However, the stock of agricultural technologies and empirical knowledge at that time indicated that the agricultural frontier – the "Brazilian Cerrado" – could, at best, accommodate only subsistence farming.

The government rejected the subsistence farming alternative and started a huge effort to transform traditional tropical agriculture toward one based on science and anchored on productivity gains instead of area expansion. The applied agricultural science unveiled the constraints imposed by the poor acid soils of the Cerrado. New crop varieties, adapted to low latitudes and to soil and climatic conditions of the tropics, and modern inputs were increasingly incorporated into novel production systems. The intensification of agricultural mechanization, particularly in grain production, was also an important part of the development of Brazilian agriculture.

In sum, the increase in agricultural production was to be achieved through the expansion of the cultivated area, increase in productivity or, more frequently, a combination of both. In the decades following the Second World War, food production in Brazil relied heavily on area expansion. However, from the mid-1970s onwards, and especially after the mid-1990s, gains in food production were mainly explained by productivity gains. The technologies developed by Embrapa, state agricultural research organizations, universities and other public and private partners (in Brazil and abroad), with the support of sectoral and more general public policies, and especially of farmers, have made it possible for Brazilian agriculture to be transformed and to present high-impact outcomes.

12.2.3   The Response of Agricultural Supply[10]

In the 1976–2011 period, grain and oilseeds area increased 32 percent whilst production increased 240 percent and yields increased 2.57 times (Table 12.1). Sugarcane production showed strong expansion between 1975/76 and 2009/10, from 89 million metric tons to 696 million metric tons. In the same period, sugar production increased 369 percent, from 6.72 million tons to 31.51 million tons. Total ethanol production (including both anhydrous and hydrated ethanol) grew from 0.60 billion liters in 1975/76, to 25.56 billion liters in 2009/10.

Similar trends were observed in the meat sector. Beef, pork and poultry production increased steadily from 4 270 000 metric tons in 1978, to

Table 12.1   *Production, area and productivity annual growth rates in*
              Brazilian agriculture, 1975–2010

	Rice	Maize	Beans	Soybeans	Wheat
Harvested area					
1975–2010	−2.38	0.38	−0.64	3.58	−1.63
1980–89	−0.97	1.72	1.35	3.35	5.08
1990–99	−3.25	−0.95	−3.04	2.66	−6.15
2000–10	−2.07	1.53	0.13	5.05	3.09
Production					
1975–2010	1.05	3.43	1.52	5.55	1.35
1980–89	2.98	2.98	1.13	4.16	14.76
1990–99	0.82	3.54	0.28	6.80	−2.09
2000–10	1.31	4.38	2.63	6.06	5.96
Productivity					
1975–2010	3.51	3.04	2.18	1.90	2.92
1980–89	3.99	1.24	−0.22	0.79	9.21
1990–99	4.20	4.53	3.43	4.04	4.32
2000–10	3.45	2.80	2.50	0.96	1.79

Source: Conab and IBGE's databases, elaborated by Contini et al. (2010).

25 496 000 metric tons in 2010/11. In the 1978–2011 period, poultry production increased from 1 096 000 tons to 12 928 000 tons (11.8 times), pork production increased from 1 060 000 tons to 3 384 000 tons (3.2 times), and beef production increased from 2 114 000 tons to 9 184 000 tons (4.3 times). In the 1978–2011 period, yearly growth rates registered for beef, poultry and pork were, respectively, 4.70 percent, 8.02 percent and 3.70 percent. Milk production also deserves to be highlighted, as production significantly increased from 11.16 billion liters in 1980, to 30.3 billion liters in 2009.

12.2.4   Agricultural Exports

Exports of agricultural products such as sugar, cotton and coffee have been historically important for Brazil's economy. In 1965, agribusiness exports accounted for 84.4 percent of total exports (Rodrigues, 2008). In 2010, exports totaled US$76 billion and represented 38 percent of exports. Current agribusiness exports reflect a higher participation of soybean, meat and sugar–ethanol complex products, as well as of the forestry sector (Agrostat-Brasil, 2011).

With the increased importance of Brazil in the international agricultural market, domestic food supply was not affected (Figure 12.1). Productivity

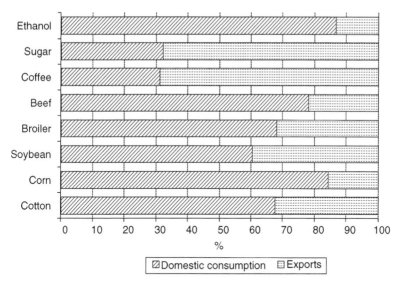

Source: MAPA (2010).

Figure 12.1 Domestic consumption and exports (2009), Brazil

will continue to be the main driver of food and feed production expansion. Production is expected to grow 2.88 percent per year, and productivity is projected to explain around 70 percent of the increased agricultural output. Cropland area is likely to increase by 9.3 million hectares (MAPA/AGE, 2010). This area, however, represents only 5.9 percent of the current pasture area in Brazil, clearly indicating that future land-saving effects arising from even small increases in pasture productivity can easily accommodate crops' demand for land (Martha and Vilela, 2009).

12.2.5 Total Factor Productivity in Brazilian Agriculture

The total factor productivity (TFP) of the Brazilian agriculture increased steadily and continuously in the 36 years of 1970–2006. Compared to 1970 (index 100), the TFP increased 124 percent, the product rose 243 percent and inputs grew 53 percent (Table 12.2). These figures reinforce the style of development of Brazilian agriculture, prioritizing productivity gains instead of land area expansion. Investments in research have been very important for these achievements. Gasques et al. (2009) estimated that a 1 percent increase in Embrapa's research expenditure increases the agricultural TFP by 0.2 percent.

In the last decade of this period (1995–2006), productivity indicators

Table 12.2   Product index, inputs index and TFP – Brazil

Years	Product index	Input index	Total factor productivity (100)
1970	100	100	100
1975	139	122	114
1980	173	142	122
1985	211	149	142
1996	244	137	178
2006	343	153	224

Source: Gasques et al. (2010).

Table 12.3   Growth rates for product index, inputs index, TFP, land productivity and labor productivity – Brazil

Specification	2006/1970	2006/1996
Product index	3.48	3.14
Input index	1.19	0.99
Total factor productivity	2.27	2.13
Land productivity	3.32	3.16
Labor productivity	3.53	3.40

Source: Gasques et al. (2010).

(TFP, land productivity and labor productivity) represented approximately 95 percent of the values registered in the 1970–2006 period. In comparison with the 36-year period, input and product indexes in the 1995–2006 period dropped to 83 percent and 90 percent, respectively (Table 12.3). Gains in productivity represented 65 percent of the agricultural output in the 1970–2006 period, while inputs explained 35 percent. In the decade to 2006, productivity was even more important and represented 68 percent of the production increase. The annual growth rate in the area theoretically worked per farmer (that is, labor productivity rate − land productivity rate; Table 12.3) was 0.21 percent from 1970–2006 and 0.24 percent in the decade to 2006. This slow increase indicates that there is great potential to increase agricultural mechanization in Brazil.

At the regional level, there is considerable variation in the TFP. Figure 12.2 shows that five out of seven states in the North showed lower TFP than the country average of 224 in 2006. Amazonas and Tocantins states raise concerns, because their TFP is close to Brazil's average in 1970.

Traditional agricultural states in the Southeast (SP, São Paulo; MG,

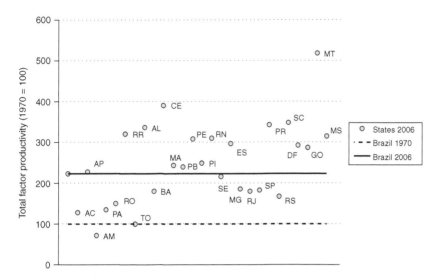

Notes: Index 100 was set in 1970, except for Mato Grosso do Sul (1975 = 100) and Tocantins (1985 = 100). North: AC – Acre, AP – Amapá, AM – Amazonas, PA – Pará, RO – Rondônia, RR – Roraima, TO – Tocantins; Northeast: AL – Alagoas, BA – Bahia, CE – Ceará, MA – Maranhão, PB – Paraíba, PE – Pernambuco, PI – Piauí, RN – Rio Grande do Norte, SE – Sergipe; Southeast: ES – Espírito Santo, MG – Minas Gerais, RJ – Rio de Janeiro, SP – São Paulo; South: Paraná, RS – Rio Grande do Sul, SC – Santa Catarina; Midwest: DF – Distrito Federal, GO – Goiás, MT – Mato Grosso, MS – Mato Grosso do Sul.

Source: Gasques et al. (2010) data, authors' elaboration.

Figure 12.2   Total factor productivity in Brazil (2006), by state

Minas Gerais) and in the South (RS, Rio Grande do Sul) had TFP below the Brazilian average in 2006, which might probably be explained by the initial higher baseline figures. The dynamic agricultural states in the Cerrado – namely Mato Grosso (MT), Mato Grosso do Sul (MS) and Goiás (GO) – expressed higher TFP than Brazil. Several states in the Northeast expressed higher TFP values than the national average in 2006 (Figure 12.2).

12.3   EMBRAPA[11]

Embrapa is a case of successful institutional innovation whose main characteristics are: a public corporation model of organization; scale of operation at the national level; spatial decentralization; specialized research units; enhanced training and remuneration of human resources; and a vision of an agriculture based on science and technology.

Embrapa's strategy thus considered the importance of a research portfolio capable of providing short-term deliverables while the (long-term) research with more significant outcomes was under way. Furthermore, it also gave special attention to the dissemination of existing results.

12.3.1 The Embrapa Model

Embrapa was created when conditions were favorable for its success. There was pressure to reform public research in agriculture, and the necessary understanding to move forward to accomplish this task; a typical case of induction of institutional reform, as provided by Hayami and Ruttan (1971).[12] To facilitate the interaction with farmers and society, the model chosen was decentralized in the territorial dimension and organized by priorities in the following order: product level, resources and themes. At a national level, the model requires strong interaction with decision-makers, at the level of the presidency of the Republic, Congress and ministries. In addition, Embrapa gave priority to transparency, to assessing the social and economic impact of its investments and, as previously indicated, gave special attention to the media.

The option to organize Embrapa as a public corporation was intended to release it from the bureaucratic rules used in the public administration, and thus give it the flexibility to administer resources and personnel, to plan, to assess performance, to implement the budget and to disseminate results in a transparent manner. Choosing CLT[13] gave Embrapa much more flexibility in the administration of personnel, construction of several careers – especially that of researcher – and in designing and implementing a personnel evaluation policy. As a public corporation, the relationship with the outside world and with the private initiative is much easier. Furthermore, the model allowed Embrapa to develop its own personality, which has characterized it at the national and at the international scenario as a unique example in the field of public research.

A concentrated and decentralized research model

In a country of continental dimensions, such as Brazil, it was soon realized that the success of Embrapa would depend on its size and on an accumulated critical mass of researchers, who should be diverse in talent and dispersed throughout the national territory.[14] It was also understood that Embrapa needed its own research network so that it could be directly responsible for its results, allowing it to be well known and evaluated on its own merits. Once it was large, diverse and decentralized,

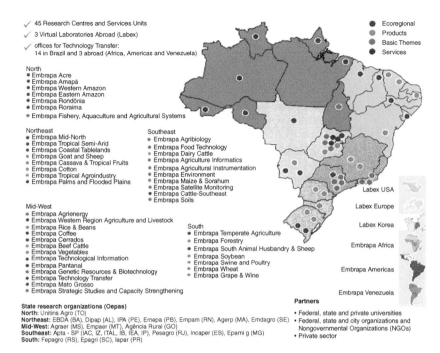

√ 45 Research Centres and Services Units
√ 3 Virtual Laboratories Abroad (Labex)
√ offices for Technology Transfer:
14 in Brazil and 3 abroad (Africa, Americas and Venezuela)

● Ecoregional
● Products
● Basic Themes
● Services

North
● Embrapa Acre
● Embrapa Amapá
● Embrapa Western Amazon
● Embrapa Eastern Amazon
● Embrapa Rondônia
● Embrapa Roraima
● Embrapa Fishery, Aquaculture and Agricultural Systems

Northeast
● Embrapa Mid-North
● Embrapa Tropical Semi-Arid
● Embrapa Coastal Tablelands
● Embrapa Goat and Sheep
● Embrapa Cassava & Tropical Fruits
● Embrapa Cotton
● Embrapa Tropical Agroindustry
● Embrapa Palms and Flooded Plains

Southeast
● Embrapa Agribiology
● Embrapa Food Technology
● Embrapa Dairy Cattle
● Embrapa Agriculture Informatics
● Embrapa Agricultural Instrumentation
● Embrapa Environment
● Embrapa Maize & Sorahum
● Embrapa Satellite Monitoring
● Embrapa Cattle-Southeast
● Embrapa Soils

Mid-West
● Embrapa Agrienergy
● Embrapa Western Region Agriculture and Livestock
● Embrapa Rice & Beans
● Embrapa Coffee
● Embrapa Cerrados
● Embrapa Beef Cattle
● Embrapa Vegetables
● Embrapa Technological Information
● Embrapa Pantanal
● Embrapa Genetic Resources & Biotechnology
● Embrapa Technology Transfer
● Embrapa Mato Grosso
● Embrapa Strategic Studies and Capacity Strengthening

South
● Embrapa Temperate Agriculture
● Embrapa Forestry
● Embrapa South Animal Husbandry & Sheep
● Embrapa Soybean
● Embrapa Swine and Poultry
● Embrapa Wheat
● Embrapa Grape & Wine

Labex USA
Labex Europe
Labex Korea
Embrapa Africa
Embrapa Americas
Embrapa Venezuela

State research organizations (Oepas)
North: Unitins Agro (TO)
Northeast: EBDA (BA), Dipap (AL), IPA (PE), Emepa (PB), Empam (RN), Agerp (MA), Emdagro (SE)
Mid-West: Agraer (MS), Empaer (MT), Agência Rural (GO)
Southeast: Apta - SP (IAC, IZ, ITAL, IB, IEA, IP), Pesagro (RJ), Incaper (ES), Epami g (MG)
South: Fepagro (RS), Epagri (SC), Iapar (PR)

Partners
• Federal, state and private universities
• Federal, state and city organizations and Nongovernmental Organizations (NGOs)
• Private sector

Figure 12.3   Embrapa Research Units in 2010. In 2011, a new Labex was open in China (courtesy of Embrapa's Secretariat for International Affairs)

Embrapa would have the ability to represent the federal government in an area as important as agriculture, and to receive priority both in the allocation of resources and with regard to institutional development (Figure 12.3).

This model also allowed Embrapa to seek cooperation with universities, research institutes, private sector companies and overseas partners, as equals. In the mid-1980s, states' responsibility in agricultural research and science generation at agricultural colleges was further strengthened through the creation of the National Agricultural Research System, under Embrapa's leadership.

Embrapa's inception was founded on two pillars: (1) a focused research model, concentrated on products and areas of fundamental importance for the development of the country, and which constitutes an objective way of identifying research priorities; and (2) human resource capacity building, based on strong training programs in centers of excellence around the world.

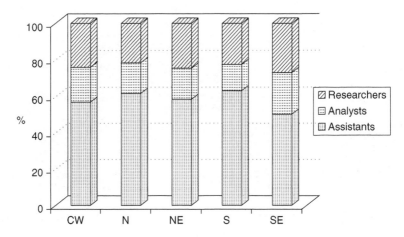

Note: CW – Center-West, N – North, NE – Northeast, S – South, SE – Southeast.

Source: Data courtesy of Embrapa's Financial Administration Department, authors' elaboration.

Figure 12.4   Distribution of Embrapa's employees according to categories (2009), by regions

Embrapa research units are thus distributed throughout the national territory and are specialized in products (maize and sorghum, dairy cattle, and so on), resources (*cerrado*, semi-arid, and so on) and themes (environment, satellite monitoring, and so on).[15] This structure allowed farmers and, more recently, the entire society to obtain objectively (and more efficiently) specific information and results for their demands. Similarly, researchers have a better notion of their responsibilities, minimizing ambiguities regarding goals and necessary actions.

Human resources
The human resources policy is one of the main reasons for Embrapa's success. From the beginning, Embrapa invested heavily in institution building. Across geographic regions, there is an approximately equal distribution among assistants (high school education), analysts (Bachelor's degree posts, a small percentage of which have a Master's degree, and only a few of which have PhDs) and researchers (Figure 12.4). The share of PhDs among researchers has been increasing rapidly, but the researchers in the Northern units lag behind (Figure 12.5).

The human capital policy at Embrapa, in brief, has been based on the following points:

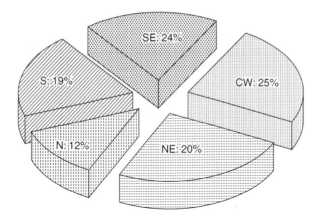

Note: CW – Midwest, N – North, NE – Northeast, S – South, SE – Southeast.

Source: Data courtesy of Embrapa's Financial Administration Department, authors' elaboration.

Figure 12.5   Distribution of Embrapa's researchers with PhD (2009), by geographic regions

1. The establishment of a career that stimulates the desire to study and progress.
2. A competitive salary compared to universities and other research centers.
3. A retirement plan to supplement public social security.
4. A health insurance plan that helps researchers and their families with expenses in healthcare, preserving employees' health, which is the most important capital of the corporation.
5. A promotion system based on merit, ranging from the individual up to the research group/unit level. Thus, there are two products that Embrapa has to deliver: increasingly competent employees and technologies.
6. A training program at postgraduate and postdoctorate levels that meets the interests of the corporation and of researchers, and which seeks to train them at the same levels as the best centers abroad.
7. The corporation recognizes that the technology generated incorporates the effort of all of its employees. Thus, the training program is available for everyone; postgraduate training (MSc, PhD) focuses on researchers, but it is not exclusive to them.
8. Each research unit has a critical mass of researchers. They are organized around a specific target audience, a clear main problem to solve and according to the team's responsibility towards society.

9. Embrapa seeks to encourage researchers to be entrepreneurs in their field, to seek resources, to interact with the outside world and to ensure the dissemination of technologies.
10. Embrapa's communication program aims at providing accountability for work, actions to disseminate research results, giving the corporation visibility and transparency, and valuing its employers.
11. Although the corporation is always looking for opportunities to improve its human capital, one has to plan for the future and the principle of researcher replacement has prevailed.[16]
12. Ongoing efforts focus on keeping and developing "the Embrapa spirit" among the newest members of staff, firmly reinforcing the need not to overlook this point. An issue to some extent related to this one is that in research it is natural for seniority to develop over the course of time, solidifying leadership founded on knowledge and recognition among peers. An institutional goal is to find mechanisms to promote those who can work in teams, spread their knowledge, and to motivate other colleagues to cooperate comfortably in such a view.

International opening

Embrapa was open to international cooperation very early in its life, even when the external exposure of the Brazilian economy was still very small. This openness enabled it to: (1) create a positive image abroad, thus facilitating the relationship with donors, universities, and research organizations in other countries; this, in turn, was positively perceived by the federal government, which responded with increased support; (2) have an international dimension in terms of the quality of research and in measuring scientists' performance; (3) help Brazil, as an instrument of foreign policy; (4) understand that in a globalized world, science is also globalized and that it is crucial for its very existence to improve the mechanisms of interaction with other countries, universities, funding bodies, broader types of organizations and, of course, other scientists.

In addition, Embrapa, throughout its life, has kept a strong postgraduate program, sending researchers to several countries, the vast majority to the United States, and lesser numbers to the United Kingdom, Canada, Spain, the Netherlands, Germany and Australia. The good performance of students helped to form important relationship bridges with the academic world abroad. Moreover, projects financed by international agencies were important to equip Embrapa better and to help it finance training programs abroad. Because these activities were well implemented and conducted, they helped to solidify the image of Embrapa as a serious and responsible corporation.

Since the late 1990s, Embrapa has expanded its participation in international cooperative projects. In the late 1990s it created the Virtual Labs Abroad (Labex). The first Labex was established in the United States, through an agreement with the US Department of Agriculture's Agricultural Research Service (USDA-ARS), and then other initiatives were implemented in Montpellier, France (Labex Europe Headquarters), with offices in the Netherlands and in the United Kingdom, and more recently in South Korea and China. The Labex structure has allowed Embrapa to have senior scientists working together with foreign scientists, and also to seek to establish permanent cooperation links between the parties.

The success of Brazilian tropical agriculture motivates poor countries to seek information and support for technology transfer from Embrapa. Besides the traditional instruments of support, Embrapa decided to have researchers in less developed countries, creating Embrapa Africa, in Accra (Ghana);[17] Embrapa Venezuela, in Caracas; and Embrapa Americas, in Panama. The goal in this initiative is to transfer knowledge and technology in tropical agriculture and to look for opportunities in licensing Embrapa's technology.

Both the Labex model – cooperating in research programs with developed countries – and the structures for transferring technologies to developing countries are flexible models that can be expanded with new scientists or through occasional transfers of scientists among countries, according to the interests of Embrapa. The goal is both to benefit the development of sustainable and competitive agriculture in recipient countries, and to help them find sound solutions to improve food security for their people.

Brazilian government support

Total government spending for Embrapa grew rapidly in the period 1974–82, reaching a ceiling in 1982, and experiencing a fall between 1983 and 1984. It subsequently increased in the decade starting in 1985, peaking at 1996. Government support fell in the period 1997–2002, but this was greatly influenced by the macroeconomic adjustments of the Real Plan. In 2003, government spending on Embrapa resumed a growing trend, peaking in 2009. Payroll expenses typically represented 65–75 percent of Embrapa's total expenditure.

Embrapa's spending, in its earlier years, focused on the Midwest region (Figure 12.6). This was consistent with the need to incorporate the Brazilian Cerrado into the productive process. Huge investments were made in plant genetics and in improving resource use (soil, water) to allow for better production systems. Indeed, changing the production

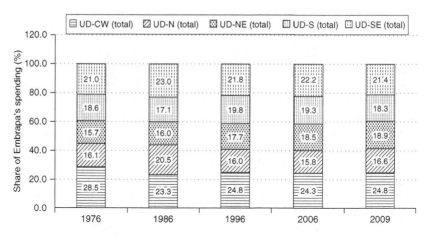

Note: CW – Midwest, N – North, NE – Northeast, S – South, SE – Southeast.

Source: Courtesy of Embrapa's Financial Administration Department.

Figure 12.6   Share of Embrapa's total spending among geographic regions

environment for taking full advantage of the Cerrado's potential was perceived as a strategy to be explored in order to make the enterprise competitive with traditional production regions in the country. Consequently, an ever-increasing input use in grain-producing systems (improved seeds, fertilizers, pesticides, and so on) was observed.

Beef production in Brazil, for instance, is often criticized as a sector of low productivity that is viable as an economic alternative only through the expansion of pasture area. This is, however, a wrong view of the sector. Based on official statistics (IBGE), Martha et al. (2012) found that productivity improved from 10.1 kg/ha of carcass-weight equivalent in 1950, to 43.4 kg/ha of carcass-weight equivalent in 2006. Productivity gains explained 79 percent of the production growth rates in the 1950–2006 period, while pasture area expansion in the 1950–2006 period, which varied from 107.6 to 158.75 million hectares, was responsible for less than 21 percent of the production increase in the 1950–2006 period.[18] The observed land-saving effect arising from productivity gains in beef production in Brazil, of around 525 million hectares, was simply astonishing. Without this land-saving effect, an additional pasture area that is 25 percent larger than the Amazon biome in Brazil would be needed to meet the current levels of Brazilian beef production.

The significant investments of the Brazilian government on infrastructure and on development programs for the region (during the 1970s and early 1980s), the availability of forage species adapted to the climate and soil conditions of the Cerrado, and the low-priced land, allowed cattle enterprises to be economically competitive despite their low productivity and economic output. These systems, which were also regarded as a capital reserve (because of cattle and land ownership, and due to the expectation of land valorization in the coming decades) ensured real economic gains to cattle farmers (Martha et al., 2007).

While the share in spending for the research units in the North, South and Southeast regions were more or less in balance from the 1970s to the 2000s, the money directed to Northeastern units as a share of total spending increased in recent years. The increased Embrapa spending effort in the Northeast is consistent with the fact that the region accounts for 47.4 percent of the farms and 47.1 percent of the rural population. The annual income per farm in the region (R$11 578.44) represents only 41 percent of Brazil's average (R$27 789.50), clearly indicating the need for greater assistance (Alves and Rocha, 2010). With the increasing importance of the environmental agenda, and considering that land-use changes, especially in the Amazon, are the main factor responsible for greenhouse gas emissions in Brazil, the spending share directed to research units in the North will eventually increase.

12.3.2 Pay-offs to Embrapa's Research

Varietal innovation played a key role in the development of the Brazilian Cerrado and, hence, in the history of Embrapa. Soybean production, by the 1960s, had been confined to the southern portion of the country, which has a temperate climate; given the research effort in genetic improvement in the following decades commissioned by Embrapa, universities, state agricultural research stations, private companies and international partners, it was possible for the crop to move north, to the border of the Amazon and Cerrado biomes, with average yields that were higher than those observed in the US and in Argentina. Simon and Garagorry (2005) found that latitudinal movement of the centroid of soybeans in Brazil moved from 26°S to 20°S between 1976 and 2001. Upland rice is another example of a breakthrough in varietal improvement in Brazil (Martha et al., 2006).

Whilst there is little doubt that the pay-offs to agricultural research and development (R&D) have been high (Alston et al., 1998; Pardey et al., 2006; Avila et al., 2010), much of the literature has been centered in varietal improvements. There is imprecise evidence regarding regional impacts of research and the impacts of an ample array of technologies. In part this reflects the difficulties in assigning adequate weights to benefits and costs among different agents involved in the process.

Pardey et al. (2006) presented a detailed study evaluating the impact of soybeans, dry beans and rice varietal improvement at Embrapa as compared to non-Embrapa investments. In the aggregate, varietal improvement in these crops from 1981 to 2003 yielded benefits of US$14.8 billion (1999 prices). Attributing all of the benefits to Embrapa, the benefit–cost ratio would be 27 for upland rice, 15 for dry beans and 149 for soybeans. Under alternative distribution rules, which indicate that Embrapa was given partial credit for the varieties developed jointly with other partners, the ratios would drop to 5, 3 and 31, respectively.

At the regional level, Embrapa assessed its impact from the 1970s to 1980s. While for Embrapa as a whole the registered internal rate of return ranged from 34 percent to 41 percent, the internal rates of return were comparatively smaller for the North (24 percent; Kitamura et al., 1989) and for the Northeast (25 percent; Santos et al., 1989), and were higher for the Midwest and Southern regions (both with 43 percent; Lanzer et al., 1989; Teixeira et al., 1990). In the 1990s, regional impact could be indirectly estimated through the research impacts in grain and oilseed varieties, because of regional distribution of these crops in the country. In the study of Evenson and Avila (1995), for example, the internal rates of returns for soybean, corn, rice and wheat were 40 percent, 58 percent, 37 percent and 40 percent, respectively.[19] These crops are mainly concentrated in the Center-South region.

12.4   AGRICULTURAL TECHNOLOGY AND SOME FUTURE DEMANDS

The role of agriculture in fostering development and as an effective tool to guarantee food and energy security requires a systemic approach, adequate investments and coordinated efforts – which are often carried out by agents that have conflicting opinions about a given matter – to find sound solutions for the different challenges in the economic, social and environmental dimensions (Mueller and Martha, 2008). In the coming decades, although food production will still be the main focus, the production process will bring forth additional issues. Brazilian and world societies are becoming increasingly concerned about other issues to be included in the "production function", such as environmental, food quality and safety issues.

A main future challenge for research, given the ample array of stakeholder pressure and funding possibilities, is clearly and objectively identifying the sequence of relevant problems that shall be solved by research in order to increase welfare in society. Classifying research deliverables according to results, and eventually incorporating computable externalities, could be an interesting method (Antle and Wagonet, 1995; Alves, 2008). Of course, in this view, it is important to consider the need to advance continuously in a sustainable agricultural growth path.

It must be noted, however, that no concise, universally acceptable definition of sustainable agriculture has yet emerged. However, it is well accepted that technical, economic, social and environmental sustainability dimensions should be pursued (Cunha et al., 1994). Sustainability dimensions have strong interdependence linkages and, ideally, should be met simultaneously. In other words, focusing on a single dimension, such as the economic or environmental, will not reflect the multiple dimensions of sustainability. Rather than this limited view, agricultural production systems, and thus agricultural research, should design strategies that create win–win situations, that is, simultaneous gains in all sustainability dimensions. When this ideal condition is not an option, small loss, big gain situations should be targeted. And in this view, sometimes one dimension, such as the economic, must be favored at the expense of a second, such as the environmental dimension, and vice versa; that is, under certain circumstances the environmental dimension shall be favored over the economic (Martha et al., 2010b).

It seems inevitable that a science-based era will be strengthened in the future. The research response in terms of technology generation will be strong. In the example of sustainability, the development and/or adaptation of resource-saving (for example, land-, water- and nutrient-saving) technologies will be prioritized. Regional characteristics will obviously be a matter of concern. Because of high agro-ecological and social heterogeneity in Brazil, locally specific approaches will have to be designed, which will thus require an in-depth review of the R&D agenda goals.

Embrapa is an institution with the ambition of persisting for a long time into the future, serving Brazilian and world societies. In this sense, it will be prepared for the unknown and, thus, it will invest heavily in human capital, and probably more than necessary to accomplish immediate needs (Alves, 2008).

In spite of the highly favorable economic result, the investments made in agricultural research are large and it takes a long time to repay them: usually 15–20 years depending on the technology. A relevant question is how to promote a continuous stream of institutional innovation capable of sustaining a virtuous R&D and innovation cycle in agriculture. Furthermore, as knowledge advances, it is necessary to integrate diverse datasets which, when jointly analyzed, will provide important input for different disciplines as well as for research planning and policy analysis (Antle and Wagonet, 1995).

Finally, the partnership between public and private research can help to increase investments in research, thus expanding the universe of knowledge and technologies available to farmers. This partnership might additionally be interesting to society when the pragmatism of private research helps public research to contribute more objectively to meeting society's demands (Alves, 2008).

NOTES

1. Mariana Medeiros (Embrapa Studies and Training) provided insightful comments on an earlier draft, and Renner Marra (Embrapa Strategic Management Secretariat) helped in data collection.
2. Using historical data on food prices from Dieese (Inter-Union Department of Statistics and Socio-Economic Studies), concerning a food basket for the city of São Paulo, it was found that the price of this food basket in April 2010 represented, in real terms, around 53 percent of the price paid by consumers in January 1975. In 35 years, the food price to consumers decreased by half, greatly reflecting the expansion of agricultural production in Brazil. Even when the food price peaked in 2008 it had a very small impact on the prices paid by consumers (Martha et al., 2010a).
3. Barros (2006) estimated that, in the decade that followed the Real Plan, this transfer might have exceeded R$1 trillion. According to Barros, income transfer from the rural area to consumers seems to have stabilized at around R$150 billion annually.
4. Estimates by the Brazilian Confederation of Agriculture and Livestock for 2008 (Medeiros et al., 2005) indicated that Brazilian agribusiness employs 17.7 million people (37 percent of the national jobs). USP/CEPEA (2011), in turn, found that agribusiness contributed US$497.6 billion to the country's 2010 gross domestic product (GDP) (25.2 percent of the total). In 2010, Brazilian agribusiness exports amounted US$76.4 billion, representing 37.9 percent of total Brazilian exports (Agrostat-Brasil, 2011).
5. For additional details see Baer (2008) and Contini et al. (2010).
6. The increased opportunity cost of labor for the farmers and the massive rural exodus scenario led to a favorable environment for agriculture growth and modernization.
7. According to the Instituto Brasileiro de Geografia e Estatística (IBGE) (2010), the Brazilian population in 1960 was 70 million people, of which 45 percent were considered urban. In 1980 the population had increased to 119 million and 68 percent were urban. In the period 1960–1980, the gross domestic product (GDP) had an impressive yearly growth rate of 7.54 percent, which caused the demand for food, especially by those that positively responded to income increase (especially the poor), to increase even more.
8. Exchange rate R$1.75/US$1.00.
9. Data from the Brazilian Central Bank (Bacen). Values were deflated to 2009 prices using FGV (Getulio Vargas Foundation) IGP-DI. The figures do not include rural credit for family agriculture – PRONAF (the Programa Nacional de Fortalecimento da Agricultura Familiar, or Program for Strengthening Family Agriculture) – which received increased resources after the late 1980s and especially in the 2004–11 period.
   It is important to note that in spite of this increase in rural credit, Brazilian agriculture receives minor incentives for production. An index that reflects the amount of incentives in the sector, the producer support estimate (PSE) calculated for Brazil by the OECD, revealed a net transfer of resources from agriculture to other sectors in the economy until the late 1990s. Between 1995 and 2007, the average PSE for Brazilian agriculture was 3.25 percent of the gross value of production. This amount is substantially less than those estimated for the US (16.62 percent) and the OECD countries (29.81 percent) in the same period.

10. Discussion based on Conab database.
11. This section benefited greatly from a previous paper by Alves (2010). See, additionally, Embrapa (2006).
12. The theory of induced innovation emphasizes the interaction of farmers with researchers; this interaction indicates the priorities for research within public research institutions. For private research institutions, the market acts directly, otherwise the technology developed would not find buyers. In public research, the market influence is indirect. It creates, among farmers, demand for a certain type of technology, for example land-saving technologies, and in response to that demand farmers indicate their needs to researchers, who respond with the adaptation and/or generation of technologies that increase land productivity (Alves, 2010).
13. CLT (Consolidação das Leis do Trabalho) allowed the hiring of personnel using laws governing the private sector instead of civil service laws.
14. This presence of Embrapa throughout the national territory was important in order to attract the sympathy of the state governments and the National Congress. Embrapa has a marked presence in the Federal District and this proximity of power has played an important role in establishing and solidifying the image of the corporation near the central power and also the international market (Alves, 2010).
15. Regarding the distribution of Embrapa's research units, 23 percent are in the Southeast, 25 percent are in the Midwest, 17 percent are in the North, 17 percent are in the Northeast and 18 percent are in the South.
16. In Embrapa's case, the goal is to maintain an average of 45 years of age for PhD holders, imagining the following guideline: on average, researchers should finish their PhDs at around the age of 30, which would leave them with a horizon of around 30 years of productive work. Half of this is 15. So, 15 years should be added to 30, comprising 45 years. Thus, on average, a young researcher has 15 years of work alongside senior researchers. A complementary strategy would be the creation of conditions that would allow for competent and outstanding retiring researchers to continue doing work with Embrapa. However, there is much to be done in this regard.
17. In past decades, Embrapa's activity in Africa has focused on specific cooperation projects for technology transfer on specific products, at the request of the governments concerned. Recently, Embrapa has increasingly offered training courses for professionals from African countries in its research centers, with funding from the Brazilian government (ABC – Agência Brasileira de Cooperação (Brazilian Cooperation Agency)), international agencies or foreign governments. To meet such growing demand, Embrapa has restructured its international cooperation and has created a frame for "structuring projects" (which have more resources and last longer), aiming at better results. In late 2010, Embrapa had a total of 38 projects that were either being implemented or were under final negotiations with 16 African countries. Total resources amounted to US$16.2 million, out of which nearly US$9 million were from the Brazilian government.
18. Beef production systems, in turn, were heavily based on pasture area expansion until 1975, while productivity gains became the main channel of growth from 1985 onwards; the expansion of the cultivated pasture area mainly with *Brachiaria*, was key to the success of the Brazilian beef industry (Martha et al., 2012).
19. For an additional discussion on impact assessment, please see Avila and Souza (2002).

REFERENCES

Agrostat-Brasil (2011), Ministry of Agriculture, Livestock and Food Supply, International Relations Secretariat, online database (compiled from Secex/MDIC), www.agricultura.gov.br//internacional/indicadores-e-estatisticas (accessed 23 May 2011).

Alston, J.M., G.W. Norton and P.G. Pardey (1998), *Science under Scarcity: Principles and Practice for Agricultural Research Evaluation and Priority Setting*, Wallingford: CABI Publishing.

Alves, E. (2008), "Alguns desafios que a Embrapa enfrentará", Seminário Fertbio, Londrina, 17 de setembro.

Alves, E. (2010), "Embrapa: a successful case of institutional innovation", *Revista de Política Agrícola*, **19**, special issue, 64–72.

Alves, E. and D.P. Rocha (2010), "Ganhar tempo é possível?" in J.G. Gasques, J.E.R. Vieira Filho and Z. Navarro (eds), *Agricultura brasileira: desempenho, desafios e perspectivas*, Brasília: IPEA, pp. 275–290.

Alves, E., M. Lopes and E. Contini (1999), "O empobrecimento da Agricultura Brasileira", *Revista de Política Agrícola*, **8** (3), 5–19.

Antle, J.M. and R.J. Wagenet (1995), "Why scientists should talk with economists", *Agronomy Journal*, **87**, 1033–1040.

Avila, A.F.D. and G.S. Souza (2002), "The importance of impact assessment studies for the Brazilian agricultural research system", paper presented at the International Conference on Impacts of Agricultural Research and Development: Why Has Impact Assessment Research Not Made More a Difference? San José, Costa Rica, 4–7 February.

Ávila, A.F.D., L. Romano and F. Garagorry (2010), "Agricultural productivity in Latin America and the Caribbean and sources of growth", in P.L. Pingalli and R.E. Evenson (ed.), *Handbook of Agricultural Economics*, Vol. 4, Amsterdam: North-Holland, pp. 3713–3768.

Baer, W. (2008), *The Brazilian Economy*, 6th edn, Boulder, Co: Lynne Rienner Publishers.

Barros, G.C.S. (2006), *Agronegócio brasileiro: perspectivas, desafios e uma agenda para seu desenvolvimento*, Piracicaba: USP/Esalq/Cepea.

Coelho, C.N. (2001), "70 anos de política agrícola no Brasil (1931–2001)", *Revista de Política Agrícola*, **10**, edição especial, 3–58.

Contini, E., J.G. Gasques, E. Alves and E.T. Bastos (2010), "Dynamism of Brazilian agriculture", *Revista de Política Agrícola*, **19**, special issue, 42–63.

Cunha, A.S., C.C. Mueller, E.R.A. Alves and J.E. Silva (1994), *Uma avaliação da sustentabilidade da agricultura nos cerrados*, Brasília: IPEA.

Evenson, R.E. and A.F.D. Ávila (1995), "Productivity change in the Brazilian grain sector and agricultural research role", *Revista de Economia e Sociologia Rural*, **34**, 93–109.

Gasques, J.G., E.T. Bastos, M.R.P. Bacchi and C. Valdes (2010), "Produtividade total dos fatores e transformações da agricultura brasileira: análise dos dados dos Censos Agropecuários", in J.G. Gasques, J.E.R. Vieira Filho and Z. Navarro (eds), *Agricultura brasileira: desempenho, desafios e perspectivas*, Brasília: IPEA, pp. 19–44.

Hayami, Y. and V.W. Ruttan (1971), *Agricultural Development: An International Perspective*, Baltimore, MD, USA and London, UK: Johns Hopkins Press.

Instituto Brasileiro de Geografia e Estatística (IBGE) (2010), "População", http://www.ibge.gov.br/home/estatistica/populacao/contagem2007/default.shtm (accessed 15 June 2010).

Kitamura, P.C., A. Souza, A. Conto, F.M. Rodrigues, J. Oliveira, J.C. Rezende, N. Vilela, P. Tinoco, P.M. Alves, R. Braga and R.A. Carvalho (1989), *Avaliação regional dos impactos sociais e econômicos da pesquisa da Embrapa: Região Amazônica*, Embrapa-SEP, Documentos, 38, Brasília: Embrapa-DPU.

Lanzer, E.A., I. Ambrosi, D. Dossa, L.M. Freire, A. Girotto, V. Hoeflich, P. Reis, V.F. Osório, V.H.F. Porto, S.X. Souza and A.M. Trindade (1989), *Avaliação regional dos impactos sociais e econômicos da pesquisa da Embrapa: Região sul*, Embrapa-SEP, Documentos, 45, Brasília: Embrapa-DPU.

Liapis, P.S. (2010), "Trends in agricultural trade", presented at Joint ICTSD-FAO expert meeting, Geneva, 25–26 March.

MAPA (2010), "Brazilian exports", Ministry of Agriculture, Livestock and Food Supply, International Relations Secretariat.

MAPA/AGE (2010), Ministério da Agricultura, Pecuária e Abastecimento. Projeções do Agronegócio: Brasil 2009/10 a 2019/20. Assessoria de Gestão Estratégica, Brasília. Disponível em: www.agricultura.gov.br (accessed 2 May 2010).

Martha Jr, G.B., E. Alves and E. Contini (2012), "Land-saving approaches and beef production growth in Brazil", *Agricultural Systems* (in press).

Martha Jr, G.B., E. Alves, E. Contini and S.Y. Ramos (2010a), "The development of Brazilian agriculture and future challenges", *Revista de Política Agrícola*, **19**, special issue, pp. 91–104.

Martha Jr, G.B., E.O. Krebsky and L. Vilela (2010b), "Produção sustentável de bovinos em pastagens", in O.G. Pereira, J.A. Obeid, D. Nascimento Jr. and D.M. Fonseca (eds), *Simfor 5*, Viçosa: UFV, pp. 93–136.

Martha Jr, G.B. and L. Vilela (2009), "Efeito poupa-terra de sistemas de integração lavoura-pecuária", Embrapa Cerrados, Comunicado Técnico, 164, Planaltina: Embrapa Cerrados.

Martha Jr, G.B., L. Vilela and A.O. Barcellos (2006), "A planta forrageira em pastagens", in Simpósio Sobre Manejo da Pastagem, 23, Proceedings Piracicaba: Fealq, pp. 87–137.

Martha Jr, G.B., L. Vilela and D.M.G. Sousa (2007), *Cerrado: uso eficiente de correctivos e fertilizantes em pastagens*, Planaltina: Embrapa Cerrados.

Medeiros, E.A., M. Araújo, M.F. Belloni, R.B.A. Leonardi, E.T. Bastos, L.M. Santos, P.S.V. Fresneda and E. Contini (2005), "Prioridades estratégicas do Mapa 2005–2006", *Revista de Política Agrícola*, **14** (3), pp. 5–13.

Mueller, C.C. and G.B. Martha Jr. (2008), "A agropecuária e o desenvolvimento socioeconômico recente do Cerrado", in F.G. Faleiro and A.L. Farias Neto (eds), *Savanas: desafios e estratégias para o equilíbrio entre sociedade, agronegócio e recursos naturais*, Planaltina: Embrapa Cerrados, pp. 35–99.

OECD/FAO (2010), *OECD–FAO Agricultural Outlook 2010–2019*, Paris.

Pardey, P.G., J.M. Alston, C. Chan-Kang, E.C. Magalhães and S.A. Vosti (2006), "International and institutional R&D spillovers: attribution of benefits among sources for Brazil's new crop varieties", *American Journal of Agricultural Economics*, **88**, 104–123.

Rodrigues, R. (2008), "Facing energy security in the Americas through agro-energy sources", presented at Thirtieth Conference in the Organization of American States' (OAS) Lecture Series of the Americas, Washington, DC, 28 October (available at http://www.der.oas.org/lecture.html, accessed 15 December 2008).

Santos, R.F., G. Calegar, V. Silva, M.A. Barros, J.O. Lima, J. Motta and J.S. Neto (1989), "Avaliação socio-econômica das pesquisas da Embrapa na região nordeste", Embrapa-SEP, Documentos, 37, Brasília, Embrapa-DPU.

Simon, M.F. and L.F. Garagorry (2005), "The expansion of agriculture in the Brazilian Amazon", *Environmental Conservation*, **32**, 203–212.

Teixeira, S.M., G.C. Gomes, F.P. Costa, E.P. Santana, A.M. Machado, N.A. Santos, J.M. Kruker, L. Coradin and R.C. Vieira (1990), "Avaliação socio-econômica das pesquisas da Embrapa na Região Centro-oeste", Embrapa-DPL, Documentos, 09, Brasília: Embrapa-DPL.

USP/CEPEA (n.d.), "Brazilian agribusiness GDP", Center for Advanced Studies on Applied Economics (CEPEA) (available at http://www.cepea.esalq.usp.br/pib/, accessed 23 May 2011).

13. The regional impact of federal government programs in Brazil: the case of Rio de Janeiro

Thomas J. Trebat and Nicholas M. Trebat

13.1 INTRODUCTION

Regional studies have a very long tradition in Brazil, a country of continental dimensions (Baer, 2008, esp. pp. 243–276). Many studies have focused on the notorious regional inequalities and, therefore, on the Northeast region and the yawning income and welfare gaps between the Northeast and the more developed areas of the Southeast. It is right that academic and policy attention focuses on the Northeast, given that region's relative backwardness and the enormous proportion of Brazil's poor that it holds.

The aim of this study is to review our knowledge of the regional impact of federal government policies in a relatively more developed region of Brazil which also happens to contain a large number of poor and extremely poor citizens. The case chosen is that of Rio de Janeiro; the iconic city itself, in particular, and also the surrounding state which has taken the same name.

What makes this case study of Rio de Janeiro so interesting and potentially instructive in terms of the impact of federal policies on regions? In large part, the justification comes from the important role that the federal government, broadly understood to encompass state-owned enterprises, has played in Rio and continues to play. We believe that examination of the case of Rio de Janeiro can show that the best regional policy for the federal government to pursue might not be a regional policy at all, but rather better coordination between the policies of the federal, state and local governments.

Rio is also a fascinating laboratory for the analysis of development policy. The city and state rank among the highest per capita income areas in Brazil, responsible for close to 12 percent of Brazil's gross domestic product (GDP) in the late 2000s, and yet these areas are beset with severe problems of poverty, informality, low productivity, crime and violence. The educational system is consistently among the worst of Brazil's major urban areas. Rio is plagued by urban problems of every type, and has a history of poor political management and also of poor political coordination with the federal government, at least until recent years. Though boosted since the early 1990s by the discovery of oil in offshore waters of the state, the regional economy of Rio de Janeiro underperformed the rest of the nation for decades and its economic future is still highly uncertain despite the beguiling promise of oil wealth and the prospect of the Olympic Games in 2016.

Our working hypothesis is that if we can understand the complex interactions between federal and local policies in terms of development in a relatively rich and well-endowed region such as the city and the state of Rio de Janeiro, lessons can be extracted for the proper coordination of government policies elsewhere in Brazil.

13.2   CASE STUDY BACKGROUND: THE ECONOMY OF RIO DE JANEIRO

Rio de Janeiro is among Brazil's richest states, with a GDP of about $215 billion in 2010 which is about 12 percent of the country's GDP and approximately the size of the economy of Portugal. Rio is also one of the most populous of Brazil's states, with 96 percent of the population living in urban areas and 75 percent in the metropolitan area of Rio de Janeiro.[1] Brazil's federal constitution of 1988 grants specific attributions to municipal governments (*municipios*). These units of subnational government are recognized as autonomous, independent entities within the Brazilian federation. Municipal governments are the main providers of many essential public services, including education (to the ninth grade), health, sanitation, garbage collection and general urban infrastructure. The provision of federal funding in each of these areas allows for federal influence, but actual policy implementation depends upon the municipality. State governments also enjoy an important degree of autonomy from the federal government and are responsible for such critical services as secondary education, much of the health delivery system, and business registration. Hence, successful performance at the state and municipal levels is critical to promoting growth and reducing poverty.

Despite the city of Rio's many advantages related to infrastructure, human and natural resources, the economy of the city lagged behind other major urban areas of Brazil for a long time, starting in the mid-1980s and through the early 2000s. While this was a period of slow growth for Brazil

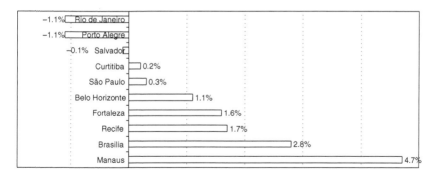

Source: World Bank (2010), Report No. 51690-BR, 10 June, p. 9 (available at www. worldbank.org).

Figure 13.1   Real annual GDP growth of Brazil's largest cities, 1985–2003

as a whole as the national economy suffered from debt-induced external shocks, Rio de Janeiro fared particularly poorly. The municipal economy declined at an annual average rate of more than 1 percent, worse than São Paulo and far worse than the performance of most Brazilian cities in the North and Northeast (see Figure 13.1).

Rio de Janeiro city is highly dependent on services, having suffered over decades from a hollowing-out of its industrial base. From the late 1930s to the early 1980s, Rio city's share of national industrial output declined from about 30 percent to 10 percent before stabilizing. More than two-thirds of regional output in the late 2000s was being generated by services, including a large informal services sector. With much of industry migrating to São Paulo and other states over many decades, industrial activity in the city accounts for only about 10 percent of GDP and this has contributed to the flight of the financial services sector.

In many respects, the above comments seem to relate to a closed chapter in Rio's economic history. A much more optimistic outlook for the city and the state now seems within reach. In fact, recent data (Figure 13.2) show that Rio is beginning to grow faster than the rest of Brazil in per capita terms, even while it may still be a laggard with respect to São Paulo and other cities in the South.

Why the change in outlook for this apparently beleaguered region of Brazil? A tectonic shift in the development model in Rio began in the early 1990s with the discovery of major oil reserves in the offshore Campos Basin, leading to a gradual rise in oil output and proven reserves in the state of Rio. Total oil production of around 1.7 million barrels per day is the equivalent of about 80 percent of Brazil's total oil output. Discovery of much larger

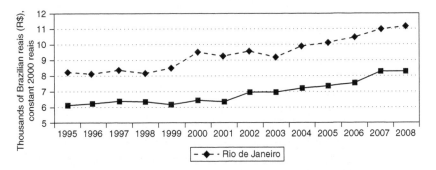

Source: Instituto de Pesquisa Econômica Aplicada (IPEA), www.ipeadata.gov.br.

Figure 13.2 GDP per capita, Rio de Janeiro vs. Brazil, 1995–2008

fields, the so-called "pre-salt" deposits in deep waters off Rio de Janeiro, will accelerate oil-driven growth, perhaps even resulting in a doubling or more in the rate of oil production. For Brazil as a whole, the pre-salt oil deposits offer the enticing prospect of oil independence and, more than that, the emergence of Brazil as a global energy player of the first order.

It seems almost inevitable, therefore, that the city and surrounding state of Rio de Janeiro will benefit from the injection of enormous amounts of federal government and private sector investment which will be required to develop oil and gas and also related industries (petrochemical complexes and steel, and infrastructure; new ports, roads and energy facilities). This "big push" will solidify the underlying trend in Rio, which is steady morphing into a natural-resource-based economy. All ten of the largest companies in the state already are natural-resource companies and five of the largest ten companies are in petroleum and oil-related industries. Of course, the mega-company in the Rio mix is Petrobrás, long headquartered in the state and now with its business activities in oil and gas increasingly concentrated there.

Thus, Rio de Janeiro in the early 2000s seemed ready to rebound from decades of malaise, on the back of strong domestic and international demand for oil and gas and oil-related services. With the likelihood of a bonanza drawing ever nearer, some of Rio's long-standing characteristics now appear to be more valuable in terms of aggregate spending and economic activity. These would include Rio's large population of relatively well-educated federal retirees, the large and expanding state-owned enterprises based in Rio (Petrobrás, the National Bank for Economic and Social Development, and others), and likely strong performance in collections of municipal and state tax revenues. Rio would seem to be well placed for an expansion of tourism (in part stimulated by hosting international sporting events), telecommunications and knowledge-based industries tapping into the city's substantial networks of universities, think tanks and specialized research centers. The Soccer World Cup of 2014 and the Summer Olympics of 2016 may not have a dramatic effect on economic growth in Rio, but they will allow for some front-loading of economic infrastructure which should contribute positively to growth over time.[2]

13.3 CASE STUDY BACKGROUND: SOCIAL CONDITIONS IN RIO DE JANEIRO

Rio de Janeiro is a microcosm of Brazil with its notorious social and economic inequalities. Again according to the World Bank, approximately 13 percent of the population of the city (conditions are worse in the surrounding state) is poor, with about 19 percent of the population living in slum communities or *favelas*. About 50 percent of the Rio workforce is employed in the informal sector where productivity and salaries are generally low. *Favela* communities are characterized by inadequate water, sewerage, road access, schools and health facilities. Human Development Index (HDI) scores for the city and state show a very high dispersion of outcomes, though HDI scores are generally higher than the average for the impoverished states of the Brazilian Northeast. While generally declining, homicide rates are very high in Rio compared to many other global urban centers. Health results, measured by such indicators as maternal mortality rates and mortality rate by heart attack, show that Rio de Janeiro state lags behind São Paulo and other states of Brazil's Southeast.

Educational indicators for the city reveal that Rio's school performance is above average for municipal systems across Brazil, but lags behind results in other large public systems in the South and Southeast. Average school year repetition rates in Rio are well above those in São Paulo, Curitiba and Belo Horizonte. This is measured in terms of student learning levels, grade repetition and dropout rates in primary school. Educational outcomes for the city are far better than for the surrounding state, where performance in schools has been characterized as "truly awful" by the World Bank on the basis of student test scores on standardized tests that fall well below national benchmarks in mathematics and in Portuguese.[3] Particular problems affecting the school system in the city of Rio de Janeiro involve delivering educational services to students living in high-crime areas of the city. Also, the city is falling very short of meeting the demand for pre-school education and daycare facilities for school-age children. While responsibility for primary education is that of the city,

coordination with the state authorities who are responsible for secondary education is improving. The federal government is also influential in
Rio's schools and supports eight separate programs in the city to improve
educational outcomes.[4]

13.4   CASE STUDY BACKGROUND: POLITICS IN THE CITY AND STATE

The political context is obviously important to an understanding of how
federal policies affect regional development in Rio de Janeiro. The city
and state have had a history of conflictual relations between city and state
officials because of differing political affiliations, and both levels of government in the past were often in political rivalry with the federal government in Brasília. As Nader (2009) notes, from 1982 through 2006, "lack of
political alignment between state authorities and the federal government
created a situation in which no significant federal resources were invested
in Rio de Janeiro" (p. 89). Things changed in 2006, when Sérgio Cabral of
the Partido do Movimento Democrático Brasileiro (PMDB) was elected
Governor of the State of Rio. His party fashioned a strong alliance with
President Lula which has extended into the administration of President
Dilma Rousseff.

It is not a surprising outcome that the stronger working relationship
between the government of the state and the federal government in Brasília
has increased federal assistance to Rio in such areas as housing, urban
infrastructure and education. Federal provision of financing, virtually guaranteeing the city's ability to pay for the Games, was an instrumental factor
in Rio's winning bid to host the Olympics in 2016. Cabral helped to assure
the victory of a close political ally, Eduardo Paes, to the mayoralty of the
city in 2008. Thus, by the late 2000s, the two highest elected officials in the
city and the state were in close political alliance with one another and also
aligned politically with the federal government in Brasília. Our hypothesis
is that this political convergence has laid the groundwork for more effective
coordination between state, municipal and federal levels of government on
behalf of regional development problems and issues in Rio de Janeiro.

13.5   IMPACTS OF FEDERAL POLICIES ON REGIONAL GROWTH IN RIO

While it is difficult to point to any particular federal government development policy specifically aimed at the region of Rio de Janeiro, federal

policies even without being specifically designed for the region have had, and are having, a significant impact on regional growth in Rio de Janeiro. Some of these policies have been mentioned already. The Growth Acceleration Program of the Lula and Dilma administrations has as one of its objectives upgrading housing conditions in degraded urban areas, and Rio has been a principal beneficiary of such funding beginning in the late 2000s. At least eight federal programs in the field of public education are providing assistance to local educational officials in the city of Rio. Federal military assistance has been used effectively by the city and state governments to quell violence and restore order in poor communities in the city of Rio. All of these federal programs, and many others, have had important regional impacts in Rio, and a careful analysis of the economic impact of such policies would need to be included in a more comprehensive assessment of federal policies.

We have selected for examination the following three broad examples of federal policies with significant regional development impact in Rio de Janeiro:

1. Federal government policies to reform and reorganize state and local finances, with special emphasis on the Law of Fiscal Responsibility.
2. Federal policies involving intergovernmental fiscal transfers, with emphasis on tax revenues and royalties generated by oil and gas activities and how these are shared among the different states of the Brazilian federation.
3. State-owned enterprise investment in the state of Rio to develop extensive oil and gas reserves and also to build infrastructure in petrochemicals and oil-related service industries.

13.5.1   Example 1: Law of Fiscal Responsibility and Rio's Fiscal Positions

After many years of mismanagement of city and state finances and low levels of investment, the financial situation at both levels of government has been improving steadily in recent years. The tax base has been broadened. Runaway liabilities for pensions for former workers have been brought under greater control (Villela and Tafner, 2011). The data describe a generally improving fiscal situation with rising primary fiscal balances due to improved management practices, the positive effect on tax revenues of higher economic growth, and declines in investment spending. The improvement in fiscal finances has been substantial. For example, the debt of the State of Rio de Janeiro was classified as investment grade by Standard & Poor's in 2008. This has allowed both the state and city governments to leverage their respective balance sheets to

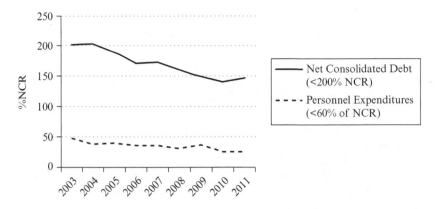

Source: Secretaría de Fazenda of the State of Rio de Janeiro, http://www.fazenda.rj.gov. br/portal/index.portal?_nfpb=true&_pageLabel=boletim.

Figure 13.3 Evolution of the fiscal responsibility law indicators for the state of Rio de Janeiro

borrow abroad and to provide counterpart funding for federal programs in the region.

Much of the impetus for the improvement in state and local finances in Rio came from efforts of the federal government starting in the late 1990s to bring order to the finances of state and local governments. A persistent pattern prior to this period was for state and local governments to issue debt to fund the costs of their operations and then to pass on the debt to the federal government (Fishlow, 2011, p. 27). At one point in the late 1990s, 25 of the 27 Brazilian states, including Rio de Janeiro, were unable to service their debts, leading to a massive bailout by the federal government.[5] This and subsequent federal operations sought to strengthen the finances of subnational governments, in particular, by placing limits on their indebtedness, requiring regular audits, and prohibiting debt refinancing between different levels of government. Eventually, the new framework of "constrained federalism" was codified in the Law of Fiscal Responsibility (LFR) of 2000 which set limits on the expenditures allocated to personnel as well as on borrowing and overall indebtedness of subnational governments (Fishlow, 2011, p. 27).

Improvements in the fiscal situation of both the state and city of Rio date back to the institutional reforms embodied in the LRF. The state of Rio, for example, was bailed out three times in the decade prior to the reforms in the early 2000s, and in the decade since has amassed a record of rising revenues and contained expenditures leading to steady increases in the primary fiscal surplus and strict adherence to the various benchmarks of the federal law, including indebtedness. The state's fiscal performance continued to improve after the election of Cabral in 2006 and subsequent fiscal reforms. The state budget was further aided by the rise in economic activity and in oil and gas prices. However, it can safely be said that the state's improvement in fiscal finances can be traced to federal policies and the new form of fiscal federalism.

Meanwhile, a parallel process of debt renegotiation in the early 2000s also occurred at the municipal level in the context of the LFR. As has been the case with the state government, the city of Rio has also been able to adhere to the various benchmarks of the LFR in the context of rising municipal revenues and controlled expenditure growth, aided by the same external factors (for example, oil prices) that have also benefited the state coffers. And as in the case of the state of Rio, the improvement in fiscal finances led to an investment grade rating for the debt of the city of Rio in 2010.

City and state financial officials credit the fiscal reforms ushered in by the LFR with increasing the capacity of both subnational governments to contract new debt safely and to leverage resources from the federal government that were previously unavailable due to the lack of counterpart funds at the local level (Villela and Tafner, 2011, p. 21). For example, the city of Rio de Janeiro received a $1 billion loan from the World Bank in 2010 for purposes of long-term debt renegotiation on the basis of fiscal and management reforms. As if to underline the dramatic improvement in the city's financial structure, this was the first loan to a municipal government in the history of the World Bank (ibid.). The state of Rio has also been able to increase its borrowing with multilateral organizations and with federal government banks to a significant extent, adding to fiscal capability while remaining within the indebtedness guidelines of the LFR (ibid.).

The City of Rio's budget faces still many challenges: personnel expenditures, mandated expenditures in health, education, pensions and debt servicing exert multiple pressures. In common with many governments in Rio, pension benefits for retired civil servants consume an enormous proportion of personnel expenses. Pensions for retired workers take more than 40 percent of the total wage bill. The pension deficit is increasing steadily and is projected to reach 10 percent of Rio's net current revenues by 2015–20. Also, because of past debt, debt service is a significant part of Rio's expenses.

Still, the city and state have benefited enormously from the federal government's programs, of which the Law of Fiscal Responsibility is the most important. By 2009, the city's macroeconomic and fiscal situation was strong and in compliance with the prudential limits set out in the LRF. Net consolidated debt decreased significantly from 79 percent of net current revenues in 2004 to 25.4 percent five years later.[6]

13.5.2   Example 2: Taxation of Oil and Gas Revenues

One of the most important current issues in fiscal federalism in Brazil is the debate about the division of royalties and other tax revenues that will be produced as a result of the development of the "pre-salt" or "sub-salt" deepwater oil and gas reserves off the coast of Rio de Janeiro. Given the potential impact of oil-generated fiscal revenues, some brief contextual remarks on the finances of Rio de Janeiro would be useful.

The main source of fiscal revenue for the state of Rio, as for all Brazilian states, is a state turnover tax on goods and services produced within state boundaries; the tax is known by its Portuguese acronym as the ICMS.[7] The product coverage of the ICMS is narrower in Rio de Janeiro than in other states because of the unique tax regime applied to petroleum. Unlike the taxation of other goods and services, petroleum is taxed at the point of sale rather than at the point of origin. This can be seen as putting producer states, such as Rio, in a disadvantageous position with regard to fiscal capacity.

However, the state and the city of Rio both derive revenues from royalties paid by oil companies operating within the state. This is in compliance with the Brazilian Constitution of 1988 which provides for such payments to producing states and producing municipalities, while allocating a large share of such revenues to the federal government. Revenues from this source to the state of Rio de Janeiro have been significant in the present era, but also volatile in accordance with global oil price fluctuations. Royalties and other oil and gas-related revenues accounted for between 12 and 16 percent of state revenues in recent years from 2007 to 2010[8] (Figure 13.4). Dependence on oil royalty revenue is much higher in the largely impoverished oil municipalities in the north of the state, such as Campos dos Goytacazes, Quissamã, São João da Barra and Rio das Ostras. Typically, royalties account for anywhere between 50 and 80 percent of the municipal revenues of these cities. Moreover, with the exception of Macaé and Rio das Ostras, oil dependence has increased in the *norte fluminense* region since the early 2000s.[9]

The finances of the city of Rio de Janeiro are closely linked to revenues that are collected at the state and federal levels and then passed on through fiscal transfers to the city. For example, the municipality of Rio receives transfers from state revenues collected via the ICMS (the state turnover tax, discussed above), and oil royalties collected at the state

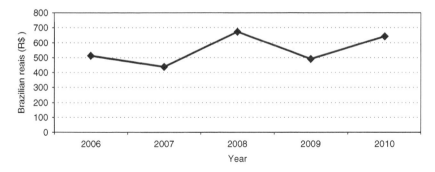

Source: Secretaria da Fazenda, Governo do Estado do Rio de Janeiro; http://
www.fazenda.rj.gov.br/portal/instituicao/contadoria.portal?_nfpb=true&_
pageLabel=instituicao_contadoria_home_normasOrientacoes_principal&file=/
relatoriosContabeis/demonstrativo/demonstrativo_resu_desp_rec/receita/index.shtml.
Accessed Sept. 26, 2011.

*Figure 13.4 Public oil and gas revenues (royalties and taxes) in the state
of Rio, 2006–10*

level and passed through to the city budget. The city of Rio also receives
important educational financing from the federal government through a
fund for the improvement of basic education in the nation and known
as FUNDEB.[10] In all, transfers from the federal and state governments
account for about 36 percent of the municipal revenues of Rio de Janeiro
in recent years.[11]

With these comments as background with which to understand some of
the fiscal interaction between the federal, state and local governments, a
major new policy issue is on the horizon, given the likelihood of a substantial
increase over the next ten years in the amount of oil to be produced in the
state of Rio de Janeiro. The fiscal and political issue confronting the federal
government is to broker among the 27 Brazilian states an equitable and
politically acceptable agreement on the division of tax revenues from the
pre-salt oil deposits, 75 percent of which are located in waters off the coast of
Rio.[12] Until this intergovernmental fiscal transfer issue is resolved, it is difficult to imagine that the physical development of the oil deposits can proceed.

The fiscal transfer issue is made complex by the constitutional guar-
antees that grant royalty and other tax rights to producer states and to
producer municipalities. As long as total revenues from oil drilled in Brazil
were fairly modest and oil output was low, the distribution of oil royalties to the state and municipalities in a way generally favorable to Rio de
Janeiro (and four other producer states) was not controversial. This is no
longer the case and the matter is being hotly debated, especially since the

*Table 13.1   Division of oil-related royalties among government levels:
actual versus proposed as of September 2011*

	Federal government (%)	Producer states (%)	Producer local govt. (%)	Non-producer states (%)	Other (%)	Totals (%)
Actual legislation on existing fields	30	26.5	26.25	8.75	8	100
Proposed legislation for pre-salt deposits	20	25	6	46	3	100

Source: Garman (2011).

non-producer states include all of the poorest states of the Brazilian federation. If present tax-sharing legislation applicable to existing oil fields is left in place, Rio and other producer states will see a multiplication of their revenues. A consensus has emerged that a new revenue-sharing formula must be devised.

Needless to say, the politics behind this matter are complicated. If the Brazilian Congress decides the issue, producer states such as Rio and São Paulo are going to be clearly outvoted and forced to accept legislation that diminishes, perhaps drastically, their share of future oil revenues on the basis that the oil resources belong to the nation and not to individual states in which they are located. On the other hand, legislation approved by the Brazilian Congress, but unacceptable to the producer states, could wind up in court proceedings that might drag on, harming not only aggregate fiscal revenues but also the very development of the pre-salt fields themselves. It would seem incumbent for the federal government to set policy in this issue by brokering some sort of arrangement among the states.

As of this writing, this issue is still in flux, but the broad outlines of what might be an acceptable agreement are beginning to appear in various press and other non-official accounts (Garman, 2011). The essence of what is being reported, and summarized in Table 13.1, is that the federal government will gradually reduce its own share of oil revenues in order to broker a deal acceptable to Rio de Janeiro, in particular, and to the non-producer states.

The amounts of revenues involved are significant, something like R$2–3 billion (about US$2 billion) per year in additional annual revenues at current (mid-2011) oil prices for non-producer states.[13] The big loser in the proposal would be the federal government, whose share in revenues would decrease from 30 to 20 percent. Producer municipalities, for example, the poor municipalities in the north of the state of Rio, would be severely disadvantaged; their revenue share would shrivel over time to less than 10 percent. These municipalities can be expected to challenge this in court. Moreover, the state of Rio de Janeiro, while relatively favored in the proposal as its share would diminish only marginally, also may have grounds to challenge the legislation in court. The argument is that the changes should not affect existing licenses, only new ones to be issued as the pre-salt reserves are developed.

The proposal for the division of fiscal revenues from oil is a significant departure from traditional rules for sharing federal taxes among the states. Taxes collected at the federal level are usually distributed to states in inverse proportion to their GDP per capita, an arrangement that obviously has favored the poorer states of the North, Northeast, and Center-West of the country. At the other extreme, Rio de Janeiro with its very high per capita income has traditionally had a very small share (about 2.4 percent) of taxes collected at the federal level and then transferred to state governments.

In sum, econometric modeling might be useful to make the implications of the proposed legislation clearer to policymakers, but the federal government is being asked to broker a political deal among subnational units competing for scarce resources. We submit this issue of the proposed division of oil revenues as an example of how federal policy affects regional development even when not explicitly cast as regional policy.

13.5.3   Example 3: State-Owned Enterprise Investment in Rio de Janeiro

Ultimately, the most important impact of federal policies on regional development in Rio de Janeiro may be the increase in Petrobrás's investments in the development of the pre-salt fields. These offshore drilling investments will be magnified by the impact of complementary private sector investment in many areas of oil-related manufactures and services, such as steel and petrochemicals. Furthermore, the impact of the federal government's ambitious local content requirement for equipment and infrastructure needed to support the pre-salt development suggests a heightened impact on businesses located in and near the region of Rio de Janeiro.

Some of the background on oil in the state of Rio is useful. While important oil discoveries were made in the Campos basin region of the state in the early 1990s, the modern history of oil and gas in Rio can be traced

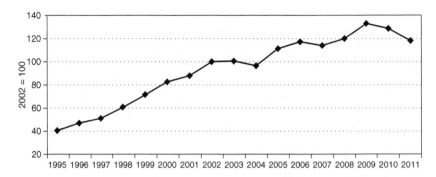

Source: Instituto de Pesquisa Econômica Aplicada (IPEA), www.ipeadata.gov.br.

*Figure 13.5   Index of minerals production state of Rio de Janeiro,
1995–2011*

to later federal reforms which altered the structure of the oil industry. These reforms include a constitutional amendment in 1995 which ended the state oil monopoly in place since the early 1950s, and the Petroleum Law of 1997 which created the regulatory framework for the sector, especially the Agência Nacional de Petróleo. As expected at the time of the reforms, the legislation permitted an expansion of private sector involvement in the industry and exposed Petrobrás to competition. However, the most important by-product of the reforms may have been the unleashing of Petrobrás itself, which has emerged in subsequent years as a much-admired company and a strong competitor in global oil markets. Fifteen years after the opening of the petroleum sector, state-owned Petrobrás remains by far the largest producer and investor, accounting for some 90 percent of total investment in the sector. Furthermore, new legislation affecting the pre-salt deposits gives a privileged position to the state-owned company, assuring that Petrobrás will be the dominant actor in the oil and gas market in the future, although with ample scope for a much larger role for the private sector than ever could have been imaginable before the end of the oil monopoly.

This is not the place for a fuller analysis of the impact of Petrobras's investment program and its impact on its suppliers, though some work is beginning to emerge on this issue (IPEA, 2010). Preliminary data and early indicators suggest a very substantial expenditure impact has already occurred in the confines of the state of Rio and that a much larger impact could be anticipated to occur in the future. As Figure 13.5 illustrates, the state of Rio's economic growth since 1995 has taken place simultaneously with a significant increase in mineral (mainly oil) production. Figure 13.6

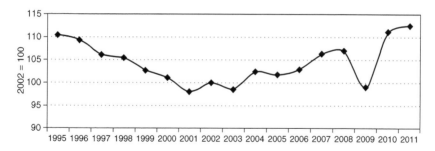

Source: Instituto de Pesquisa Econômica Aplicada (IPEA), www.ipeadata.gov.br.

Figure 13.6   *Manufacturing output in Rio de Janeiro, 1995–2011 (volume index)*

suggests that manufacturing output in the state only began to grow significantly after 2005 or so, more or less in line with the start of a surge in investments by Petrobrás in response to the sharp increase in world oil prices in the early to mid-2000s and the steady increase in proven oil and gas reserves even prior to the discovery of the pre-salt deposits. Note the very sharp rebound in manufacturing activity in the state of Rio after 2009 and how closely correlated this appears to be with a similar pattern in Petrobrás's investment program in 2008–09, that is, in the immediate aftermath of the pre-salt discoveries (Figure 13.7). We believe that it is reasonable to conclude that the increase in Rio's share in domestic oil and gas production as a result of the oil discoveries is translating into significant demand for manufacturing within the borders of the state. Private sector data on projected (2010–12) levels of private sector investment spending suggest both the large size and diversified impact on sectors of manufacturing and infrastructure that will follow as complementary investments to the initial thrust by Petrobrás.

While the emphasis is on Petrobrás and its impact on development in Rio, it is worth mentioning the almost exactly parallel role being played in the state of Rio de Janeiro by the federally owned National Bank for Economic and Social Development (BNDES) in providing long-term, low-cost financing to sustain Petrobrás's investment spending as well as to finance the investments of many firms engaged in complementary investment efforts (Figure 13.8). In some cases, such as shipbuilding and oil services firms, most of which are located in the city of Rio de Janeiro, 100 percent of investment needs have been financed by the BNDES on favorable terms in order to accelerate the pace of building oil rigs and offshore drilling platforms for Petrobrás.

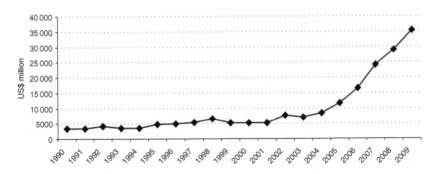

Source: Petrobrás website, www.petrobras.gov.br.

Figure 13.7 Petrobrás investments, 1990–2009 (2009 dollars)

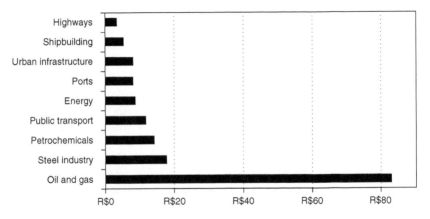

Source: FIRJAN (2011), cited in Urani and Giambiagi (2011), p. 44.

Figure 13.8 Projected investments by sector (2010–12 in billions of reais)

The major impact of the state-led, pre-salt investment push may well be in creating a large oil services industry within the state of Rio, along with the accompanying economic infrastructure. Petrobrás might purchase or rent around US$400 billion worth of equipment and services over the next decade. Directing part of this massive spending towards Rio-based and other Brazilian companies is what authorities in Brasília had in mind when they substantially increased local content requirements for oil and gas companies. For example, the federal government in 2003 created the Program for the Mobilization of the National Oil and Gas Industry, or

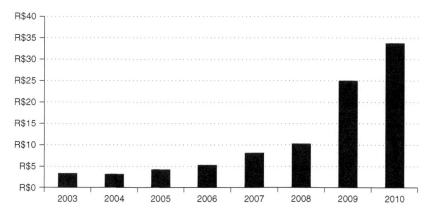

Source: BNDES, http://www.bndes.gov.br/SiteBNDES/bndes/bndes_pt/Institucional/ BNDES_Transparente/.

Figure 13.9   BNDES disbursements in Rio, 2003–2010 (billions of reais)

Prominp (Programa de Mobilização da Indústria Nacional de Petróleo e Gás).[14] Prominp invests in training programs for skilled workers and supports collaboration between oil companies, shipbuilders and university researchers in Brazil. According to government figures, Prominp helped to increase the role of domestic companies in oil and gas investments from 57 percent in 2003 to roughly 75 percent in 2010.[15] Nonetheless, it is important to add that multinational corporations based in the United States (US), Europe, Japan and South Korea still control roughly 90 percent of the world market for the most technologically advanced drilling equipment and services, such as deepwater drilling rigs, risers and the like.

Public incentives have already led to a major revival of Brazil's shipbuilding industry after a long decline in the 1980s and 1990s. As part of its Growth Acceleration Program, the federal government announced in 2005 the Program of Modernization and Expansion of the National Fleet (Promef).[16] The Promef consists mainly of the Petrobrás subsidiary Transpetro, placing orders with Brazilian shipyards for 49 new oil tankers, 16 of which will be built in Rio de Janeiro. Rio accounts for around 50 percent of national productive capacity in the shipbuilding sector.[17]

The oil-related infrastructure planned for the state of Rio includes new petrochemical complexes, of which the largest is known as Comperj in the north of the state (see Figure 13.10). New ports in the state will then link up with the petrochemical infrastructure while bypassing urban areas.

Comperj is projected to be among the largest petrochemical investments of its kind in Brazil and to be providing more than 30 percent of basic

Figure 13.10   Comperj Petrochemical project and other oil-related
infrastructure projects in the state of Rio de Janeiro

products by 2014, principally to support the production of plastics for use
in downstream industries, thereafter gradually expanding gradually into
a broad range of petroleum byproducts. It is one of the largest industrial
projects in Brazil in recent years, with an initial investment of almost $9
billion. It has the potential to increase installed capacity in the state by 10
percent or more, depending upon the efficiency and speed with which the
state can finish related infrastructure and attract firms that will use the
output of the Comperj complex.

Uncertainty about the overall project also involves uncertainty regarding the overall employment impact of this and other related investments.
Petrobrás has estimated that some 200 000 jobs nationwide will be generated, directly or indirectly, through multiplier effects, though most of
the job creation will occur during the construction phase.[18] The number
of jobs sustained during the operational phase will be far more modest,
something in the order of 30 000.

We do not take a position on what the longer-term implications of this
enormous surge in state-led, natural-resource development is going to be
for the state and city of Rio. In principle, two outcomes are possible. In
the first, the enormous investment push leads to a "crowding-in" of much
infrastructure and related private sector investment, which becomes a
driver of economic expansion in the state and the region. Another, less
benign hypothesis is that the push will ultimately create a "Dutch disease"
problem for Rio de Janeiro, crowding out investments in other, more

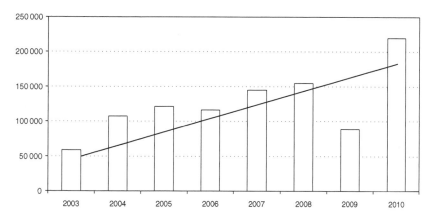

Source: Cadastro Geral de Empregados e Desempregados, http://bi.mte.gov.br/pdet/
pages/consultas/evolucaoEmprego/consultaEvolucaoEmprego.xhtml#relatorioSetor
(accessed 26 September 2011).

Figure 13.11   Formal job creation in the State of Rio, 2003–10

labor-intensive industries and services while dampening innovation. The available evidence does lend support to the "crowding-in" interpretation. Finally, we look at the pace of formal job creation in the state. While the number of new jobs created in the formal sector in Rio de Janeiro in recent years is comparable to the same nationwide indicator, the pace of formal job creation and the strong pressures driving it suggest that economic activity is likely to remain strong in the region as the federally led investment push continues (see Figure 13.11).

13.6   CONCLUSIONS

We set out to examine the impacts of federal policy in Brazil on regional development in a region, Rio de Janeiro, for which a specific regional development policy can be said barely to exist. We have tried to show how tightly interconnected federal, state and municipal policies (and politics) are, and how we must understand regional impacts of federal programs very broadly, especially taking into account those federal policies that have no explicit regional focus. One could not find a federal program for Rio de Janeiro remotely similar to the many programs mounted over the years on behalf of the impoverished regions of the North and Northeast, yet just as surely, the federal government has had an enormous impact on the state.

We have sought to emphasize state-owned enterprise investment in oil and gas infrastructure in the state of Rio de Janeiro and offshore waters as the most important federal policy with regional impact. In the process, we have left aside an analysis of other federal programs, including high-profile ones such as the World Cup and the Olympic Games. This is partly because of data and space limitations. However, our focus is more attributable to the overall impact of this wave of natural-resource investment, even if only a part of planned investments are carried out. Certainly, this is the most significant impact of federal policy on the region of Rio since the removal of the capital in the early 1960s. It will require a leveraging of public and private resources on a scale almost unprecedented in Brazilian history.

The huge investment has the potential to transform the economy of Rio de Janeiro, to create employment opportunities in highly productive areas of the economy, and to generate fiscal revenues sufficient to allow Rio to continue to address long-festering social problems. Whatever the outcome, mitigating the negative effects of a natural resource boom or managing its prosperity will require ever closer coordination between federal, state and local government policies in Rio de Janeiro in the future. The development of a framework for analysis of these complex interactions, a task well beyond the scope of this case study, could be an important tool for policymakers in the future.

NOTES

1. World Bank (2010), Report No. 52814-BR, 28 July, pp. 23–24 (available at www.worldbank.org). The urbanization rate of 96 percent overestimates somewhat the actual percentage of Rio's population living in urban areas. People residing in rural environments are often counted as urban dwellers in official statistics because they live in officially recognized municipalities. Many of these, however, lack access to paved roads, sewage facilities and other public services considered essential to urban life.
2. Source: World Bank (2010), Report No. 51690-BR, 10 June, p. 19 (available at www.worldbank.org).
3. Reference is to results in a recent (2006–08) year period in which average student scores in the State of Rio de Janeiro average about 255 points, below the minimum national benchmark of 300. Results in the mathematics scores were even worse. Source: World Bank (2010), Report No. 52814-BR, 28 July, pp. 2–3 (available at www.worldbank.org).
4. For a listing, see: World Bank (2010), Report No. 51690-BR, 10 June, p. 36 (available at www.worldbank.org).
5. World Bank, Report No. 52814-BR, op. cit., p. 20.
6. Source: World Bank (2010), Report No. 51690-BR, 10 June, p. 14 (available at www.worldbank.org).
7. Imposto sobre a Circulação de Mercadorias e a Prestação de Serviços.
8. Oil and gas revenues as a percentage of total revenues were calculated from data available on the following website of the state of Rio de Janeiro: http://www.fazenda.rj.gov.br/portal/instituicao/contadoria.portal?_nfpb=true&_pageLabel=instituicao_contadoria_home_normasOrientacoes_principal&file=/relatoriosContabeis/demonstrativo/

demonstrativo_resu_desp_rec/receita/consolidado.shtml. We added total annual revenues deriving from oil and gas production from 2008 to 2010 – royalties and other oil-related tax revenues – and divided these by total state revenues in the same years.

9. "Municípios do Rio Viram Reféns dos Royalties", *O Globo*, 20 March 2010 (available at http://oglobo.globo.com/economia/mat/2010/03/20/municipios-do-rio-viram-refens-dos-royalties-petroleo-916129509.asp, accessed 26 September 2011).

10. O Fundo de Manutenção e Desenvolvimento da Educação Básica e de Valorização dos Profissionais da Educação.

11. World Bank, on the basis of data from Secretaría Municipal de Fazenda. Source: World Bank (2010), Report No.51690-BR, 10 June, p.13 (available at www.worldbank.org).

12. For background, see Secretaría de Fazenda (2010).

13. Source: Merval Pereira (2011), "Mudança de enfoque", *O Globo*, 30 July, (available at www.oglobo.com.br). Reference is being made to revenues from royalties only on existing concessions. The special participation tax (PE) is also subject to sharing, and proposals also exist to reduce the share of the federal and producer states in order to increase that of non-producer states. According to Eurasia, the federal government would lower its share of the PE tax from 50 to 46 percent, while the state share would be shaved from 40 to 36 percent. This is could also generate an extra R\$1 billion for non-producer states.

14. http://www.prominp.com.br/data/pages/8A95489E30FCBB0B013123EAC8F279FD.htm.

15. http://www.prominp.com.br/data/pages/8A95488830FCBB0C013123EAF5943361.htm.

16. Programa de Modernização e Expansão da Frota.

17. Data on productive capacity in the industry come from the Sindicato Nacional da Indústria de Construção e Reparo Naval e Offshore (SINAVAL). See also "Indústria Naval Desenha Novo Mapa", *Diário de Pernambuco*, 1 September 2010.

18. Source: www.comperj.com.br/.

REFERENCES

Baer, Werner (2008), *The Brazilian Economy: Growth and Development*, 6th edn, Boulder, CO: Lynne Rienner.

Federação das Indústrias do Estado do Rio de Janeiro (FIRJAN) (2011), "Acompanhamento do Mercado Formal de Trabalho Fluminense no 1° Semestre de 2011", Nota Técnica Número 7, julho.

Fishlow, Albert (2011), *Starting Over: Brazil Since 1985*, Washington, DC: Brookings Institution.

Garman, Christopher (2011), "Brazil/oil: legal challenges to oil royalty bill could delay bid rounds in pre-salt", Eurasia Group, 22 September.

Instituto de Pesquisa Econômica Aplicada (IPEA) (2010), *"Poder de Compra da Petrobrás: Impactos Econômicos nos Seus Fornecedores"*, December (available at http://www.ipea.gov.br).

Nader, Glauco Lopes (2009), "O Posicionamento Estratégico de Macaé no Desenvolvimento do Estado do Rio de Janeiro", unpublished PhD dissertation, Department of Urban and Regional Planning, Federal University of Rio de Janeiro (IPPUR-UFRJ).

Ribeiro, Alcimar das Chagas (2010), *A Economia Norte Fluminense: Análise da Conjuntura e Perspectivas*, Campos dos Goytacazes: Grafimar.

Secretaría de Fazenda, Governo do Rio de Janeiro (2010), "Pré-Sal: de quanto estamos falando? Uma análise macroeconômica da produção potencial dos campos do Pré-sal brasileiro", Report SEFAZ – RJ – NT 2010.02, 26 May (available at http://www.fazenda.rj.gov.br/portal/index. portal?_nfpb=true&_pageLabel=estudoseconomicos).

Urani, André and Fabio Giambiagi (2011), *Rio: a hora da virada*, Rio de Janeiro: Elsevier.

Villela, Renato and Paulo Tafner (2011), "Finanças públicas do estado do Rio de Janeiro: modernização, eficiênica, e preparação para o desenvolvimento susten-tavel", in André Urani and Fabio Giambiagi (eds), *Rio: A hora da virada*, Rio de Janeiro: Elsevier, pp. 12–23.

Index